Fires on the Border

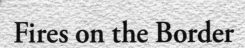

Fires on the Border

The Passionate Politics
of Labor Organizing on
the Mexican *Frontera*

Rosemary Hennessy

University of Minnesota Press
Minneapolis • London

The University of Minnesota Press gratefully acknowledges financial assistance provided for the publication of this book from the Office of the Dean for Humanities at Rice University.

An earlier version of chapter 4 was previously published as "Open Secrets: Class and the Culture of Organizing on Mexico's Northern Border," in *Researching Gender,* ed. Christina Hughes (London: Sage, 2013). An earlier version of chapter 6 was previously published as "The Value of a Second Skin," in *Intersections in Feminist and Queer Theory: Sexualities, Cultures, and Identities,* ed. Diane Richardson, Janice McLaughlin, and Mark Casey, 116–35 (Basingstoke, UK: Palgrave, 2005). An earlier version of chapter 6 was previously published as "Bio-deregulation: Bodies, Jeans, and Justice," in *Kapitalismus Reloaded: Kontroversen zu Empire und Hegemonie,* ed. Christina Kaindl, Christoph Lieber, Oliver Nachtwey, Rainer Rilling, and Tobias ten Brink, 278–304 (Hamburg: VSA-Verlag, 2007). An earlier version of chapter 7 was previously published as "Gender Adjustments in Forgotten Places: The North–South Encuentros in Mexico," in "Invisible Battlegrounds: Feminist Resistance in the Global Age of War and Imperialism," ed. Susan Comfort, special issue, *Works and Days* 29, nos. 1–2 (Spring/Fall 2011): 181–202. Portions of chapter 8 were published as "Notes toward the Political Valence of Affect," in *Gesellschaftskritik nach Marx. Philosophie, Ökonomie, politische Praxis,* ed. Rahel Jaeggi and Daniel Loick (Berlin: Akademie, 2013), and as "Bread and Roses in the Common," in *Love: A Question for Feminism in the Twenty-first Century,* ed. Ann Ferguson and Anna G. Jónasdóttir (New York: Routledge, 2013); copyright 2013 and reproduced by permission of Taylor and Francis Group, LLC, a division of Informa plc.

Published by the University of Minnesota Press
111 Third Avenue South, Suite 290
Minneapolis, MN 55401-2520
http://www.upress.umn.edu

Library of Congress Cataloging-in-Publication Data
Hennessy, Rosemary.
    Fires on the border : the passionate politics of labor organizing on the Mexican frontera / Rosemary Hennessy.
    Includes bibliographical references.
    ISBN 978-0-8166-4758-3 (hc) — ISBN 978-0-8166-7962-1 (pb)
    1. Offshore assembly industry—Employees—Labor unions—Mexican–American Border Region. 2. Labor unions—Organizing—Mexican–American Border Region. 3. Women offshore assembly industry workers—Mexican–American Border Region. I. Title.
    HD6534.O33H46   2013
    331.89'1209721—dc23
                                                        2013030706

Printed in the United States of America on acid-free paper

The University of Minnesota is an equal-opportunity educator and employer.

20 19 18 17 16 15 14 13   10 9 8 7 6 5 4 3 2 1

For Martha,
fogata de amor y guía

When we do and think and feel certain things privately and in secret, even when thousands of people are doing, thinking, whispering these things privately and in secret, there is still no general, collective understanding from which to move. Each takes her or his own risks in isolation. We may think of ourselves as individual rebels, and individual rebels can easily be shot down. The relationship among so many feelings remains unclear. But these thoughts and feelings, suppressed and stored-up and whispered, have an incendiary component. You cannot tell where or how they will connect, spreading underground from rootlet to rootlet till every grass blade is afire from every other.

Adrienne Rich, *What Is Found There: Notebooks on Poetry and Politics*

Contents

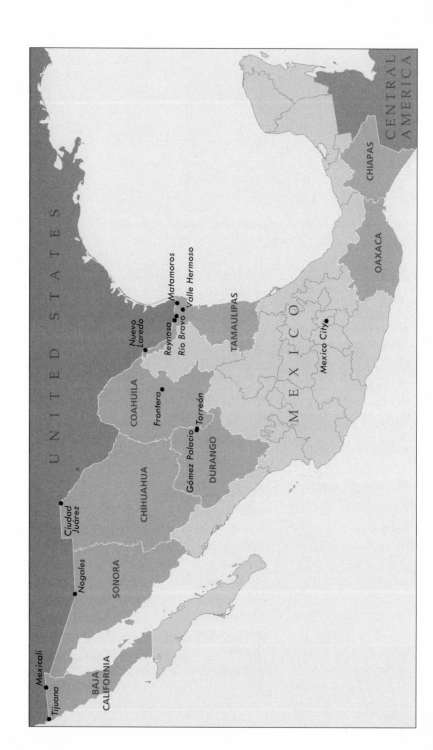

Introduction

Labor is the living, form-giving fire: it is the transitoriness of
things, their temporality, as their formation by living time.

Karl Marx, *Grundrisse*

Dignity is that native land without nationality, that rainbow
that is also a bridge, that murmur of the heart that cares not
about the blood it lives in, that irreverent rebellion that mocks
borders, customs houses, and wars.

Ejército Zapatista de Liberación Nacional (EZLN),
Primera Declaración de La Realidad

Maquiladoras are Mexican factories where workers assemble products
for export. Established in the mid-1960s as the Border Industrialization Program, the maquiladoras—or *maquilas,* as they are called—
have assured companies a huge return on investment, but they have
also offered Mexican workers a poisoned promise: poverty wages in
exchange for a life cut short. The history of the maquiladoras has been
punctuated by workers' organized resistance to their working and
living conditions. In the factory towns of Mexico's northern border
(or *frontera*), organizing propels the accomplishment of short-term
goals and animates longer-term aspirations.[1] Short-term goals often
begin with rights to collective bargaining or with health and safety
in the workplace. But in the last decade of the twentieth century,
workers extended their short-term goals to community concerns for
clean land and water, health care, and education. Longer-term goals
have been pitched at devising a coordinated social movement and
sustainable measures to claim and maintain common resources.

Labor and community organizing in this context entail intense immersion in political education, learning to strategize actions inside and outside the factory, to practice new forms of communication and leadership, and to maintain ties with allies locally and beyond. At times this political education enables workers to make connections between their short-term demands and the longer-range goals of a social movement. Embedded in these activities yet often formally unacknowledged is a dimension of organizing that not only binds people to a common cause and to one another but also at times antagonizes and pulls them apart.

Over the years of my affiliation as an ally to workers involved in organizing campaigns, I was struck by features of their struggles that are not so easy to name. They have to do with the ways organizing is propelled by attachments of affection and antagonism, belief, betrayal, identification, and frustration. Workers' stories of life on the line, of their confrontations with bosses and corrupt officials, of the price they paid for their rebellion at work and at home, and of their motivation to carry their struggle beyond the abuses of the factory were invariably punctuated by intense feelings. Whether expressed in a negative or positive register, they were a vital part of what everyone involved invariably brought into the mix of things.

I call this dimension of organizing its "affect-culture." It is not unique to the border, of course, though the forms it takes here are shaped by the particularities of local communities and institutions. The hyphen in "affect-culture" marks an awkwardness. I use it purposely as the hinge of a neologism that like a hyphenated patronymic, defies conventional prescriptions for a proper name. In this regard, it bears witness in a small way to the unsettling affects I write about. Until recently, critical attention to affect was marginalized in academic theory and ignored in the education of organizing, yet feelings are the daily medium in which concepts come to matter and organizing efforts are lived. *Fires on the Border: The Passionate Politics of Organizing on the Mexican* Frontera is a study of this aspect of labor and community organizing on Mexico's northern border and the strange attractors of sexuality and gender entangled in it.

It is generally acknowledged that people make the decision to join a collective effort because they are moved to do so. But we have only a limited conceptual vocabulary for what that moving means or how it works. People commit to labor organizing at great risk, propelled by the knowledge that the conditions of their work or community life are not right or fair and by the conviction that through a collective effort they might be otherwise. Carrying through on the risk can be a *salto mortal* (fatal leap) onto new ground in which you are forced to examine some of your deepest-rooted assumptions and called upon to express your convictions with confidence. For those who take the leap, expectations of yourself and others undergo radical revision as a collective process unfolds, at times in open confrontation with the company and the government, at other times in arduous small steps through bureaucratic traps. Keeping momentum going in the course of a long and agonizing campaign is a painstaking process of education and strategizing. The audacious rallying of human capabilities it demands requires continual reanimation to convert skepticism into commitment and anger into wise and deliberate action.

Even if we recognize that organizing a collective campaign around labor or community injustices surely makes demands upon members' feelings, questions proliferate about what that means. I am using the words "affect" and "feeling" here as if they were interchangeable, but do they signify the same thing? What precisely is the affective dimension of organizing? How is it related to culture and emotion? Are affects, feelings, and emotions an impediment or an important, even necessary element, in the process of mobilizing people to question their unjust treatment and speak out on behalf of others?

As I pondered these questions during my involvement with several campaigns on the border, I found that certain cultural categories were more affectively saturated than others. Sexuality and sexual identity are two of them; femininity is another. Though a broad range of human affects and emotions circulate in the culture of organizing—I pay attention to fear as a particularly salient one in chapter 1—my principal focus is the affective charge associated with sexuality and its gendered inflections. Sexuality is a broad-ranging historical discourse that is often gendered but not necessarily organized through gender. Though at times culturally articulated into identities, it also exceeds them. Its varied formations have been absorbed into modern understandings of the self and of lived experience accompanied by all sorts of affective intensities. Extensive research has been done on the growing investment of capital in bodies and human capacities, and a considerable archive of work exists on sexuality as a feature of that investment, some of which probes its place at the intersection of cultural and economic value. As I combed through this scholarship and sought to better understand the role of affect and emotion in organizing and of sexuality and gender as parts of them, I came to realize that relatively little is known about the values that bind affect-culture to capital and that much is still to be learned about this dimension of social movement.

One thing I did learn was that I needed a more refined vocabulary for the hunch I was following. So far, I am using the words "affect," "feelings," and "emotion" as placeholders that mark the need for more precision regarding a part of social life we are still struggling to understand. "Feelings" and "emotion" are both commonsense terms for the embodied, discursive social complex I am calling "affect-culture." In chapter 2, I more fully address some of the debates over their meanings and why I have adopted the term. Much of the rest of this book is devoted to tracing some of the ways affect-culture, often formulated through the discourses of sexuality, features in the organizing I witnessed in the maquiladora communities of northern Mexico.

Relatively recently, culture study across the disciplines has paid attention to the affective dimensions of social life,[2] and considerable research has been done on workers' living and working conditions in the Mexican assembly-for-export system.[3] But no study focuses on the affective components of organizing there and their role in the formation of collective agency. While *Fires on the Border* breaks new ground in this respect, my research is deeply indebted to the extensive body of work on gender and sexuality in the maquiladoras.[4] Many of these studies are pioneering efforts to make visible the gendered dimension of exploitation. Most take for granted, however, gender's heterosexual organization or do not address sexual identity per se. One of the arguments in *Fires on the Border* is that sexuality and homosexual identity are open secrets that punctuate the affect-culture and gender politics of labor and community organizing.

Mexico's largest cities and resorts have a well-established gay scene, and a growing, though still small, body of scholarship documents the history, culture, and politics of homosexuality in Mexico. Recent work in Latin American studies and queer migration studies investigates the changing sexual cultures of Mexico, the impact of AIDS and of tourism, and the cultures and economies of sex work.[5] Many of the studies of same-sex culture in Mexico focus, however, on cosmopolitan centers like Mexico City or Guadalajara rather than on the cities and towns in the north.[6] Little research has been done on homosexuals and gender nonconformists in the maquiladoras, and the gay or lesbian free-trade-zone worker remains illegible, even unintelligible. And yet for generations, heterosexual norms have been transgressed in the maquilas, and their transgression has colored the affect-cultures of organizing. Moreover, almost no research exists on the eroticized structure of feeling in factory and community organizing that is sometimes formulated as sexual identity and sometimes exceeds available categories.[7]

Workers' accounts of what it means to identify as gay range from descriptions of a tolerated minority to tales of being harassed at work and in the community, of being fired for being seen as homosexual, or of being driven out of organizing campaigns. Their testimonies also offer ample evidence that sexual identity (and its gendered underside) is entangled in the collective bonds that constitute the passionate politics of organizing. Over the years quite a number of key organizers in the maquilas have been lesbian or gay identified or gender nonconformists, though many of them do not claim these identities openly. For some, being lesbian or gay is an integral part of their commitment to fight for justice in the workplace, though they may not publicly acknowledge this fact, and it almost never translates into a fight for gay rights.

Sexuality and sexual identity are strong attractors; they readily become the medium of gossip and scandal that solicit potent feelings. But they do not entirely encompass the erotic energy that an organizing campaign activates. The critical knowledge generated by the political education that organizing entails is intense and laced with feelings. Part of the intensity lies in the ways people are moved to care for and collaborate with each other, yet the feelings of affection and commonality that a collective campaign can generate are complicated. Sometimes they get articulated in commonsense discourses, but workers' narratives also convey the inadequacy of familiar categories to communicate the attachments that propel their journey through work stoppages, strikes, and months-long campaigns.

In 1999 I first traveled to Mexico's northern border, where I met maquiladora workers and learned about their history of organizing, especially in the northeastern state of Tamaulipas. Soon after, I joined the international Coalition for Justice in the Maquiladoras (CJM) as the representative of the New York State higher education teachers' union, United University Professions. As a member of the coalition, I met representatives of over thirty Mexican grassroots labor and community organizations.[8] In 2003, CJM's executive director, Martha Ojeda, and I embarked on a separate but related project that involved gathering testimonies on NAFTA's impact in Mexico from workers along the northern border and from farmers and indigenous communities in central and south Mexico. These testimonies became the book *NAFTA from Below*. Before becoming director of CJM, Martha had worked for twenty years in the maquilas of Nuevo Laredo, Tamaulipas. As an organizer herself, most notably of the wildcat Sony strike she led in 1994 and then in her leadership position in CJM, she had become a legend among workers on the border, a trusted guide and teacher. Accompanying her in our visits and interviews for *NAFTA from Below* enriched my understanding of the challenges of labor and community organizing and deepened my developing relationships with workers.

As I became more involved with workers' struggles and helped to implement their action plans, I continued to visit northern Mexico's border cities several times a year, and I worked with grassroots organizations in Reynosa, Río Bravo, Valle Hermoso, Matamoros, Nuevo Laredo, Gómez Palacio, Juárez, Tijuana, Mexico City, Oaxaca, and various communities in Chiapas. I was a participant-observer in meetings and strategy sessions with groups from all of these cities, and I lived with a family in Río Bravo, Tamaulipas, for several weeks one spring. As my questions about the affective dimensions of organizing solidified, I conducted over thirty formal interviews with workers and organizers and visited thirteen communities where I had many informal conversations with workers and organizers and attended countless meetings with them.

Most of the time, however, I supported their efforts long distance by writing grants, letters, alerts, and press releases from my vantage point in a university in the United States. In the process my frame of reference as an individual, a teacher, and a culture theorist was being altered. The kinds of questions *Fires on the Border* asks and the answers it offers arise from my both up-close and distanced relationship to the organizing I became a part of, the relationships I formed, and the stories workers shared with me.

Although the burden of organizing weighs most heavily on the workers themselves, organizing campaigns also include people, like me, who support them but live far afield from a maquiladora community. I am interested in the affect-culture that circulates through these distinct yet overlapping spaces, and I use the term "bearing witness" to capture it. One of the aims of *Fires on the Border* is to draw out these attachments as they filter different but related versions of bearing witness. Witnessing is enacted not only by workers on the front lines but also by workers elsewhere. As I use it, "elsewhere" connotes a geographic and epistemic location. It gestures toward the fact that organizing sometimes recruits the support of outsiders. Perhaps as important, it points to a critical standpoint outside capitalism. This sense of elsewhere suggests that in the cooperative relationships that exceed what capital can harvest lies the potential for real social transformation. Here, too, resides the limit of knowledge, its elsewhere. Affect-culture is the arena where history's unthought and its potential is whispered.

Pursuing that limit took me into the cracks within the humanities' and the social sciences' traditional disciplines and into the fissures between them in an effort to do justice to some of the unacknowledged features of Mexican factory workers' struggles. Listening to workers forced me to wrestle with the intellectual traditions I brought to our encounters; it also helped refine my understanding of my life's history and taught me lessons in politics and humility. As an exercise in bearing witness, *Fires on the Border* issues from all of these epistemic spaces, underpinned by a commitment to the principles of materialism.

Though the book shares many aims with activist research and its methodology of collaborative reciprocity with grassroots communities, it did not directly arise from workers' explicit desire to document and analyze the affective dimensions of their organizing process, nor were sexuality and sexual identity targeted as priorities in their campaigns. That workers did not identify these issues as urgent does not mean, of course, that they did not feature in their campaigns. When I spoke with workers about my sense that affective bonds and talk about sexuality feature strongly in the cultures of organizing, they invariably agreed and had much to say on the topic. Representing the circulation of these issues in public discourse and the informal conversation of organizing, in workers' common sense and good sense, and in the unthought of cultures here and there is one feature of the book's work of bearing witness, and I discuss this dynamic in chapter 3.

In addition to the testimonies of workers themselves, the archive of feminist engagements with historical materialism and the work of lesbian, gay, and queer culture theorists have shaped my efforts to do justice to the history of organizing in the maquiladoras, and I draw upon them in the chapters that follow. In addition, I am indebted to the many ethnographic studies of communities in Mexico, as well as the work of social scientists and American and Latin American studies scholars and public intellectuals.[9] The reflections and enactments of critical solidarity by these and many other interdisciplinary researchers and journalists have influenced the relationships I formed with maquiladora workers and the substance of this book.

I began research for this project on the heels of completing *Profit and Pleasure: Sexual Identity in Late Capitalism.* In its last chapter I argue for approaching need as a conceptual reorientation to the polarized focus on either culture or society that has constrained feminist and sexuality studies. In *Fires on the Border,* I elaborate a materialist and feminist approach to affect by considering it as an integral component of the cultural forms and social relations through which needs are met. Affects are vital to the collaborative labor of production and care. They permeate relationships and propel action. They also amplify perception and cognition and infuse knowledge. Antonio Gramsci tells us that "strong passions are necessary to sharpen the intellect and help make intuition more penetrating."[10] He insightfully suggests that affect enhances that probing and predictive knowledge we call "intuition," knowledge that is both reasonable and felt. Intuition frees reason from its empiricist prison house, and perhaps because of that, it has been less recognized. But even though the disciplining of knowledge has kept intuition at bay, it respects intuition as a generator of insight that drives curiosity and prompts hunches that lead to breakthroughs and inventions. For generations workers have relied upon their intuition and good sense in organizing against the factory system's life-eroding conditions and in putting forward their claims. Their intuitions suggest the unreasonable possibility that needs can be met otherwise than through sweated labor, a possibility that depends upon what some philosophers have called "the communist hypothesis" or "the commons."[11] The aspiration to reclaim the commons has been a recent thread in the organizing on the border that ties factory-based campaigns to the squatter communities, or *colonias,* where workers live and to national and transnational movements.[12] This effort to build more sustainable communities also springs from an epistemic stance outside the way things are.

In the chapters that follow, I consider this *outside* as the basis of the strong critique of capitalism in organizing campaigns on the border and in critical work elsewhere. Every organizing campaign claims that those who labor have power and that from their collective action alternatives to the way things are can be imagined and developed. The campaigns I consider in part 2 testify to this proposal, and in this sense they fly in the face of common sense. The very fact of the preposterous suggestion that there might be an outside to capitalism creates a *meantime* between what is and what can be, a political opening where social relations and cultural categories take on new value. Over the four decades of organizing in the maquilas, this meantime has been a powerful intervention in neoliberal incursions into bodies and nature, or what has been called "biopolitics." The political education that takes place during the meantime of any campaign is uneven, messy, and provisional. Some campaigns get stuck there and achieve only minimal accomplishments, but even these provoke aspirations that keep long-term horizons in place. The dynamic animation of these aspirations constitutes what I am calling the "passionate politics" of organizing.

The epigraphs to this introduction point to the material basis for this passionate politics. Marx calls labor "the living, form-giving fire."[13] Labor gives form to a way of life, to its politics and cultural values. It also ignites collective organizing for justice when human capacities are being robbed and lives are being worn away for the benefit of a very few, usually far away, who own the means for laborers' livelihoods. Those involved in an organizing campaign also come to recognize that when capitalism reaps unpaid labor as its profit, that process depends upon another surplus that capital can never fully incorporate: the human capacities for attachment and cooperation. Though capital may harvest them, it cannot do so completely. This fact lies at the heart of my argument.

Forged in time and adhering to the transitoriness of things, this affect-saturated potential is fired up by capital's outlawing of so many human capacities and needs, and it surfaces in the passionate efforts to reclaim them as the right to well-being and dignity. In the second epigraph, the Zapatista Army of National Liberation (EZLN), representing the indigenous peoples of Mexico, refers to a sense of dignity that is rooted in indigenous tradition and that also transcends national borders. The right to *una vida digna* (a life with dignity) is a claim they make in the name of all who struggle for justice, and it is a powerful assertion that workers in maquiladora communities eventually embraced, as well. It is a measure of well-being quite distinct from the discourse of human rights in that it reclaims humanity from the dehumanizing abjection that has been projected onto certain bodies through power relations that exceed the reach of governance and institutions, saturating the relations of labor and consciousness over generations of colonial conquest.[14] Workers on the border have adopted the phrase *una vida digna* to refer to a life where living wages, health, and education would allow well-being to flourish, where one could exercise his or her capacities and be respected in interactions with others. By the mid-1990s, when the phrase circulated in the organizing efforts on the border, it came to have some of the political connotations in the EZLN's sense of it, implying the longer-term collective struggle that is needed to build and maintain the fragile bonds between indigenous farmers in the south and maquiladora workers in the north. As the heartbeat of irreverent rebellion, dignity expands the life-giving form of labor to include human affective capacities as the accompaniment of a radical politics. As intangible as a rainbow and as indispensable as a bridge from here to there, affective capacities are essential to the making of a truly living time.

Organization of the Book

The tempo of organizing in northern Mexico is spasmodic, at times lurching into high gear, at other times moving so slowly that you want to give up. With this unpredictable pulse, history, concepts, and relationships throb, often in disjointed, wrenching rhythms. *Fires on the Border* mimics this discomforting cadence. The three chapters of part 1 present key elements of the book's logic, each in a distinct narrative register. The chapters in part 2 focus on campaigns or projects of grassroots organizations who were members of CJM and with whom I worked closely. In this part, as well, as I shift from one locale and texture of organizing to another the narrative mode switches. Initially, I set out to write a book that would push outside the confining envelope of academic writing by weaving the concepts I encountered in workers' and organizers' narratives with my readings of cultural theory, but not all of the chapters take that shape or do so to the same degree. Moreover, chapters within each part sit a bit uneasily with each other. In part 1, for example, the first chapter is an empirical history; the second engages theoretical debates; and the third ultimately slips into storytelling. As you follow the changes in tone and voice, as well as my movement from one site to another, the narratives' shifts may seem a little jolting. If so, this response is just right for an account of realities that often do not neatly cohere or are at times painfully out of joint.

Together, the three chapters of part 1 provide historical background and the book's theoretical frame. Chapter 1 offers an extended introduction for readers unfamiliar with the maquiladoras or with some of the earliest labor uprisings in the factories. Chapter 2 situates the argument I make about the culture of organizing within scholarship on affect, gender, and care. Chapter 3, on what it means to bear witness, provides a bridge between the first two. Taken as a whole, part 1 provides the epistemic ground for the chapters that follow, linking history and theory, the academy and the field, to the work of organizing and my own animated and at times awkward orientation to workers' struggles for justice in northern Mexico.

Like all narratives, this one is selective. One of the principles of selection was set by my affiliation with CJM. Most of the workers I met were involved in one of the many grassroots Mexican organizations who were members of CJM and active in campaigns the coalition supported. Another distinction of my narrative is geographic. Although I address in detail organizing efforts in cities across several states—for example, some of the events surrounding the murdered women of Ciudad Juárez, which is in the state of Chihuahua, and a campaign by Levi's workers in Gómez Palacio, located in the north-central state of Durango—many of the workers I met lived and worked in the northeastern border state of Tamaulipas. This fact is significant because relatively little research on the maquiladoras has focused on this strategic area, which shares a border with Texas on the U.S. side.

Keeping this preliminary note on the book's narrative logics in mind, chapter 1 tells the story of neoliberal capitalism in Mexico as a political economy comprised of an official market and its narco supplement. The history of the maquiladora sector coincides with the emergence of neoliberal capitalism, initially born in the mid-twentieth century as a global strategy of economic restructuring in direct response to labor unrest. It dismantled state regulation of capital accumulation and sought out a workforce that could circumvent the gains won by organized labor in the overdeveloped world. It has been bolstered by narco money flooding into U.S. banks and by military investments in the U.S. war on drugs. At every step the unleashing of the free market through the maquiladora model has heavily drawn upon a culture of fear and a deeply entrenched though modifiable sex–gender system. Both have served as technologies to guarantee a good labor culture off shore. From the earliest years of the maquiladora program, organized struggles for independent unions in Mexico's factories have signaled workers' bold refusal to be cowed by this culture of fear. Women's leadership in work stoppages and strikes has also announced their resistance to the mandates of a patriarchal sex–gender system. The workers who organize today confront an exponentially compounded terror, yet some still refuse to be controlled by the explosion of criminal state violence in their cities.

Chapter 2, "The Materiality of Affect," takes up the question of affect-culture by engaging theoretical work that has circulated primarily among researchers and intellectuals in universities. I situate my argument in relation to some of the theories of affect that have proliferated over the past two decades and elaborate an explanation that grounds the slippery vocabulary of affect theory in a historical materialist analysis. My approach is quite deliberately indebted to materialist and marxist-feminist traditions.[15] As I hope the following chapters make clear, however, one of my aims in *Fires on the Border* is to stage an encounter between that knowledge and the concepts and insights in the testimonies of workers and organizers on the border.

I explain that encounter and its affective and cognitive impact as the work of bearing witness, the topic of chapter 3. Witnessing carries a weighty cultural legacy, especially in Latin America, where the practice of *testimonio* has enabled marginalized subaltern and oppressed peoples to voice their history in the public sphere. I introduce the practice of bearing witness as a way to name the political work of representation done by worker-organizers and their allies and to link labor organizing with critical practices elsewhere. I propose a strong understanding of witnessing as a potentially perilous and necessary practice that binds the individual to a collective endeavor and standpoint. In her willingness to give herself over to the other, the subject who bears witness assumes a disorienting relation to herself and to history, a stance that disengages her from familiar social relations but also claims a common ground. The critical purchase that bearing witness provides offers a risky positional advantage because in disrupting the common sense it may also undermine relations of trust on which both everyday life and solidarity depend.[16] This argument on bearing witness is the closest I come to a presentation of the book's methodology, by way of the case I make for a stance that brings together subjects from different social locations in order to risk collaborating in the humbling education that cultivating common ground entails.

In part 2, each chapter focuses on a key concept that arose from specific campaigns and organizing efforts. Chapter 4 pivots on the concept of the open secret as an ideological mechanism for the circulation of narrow ways of knowing and not knowing, at times formulated as sexual identity. Narratives of workers and organizers explain the ways homosexual identity functions as an open secret in maquiladora workplaces and communities; they also reveal some of the more unspeakable erotic bonds forged among those who participate in organizing campaigns.

In chapter 5, "The Value of a Second Skin," I consider the affect-culture that adheres to feminized sexual identities and their calculation in the value form. I suggest we think of identity as a second skin that gets folded into the value of the labor power workers exchange for a wage and that is reproduced at home. Here, I bring together research on the body as an accumulation strategy, on transsexual embodiment, and on materialist approaches to the production of value and the narratives of homosexual workers who were leaders in campaigns for better wages and working conditions. Their insights shed light on the lived and contested value of gender and sexual identity within the fundamental logic of capital by fleshing out the embodied, affective dimension of abjection that identity formation entails—a process analogous to taking on and giving over a second skin.

Chapter 6, "Feeling Bodies, Jeans, Justice," conceptualizes the impact of capital deregulation on bodies and affects as crucial components of neoliberal economy and culture by way of the multinational blue jean marketing company Levi Strauss. I read the history of Levi's movement offshore in the 1990s as it parallels the company's intensified gay marketing and philanthropy and an emerging homonormative culture in the United States. The history of runaway factories and gay marketing takes on a new valence when seen in relation to the 2005 Lajat workers' campaign against Levi Strauss & Co. in Gómez Palacio, Durango. Reading these chapters in Levi's history discloses the transnational circulation of cultural value as the deregulation of bodies takes place across the commodity chain of jeans production and the affect-cultures of international solidarity.

Chapter 7 loops back to the empirical narrative voice of chapter 1 as I trace the political horizons put forward in a series of encounters, or *encuentros,* between maquiladora workers and indigenous communities in the southern state of Chiapas. These encounters were supported through the coordination of CJM and were part of the wave of activity surrounding the Zapatistas' interventions into national politics between 2001 and 2006. The meetings were also a part of the broadened reach of CJM's organizing, which extended to include workers' initiatives outside the factory. At the same time that factory workers began taking small steps to sustain their communities autonomously, the indigenous people of Chiapas were reorienting their struggle from demands upon the state to autonomous governance. As labor organizing in the maquilas spilled from the factories into the colonias, workers' encounters with the autonomous communities in the south inspired new activities in the north around the biopolitics of *una vida digna*. In the process sex–gender categories were being adjusted. Though I address gender as a component of sexuality and sexual identity in the previous chapters, here I highlight it as a significant feature of the modifications that these meetings provoked. In so doing I extend my arguments in chapters 1 and 2 on leadership and the affect-culture of care in order to highlight adjustments to the patriarchal configuration of gender in the critical education enacted in the encuentros.

In this chapter, as throughout the book, the history I offer is selective, shaped as much by my outsider position as it is by the particular dynamics of the international solidarity that brought me and others to know and support the workers' campaigns. Labor organizing across Mexico has a long, complicated relationship with national political aspirations and other grassroots struggles—for example, those led by students and farmers or the decades of mass protests in Mexico City against the corruption of democracy.[17] The maquiladora-based labor organizing efforts I address in part 2 reached their peak intensity in the early years of the twenty-first century. The political desires provoked by the EZLN during that time shaped the hopes of many of the workers involved in these campaigns and left an imprint on their allies from elsewhere. Even if those hopes do not now resonate so widely in Mexican national politics or even on the border, their impact nonetheless lives on. It is inscribed in the stories that organizers pass on and that shape a community's sense of its history and future. It is etched in the murals on small colonia buildings that memorialize their encounters with the Zapatistas and in the living legacy they inspired in the sustainable projects that flourished in their wake.

Part 3 consists of a concluding chapter in which I return to issues that run throughout the book regarding the politics of bearing witness for the commons and that I formulate here as the question of love. I draw out some of the implications of the standpoints of witnessing by workers across working-class sectors and make a case for renarrating "love" as a name for the creative capacities of cooperation and care that are essential to social movement devoted to sustaining life.

In the coming years as the world economic crisis unfolds, unmet basic needs will impinge upon and reshape desires. Wherever organizing comes up against extreme unmet need, the hard rock of necessity will threaten to dissolve fragile collective bonds and strip the imagination of belief in possibility. In this situation, paying attention to the affective investments entangled in organizing is a strategy we cannot afford to neglect. The political education that organizing requires can be amplified by reckoning with the feelings people bring to it and the social forces that shape them because affect-culture can inspire critical insight and action or hijack passionate reason into the narrowest terms. While this book speaks to the organizing efforts of Mexican factory workers, workers in the global north are also residents of capitalism's monstrous outside. In this elsewhere lies our common cause. Smoldering here in kitchens, classrooms, and community centers are fires that can spark another possible world.

I

History, Affect, Representation

« I »

Labor Organizing in Mexico's Entangled Economies

Maquiladoras-narcos-migration—that's the triangle. If you keep these things separate you'll never understand what's happening in this city.

Julian Cardona, quoted in Ed Vuiliamy,
"Day of the Dead"

I'm a simple worker, but one thing I know: beatings make one wise. Little by little, through our experience and books, we have learned. And for us, nothing is impossible.

Rebel union leader, quoted in Peter Baird and
Ed McCaughan, "Hit and Run"

The history of organizing in the maquiladoras is rooted in the dawning of neoliberal capitalism and accompanies the restructuring of two economic sectors, one legal and the other extralegal, in the last half of the twentieth century. Manufacturing and the drug business are not usually thought together, nor is the return of free-market capitalism in the late twentieth century generally understood in terms of their intersection. But today, everyone living on the Mexican side of the border knows the economy they inhabit is controlled by the maquiladoras and the drug cartels, whose interests range over a web of overlapping investments and institutions.

Not until 2006, when Felipe Calderón assumed the Mexican presidency, did labor organizing on the border have to take into account the violence generated by warring cartels, but now that is an unavoidable if unspeakable dimension of any strategizing for labor rights. Though the history of the maquiladoras and the labor unrest it spawned precede the irruption of cartel violence, understanding them both as products of neoliberal restructuring casts into relief the intimate relationship between these two axes of transnational trade, where production, circulation, and consumption converge.

The histories of these billion-dollar-a-year trade sectors run parallel courses, each enhanced by the transnational reach of free-trade policy. In the mid-1960s a new production-for-export strategy spurred the development of the Border Industrialization Program and the establishment of a free-trade zone on Mexico's northern border. The maquiladoras supplied U.S. companies with cheap labor and Mexico with foreign investment that would allay its growing national debt. A similar shift to production for export was taking place in South America, where Colombian agribusinesses began growing coca for cocaine that would flow through the Caribbean into U.S. markets. In 1970 the U.S. Congress passed the Comprehensive Drug Abuse Prevention and Control Act that inaugurated President Richard Nixon's war on drugs. It targeted drug consumers in the United States and dealt with a restive domestic surplus labor pool there by corralling disproportionate numbers of black and Latino offenders into jail. By the mid-1980s the war claimed a major victory in the offensive on drug trafficking through Miami. Until then product had moved mostly by way of light aircraft from Colombia through the Caribbean and Florida. After the crackdown on Miami, trafficking routes shifted west to Mexico's road transporters. Mexico's well-established heroin- and marijuana-based organizations were poised to become the lead players in the cocaine business.[1] The thriving free-trade zone along the northern Mexico border would also serve as an ideal transfer point for smuggling, and soon Mexican production of methamphetamine bound for U.S. markets would boom, as well.[2]

By the early 1990s the U.S. war on drugs was vying with the North American Free Trade Agreement (NAFTA) as the leading justification for U.S. intervention in Latin America. Former DEA agent and director of the El Paso Intelligence Center Phil Jordan told ABC News in May 1997, "For the godfathers of the drug trade in Colombia and Mexico, [NAFTA] was a deal made in narco heaven."[3] The year NAFTA was passed saw a 25 percent jump in commercial vehicle smuggling across the Mexican border.[4] A year later, the U.S. and Mexican governments agreed to start training Mexican soldiers in the United States for the war on drugs. These elite commandos were called Los Zetas. Within a few years the Zetas grew into one of the most powerful cartels in Tamaulipas. After years working as a security detail for the Gulf cartel, they are now their own bosses, are vying for control of the border, and have a reputation as the most vicious killers.

This chapter tells the story of these two axes of neoliberal capitalism whose histories converge on the border. In the second decade of the twenty-first century, that convergence has increasingly set the context for maquiladora workers' lives and organizing efforts. I begin with a history of labor unrest that frames the inauguration of the maquilas and women workers' little-known organized resistance. The sweatshop economy of the maquiladora sector had set its hopes on fear as one of several tactics that would guarantee a so-called good labor culture. It was operationalized in subtle forms of intimidation and explicit threats that troublemakers would be fired and blacklisted or that organizing for better pay and working conditions would lead the factory to close and go elsewhere.

Any enduring political regime has a normative order for emotions, what William Reddy has called an "emotional regime."[5] Fear remains a key component of the emotional regime that holds sway in the maquiladora sector, and every organizing effort there has to combat that normative order with strategies that motivate people to overcome their apprehensions and act in the face of coercion and reprisals. Although fear is a powerful motivator of submission and inaction, the history of organizing in the maquilas is testimony to workers' courageous refusal to comply.

In 2006 a seemingly different, though related, emotional regime accompanied the irruption of a new reign of terror across the cities and towns of the eastern border as competition among the cartels intensified and was compounded by the militarization strategy of the newly elected National Action Party (Partido Acción Nacional; PAN) presidential candidate, Felipe Calderón. Cartel violence and government impunity in the face of a rising toll of murders and disappearances had already become the reputation of Ciudad Juárez.

Here, beginning in the mid-1990s, hundreds of women went missing and scores of mutilated corpses were found in the desert while the state and local government officials did nothing. By 2006 warring cartels were conducting shootouts in the streets, and the violence was spreading east to Nuevo Laredo, Reynosa, and Matamoros, where murders, assassinations, and disappearances were also becoming commonplace. Here, too, local and federal police were, at best, uninvolved.

Fear was going viral. It supplemented the intimidation tactics of the power brokers of labor—the companies and their allies in the official unions and the government. Narco politics also represented a new form of power exercised through control over who should die, a necropolitics that was being enacted randomly and brutally. This violent narco–necro sovereignty inaugurated a reign of terror across cities and towns on the eastern border, where ever since one or the other of the cartels has controlled every level of civic life. Workers who organize for better working conditions or exercise their right to free association still confront threats and intimidation from their bosses and their cronies in the official unions and on the labor boards, and they have to navigate, as well, the deathly politics that rules the streets and that overlaps, at times covertly and at others openly, the corporate and government sector. Organizing on the border now takes place in the cross hairs of these twin regimes.

Militant Labor and the Maquiladoras

The maquiladora sector was born as a U.S. economic strategy that developed in the mid-twentieth century to enhance profits and quell labor unrest by moving components of production offshore into a free-trade zone on Mexico's northern border. The idea was that tax breaks for the companies and low wages for the workers would make product assembly for export yield huge profit margins. This adjustment to the way manufacturing had been done was part of a transnational shift in capitalist economies across the developed and developing world that was undermining organized labor and loosening the state's regulatory check on capital accumulation. In Mexico free trade was the keystone of reforms that responded to pressure for economic liberalization from the International Monetary Fund (IMF) as a condition of its debt repayment. This new policy direction was initiated by President Miguel de la Madrid in 1983 and most fully expressed by his successor, Carlos Salinas-Gortari (1988–94), but the seeds of free-market reform that flowered in Mexico during the mid-1980s were actually sown twenty years earlier with the inauguration of an assembly-for-export model that aimed to loosen state regulation of the Mexican national economy, propel manufacturing exports, and open the country to North American investment. Ultimately, this new economic program gave multinational corporations freer reign over Mexico by brokering incentives for foreign investors and wealthy nationals, including weakened or abolished legal structures to protect workers and increased labor flexibility. The reforms of the 1980s intensified the impact of free trade as its effects registered in the erosion of social services, further immiserization of the poor, and increasingly precarious lives for the social majority.

These historical changes were not unique to Mexico. They rippled throughout economies in the developed and developing world as policies were enacted that diminished the state's active and democratic role in controlling capital accumulation and unleashed market forces that had been regulated more tightly through nationalized industries and economic planning. The movement of manufacturing outside the United States was one feature of this new direction. It is important to recognize that moving capital offshore was also a response to U.S. labor unrest that took place between 1956 and 1973. By the mid-1960s in the United States, workers' organized struggles for higher wages had spiked. Work stoppages in the U.S. garment industry were high through 1969; in electronics they peaked between 1964 and 1969, and they remained high through 1972. Significantly, electronics was the first industry to move assembly to Mexico.[6]

In 1964 Mexico's two-decades-long series of laws and agreements with the United States that was known as the Bracero Program ended. This program drew thousands of Mexican men into the United States during World War II to work in the fields and build the railroads. As opposition to the program from U.S. organized labor grew alongside the mechanization of U.S. agriculture in the 1960s, the program declined. When these men returned home, they swelled a surplus labor pool on the border that was already being augmented by peasants and farmers arriving daily from the south. In 1965 the Border Industrialization Program (BIP) inaugurated the maquiladora assembly-for-export sector, and the first industrial park opened in 1968. The BIP program took advantage of U.S. tariff schedules that allowed components to be assembled in other countries and then reexported to the United States without being taxed upon reentry.[7] U.S. firms had already been experimenting with Mexican assembly as early as 1962, when Nielsen set up a plant in Nuevo Laredo to tabulate promotional coupons.[8] Over the next decade some of the Bracero men would find jobs in the border cities of Juárez, Tijuana, and Nuevo Laredo building the factories and industrial parks. However, many men who stayed in border cities rather than return to their homes of origin were unemployed. By 1965 unemployment in some border cities was as high as 50 percent.[9] In the new factories, though, women were recruited as the preferred workforce, a strategy based on lessons from the free-trade zones in Asia, where women were considered cheaper and potentially more docile workers. Over the next twenty-five years, this workforce profile would gradually change as more factories poured into the region and companies desperate for a workforce drew men onto the assembly lines.

The concept of assembly for export began as an experiment, but it soon became a pillar of economic policy in Mexico. The aim of the maquiladora model was to draw U.S. corporations to the Mexican side of the border with the prospect of several enticing advantages. One was geographic. Even today—when competition with Asia has lured many businesses to move assembly work to China, Vietnam, and other countries where wages are lower—close proximity to U.S. markets still gives Mexico an advantage. From the inception of the maquiladora program, savings on labor were fundamental. A wide profit margin was assured from low wages and minimal overhead for worker safety or the disposal of toxic wastes. Crucial to these advantages was the complement of a promised "good labor culture" (code for a compliant workforce and union–government cooperation).

One stumbling block to that promise was, however, Mexico's federal labor law, a product of the Mexican Revolution and very favorable to workers, more favorable, in fact, than U.S. labor law.

It guaranteed the right to a living wage, the right to the eight-hour day, the right to organize and form associations, and the right to strike.[10] Fortunately for the corporations, many new factory workers were unfamiliar with their legal rights. Companies also found ways around the law, and the Mexican government began exempting the maquiladora sector from federal labor requirements.[11] Mexico had a strong union culture, but by the 1960s the national labor unions were working closely with the political party that had ruled the country since the 1930s, the Institutional Revolutionary Party (Partido Revolucionario Institucional; PRI). For this reason these unions came to be known as official or *charro* unions. The name *charro* is used derisively to refer to unions that work hand in glove with the government and the companies, and they are opposed by the movement for union democracy in Mexico.[12]

The Confederation of Mexican Workers (CTM), founded in 1938, remains the leading charro union and instrument of PRI domination. The Revolutionary Confederation of Mexican Workers and Peasants (CROC) is another official union affiliated with the PRI, and it has come to have an influential, repressive presence on the western border.[13] Both unions offer investors labor peace by drawing up protection contracts between the union and the company. In the so-called good labor culture of the maquiladoras' early years, the majority of workers were automatically enrolled under a union contract. The unions worked closely with the government but also tended to keep workers informed through monthly meetings. As part of the shift to free-trade policy in the early 1990s, President Salinas de Gortari removed many CTM leaders who were strong supporters of workers. By the mid-1990s, after NAFTA, protection contracts came to be the norm. If in the first phase of the maquilas unions were aligned with the government, then three decades later they were protecting the companies, and most workers did not even know they were represented by a union. Labor culture became more flexible, meaning that Mexican labor law would be overlooked to accommodate the companies. In addition, the labor boards (Juntas de Conciliación y Arbitraje), who heard and passed judgment on workers' complaints and consisted of representatives from the government, the company, and the union, became institutionalized. Given the alliance between the CTM union and the PRI government, however, the labor boards were always stacked against workers. By the mid-1990s under the new flexible labor culture, all three sectors of the labor boards operated as a unit protecting the companies' interests. To cite one example of how this alliance worked even in the early years, Mexican labor law stipulated that for a strike to be legal it had to be approved by the labor board, but in Juárez between 1968 and 1979, 95 percent of the strike subpoenas presented to the board concluded without a strike being approved.[14]

Profits gleaned from the erosion of workers' legal protections are compounded by the low wages in the maquilas. The average maquiladora wage is between four hundred and five hundred pesos per day, or the equivalent of forty-five to fifty U.S. dollars for a forty-eight-hour work week. In other words, maquiladora workers are paid less in a day than U.S. workers earning minimum wage make in an hour. Most workers are young, between the ages of sixteen and twenty-five, and the average time on the job is three years. Companies recognize that a worker cannot sustain the rhythms of work much longer than this.[15] Repetitive motion, toxic chemicals, and other harsh conditions in the workplace wear out a worker's body long before she or he reaches middle age.

The maquiladora model of assembly for export was a lucrative economic experiment for foreign investors, but it was also a risky one. Although women were initially considered more accommodating workers than men, within the first decade of the program organized resistance simmered and erupted in the factories as women workers came together to demand living wages, health and safety, and, above all, freedom of association and collective bargaining. The program's growth in the first period was disrupted between 1974 and 1975 by a recession in the United States that meant many Mexicans also lost jobs as factories closed, but the recession was not the only reason companies were running away. Many were also finding that the "unspoiled workforce" they were promised a decade ago had undergone some changes.[16] Company sports teams and beauty pageants fostered loyalty, but for many workers the glamour of these distractions soon wore off and they began organizing.[17]

Nuevo Laredo, Tamaulipas, quite quickly came to be known as a major trouble spot where work stoppages were common. The details of these labor disputes are worth recounting because strikes here led by women were the first serious offensives against the culture of fear cultivated by the corrupt unions and they gave birth to an autonomous union movement on the border. In the early 1970s the three major maquilas in Nuevo Laredo were Video-Craft Mexicana, a subsidiary of Pemcor, Inc. of Chicago; Sarkes-Tarzian, headquartered in Bloomington, Indiana; and Transitron Mexicana, a subsidiary of Transitron Electronics of Wakefield, Massachusetts. All were electronics sector plants.[18] Transitron began building its Mexican plant in 1966. Within four months and without any publicity, it had over 1,500 applications. The first thirty-four "girls" (as all women workers were called) were paid $2.08 per day.[19] By 1969, 1,400 workers were at the plant assembling integrated circuits, diodes, and transistors for the semiconductor markets in Europe and the United States.[20] By 1974 the workforce had grown to nearly 3,000. Transitron was the largest employer in Nuevo Laredo, and it also experienced the most labor militancy, at times coordinated with the other two factories.[21] Between winter 1973 and summer 1975, workers in all three maquilas waged an offensive against the corruption of the CTM and the political repression in the factories.[22] They demanded higher wages and benefits and better working conditions. They staged work stoppages and slowdowns, and they initiated a series of moves to democratize the union structure.[23]

The first strikes were at Sarkes-Tarzian, where the company attempted to impose temporary contracts on the "overly militant" workers.[24] The result of mediation in that case was the imposition of twenty-day renewable contracts and more flexibility for managers to set the length of the working day. Workers at Video-Craft who protested this system were fired. In 1969 workers at Transitron struck over the company's failure to pay Christmas bonuses on time.[25] Again, in December 1973, Transitron workers walked out in support of women fired for protesting fines imposed on those who opted to use private cars rather than union-sponsored taxis to get to work.[26] In May 1974 the autonomous workers' union at Transitron launched a slowdown to protest the intensification of productivity schedules.[27] In response managers fired five hundred of them for a six-month period. In December 1974 workers in the autonomous union again went on strike in support of those fired after the slowdown, and eight thousand workers gathered at the plaza to protest the charro union's practices. Between March and June 1975, worker unrest continued as the company attempted to impose temporary contracts, and when Transitron closed that summer, thousands of workers filled the streets.

Martha Ojeda tells about what happened that day. She had begun working at Transitron in 1973, where her mother, Olinda Domín-guez, was soldering and assembling television parts. One day, she says, she and her mother arrived at work only to find the factory closed: "Transitron left without warning and without paying even a penny. The administration simply disappeared. That is why we began to call the maquilas *'golindrinas,'* or swallows, because they flew away when they wanted to."[28] In response to the plant's closing, workers from the two other factories in Nuevo Laredo joined the Transitron workers who occupied the factory, guarding the machines. When they learned that the union had made a deal with the company to give them the machines, "there was a lot of disappointment among us workers," Martha says. "I was angry, upset, and I did not under-stand because I had other ideas about unions."[29] The Transitron leg-acy left its mark. In 1979 when workers assembling medical supplies at Manhattan, a subsidiary of Johnson & Johnson in Nuevo Laredo, demanded higher wages, the company closed and moved to Juárez, where they said the union culture was less strong.

Other strikes in these early years revealed cracks in the fear-mongering tactics of the companies and the official union. In 1975 workers at Zenith in Reynosa and at Mextel (Mattel) in Mexicali and in Nogales went on strike. In 1979 workers in Tijuana walked out of Rokha, a California-based garment assembly factory, protest-ing unpaid wages and overtime. That year, workers also launched a strike against Solidev Mexicana, one of the largest electronics plants in Tijuana, citing the use in production of hazardous chemicals outlawed in the United States. At Solidev workers also complained about sexual abuse by the former plant manager, who allegedly posed as a medical doctor and performed pelvic examinations on fe-male workers as a condition of employment.[30] Companies routinely threatened workers who pressed for better wages, fair benefits, or safe working conditions by telling them that if they did not behave, the plant would close. Of course, in many cases plants closed anyway, or workers branded as troublemakers were simply fired.[31]

The 1980s were the boom years of the maquiladora sector, which was carving a new economic course for the country. Mexico's devalued peso beckoned to more and more foreign investment. By the late 1980s the sector had 1,450 factories and over 300,000 workers, who were paid less than those in Korea, Hong Kong, and Singapore.[32] By 1992, 2,000 maquilas along the border employed 500,000 workers. During the 1990s and 2000s, women continued to constitute the majority of workers on the lines in many industries, and a number of them were organizing wildcat strikes.[33] Labor-organizing campaigns and strikes focused on issues like wages, the length of the work week, the right to freedom of association, and the right to health and safety in the workplace. Increasingly, however, deals between the unions and the government that favored the companies were weakening labor's leverage. More flexible arrangements, like the extension of the standard forty-eight-hour work week and the inauguration of twelve-hour shifts, were being written into union contracts and imposed on workers.

The passage of NAFTA in 1994 allowed multinational and transnational corporations to extend their factories from Mexico's northern border to the entire country, where they could continue to thrive on tax breaks and an abundance of cheap labor. From Tijuana to Matamoros, capital investors from the United States, Canada, Europe, and Asia built factories that assembled everything from wheelchairs and underwear to automotive parts, TVs, small electronics, and gift bags. NAFTA was an investment deal designed to extend and protect U.S. corporate investment in Mexico, lock in low wage rates, and raise cash for a nervous political oligarchy. Because the country was already poor, the greatest losers were ordinary people, workers and farmers whose rights, bodies, and communities had no protections. NAFTA caused a slowdown in Mexico's national economic growth that blocked the possibility of a sustainable national economy. It also devastated the environment and eroded the health of the majority of the country.[34]

Although Mexico's promise of a good labor culture was a crucial selling point for businesses ready to take advantage of NAFTA, before the treaty's passage people in the three NAFTA countries were questioning its implications for Mexican workers and provoking debate about its potential impact on them. As the movement of manufacturing to Mexico intensified, information about the horrific working and living conditions in maquiladora communities began to circulate in the United States and Canada. People in these countries started to feel responsible for the sweated labor their consumer cultures thrived upon. In 1989 the Coalition for Justice in the Maquiladoras (CJM) formed as a binational collaboration of Mexican and U.S. religious, environmental, labor, and women's organizations supporting maquiladora workers.[35] Their international support involved workers in a process of education about the hazardous chemicals with which they were working and gave an enormous boost to their efforts. One of the earliest CJM campaigns was against the Illinois-based Stepan Chemical Company, located in chemical row outside Matamoros, Tamaulipas, where clusters of anencephaly (absence at birth of all or most of the brain) had been found in children. CJM documented astronomical levels of xylene in the area, a chemical discharged by Stepan and linked to anencephaly.[36]

During the early 1990s other organizations also supported maquiladora workers and documented the negative impact of NAFTA on Mexico's people.[37] As a consequence of the strong organizing against NAFTA's passage, side agreements were drawn up to address labor and the environment. These side agreements are, respectively, the North American Agreement on Labor Cooperation and the Agreement on North American Environmental Cooperation. These agreements allow any nongovernmental organization, individual, union, or employer in any of the three countries represented in the agreement to submit a complaint against another party to their country's National Administrative Office (NAO).[38] Though NAOs do not have teeth, in that they have no power to implement fines in the case of labor violations and they offer workers no meaningful opportunities to be involved in the process, they do offer workers an international platform for publicizing injustice and help build international alliances that to some degree provide a shield against the weapon of intimidation the companies and their allies wield.

On January 1, 1994, the same day that NAFTA was officially in place, the EZLN rose up. The solidarity that grew out of their eventual alliance with maquiladora workers is a little-known part of this history. I address that alliance in chapter 6, as it bolstered workers' bravery in the face of fierce repression. In April 1994, though, just as peace talks between the EZLN and the Mexican government were ending, several thousand workers from Sony's five plants in Nuevo Laredo walked out in a wildcat strike over the right to organize. Their case was one of the first complaints under NAFTA's labor side agreements.

From the earliest years of the free-trade zone, even the most supportive analysts estimated that organizing autonomous unions in the maquiladora sector was a "harsh, dangerous, and nearly impossible task" because the organizational barriers were many and the odds were on capital's side.[39] The geopolitical mobility of capital meant that companies constantly threatened that if workers insisted on higher wages or spoke up about labor rights, there would be severe reprisals. The ruling regime had on its side the company lawyers, the corrupt charro unions, the labor boards, and, if necessary, the local police to terrorize workers into submission. All were backed by a strong patriarchal culture and a regime of fear that severely limited the possibility for the protracted organizing necessary to support autonomous struggles.[40] Nonetheless, worker uprisings continued.

Some organizing campaigns won concessions from companies, who then made minor adjustments in working conditions or were forced to award workers their severance and back pay. Campaigns like those organized by workers at the Sony plants in Nuevo Laredo; Custom-Trim in Valle Hermoso; Duro Manufacturing in Río Bravo, Tamaulipas; and Lajat (Levis) in Gómez Palacio, Durango, took precedent-setting steps toward union democracy by filing complaints under NAFTA's side agreements and obtaining the registrations for independent unions. These historic victories were the result of bitter battles that put many lives on the line. Only a few, among them the Custom-Trim workers, Duro workers, and Lajat workers, won monetary compensation. The Duro workers also won their union registration, which was later stolen by the CROC. For many of those involved, however, the victories were less tangible. Against the institutional firewall around workers' rights and a tightly controlled guarantee of a good labor culture, the organizing campaigns of these first decades of the maquiladoras testified to workers' conviction that nothing was impossible, and for each new generation of workers, they have been a foothold against fear.

Workers who become organizers have to make major adjustments in their lives. For many this means adopting a new relationship to work, home, and community. In the process what William Reddy calls the "emotive" life of individuals and what Deborah Gould refers to as the "affective habitus" of a group get reoriented as the organizing process interrupts the dominant epistemic and emotional culture. The process takes place as individuals learn by example and, at times more formally, in workshops and meetings that provide information, training, and a process for working through an alternative affect-culture. Crucial to the conversion that occurs in becoming an organizer is a new relationship to fear.

Fear is a soft weapon that a regime uses in order to get what it wants, to guard its investments, and to wield power against resistance.[41] It aims to manage the crisis that organizing provokes by forcing troublemakers into submission. Initially at least, its medium is coercion enacted through intimidation, harassment, verbal hostility, humiliation, and threats. These practices lean on people's concerns that they themselves or their family members might be physically harmed, but they also draw upon the emotional norms of the community, especially those that prescribe honor and respectability or, conversely, shame and indignity. As I address in chapters 4, 5, and 6, because sexuality and gender often feature in these norms, they too are handy mechanisms for repression.

Over the course of an organizing campaign as workers learn how to combat fear, many undergo a process of unlearning old and deeply rooted affective-emotional habits and acquiring new ones. Several of the organizers I met spoke about this process as a transformative experience. The first organizing campaign on the border with which I became deeply involved was the Duro workers' strike in 2000 over the right to an independent union. Here, I witnessed workers learning new affective responses to intimidation. Again and again, the organizing group devised strategies to disarm the threats directed at them. One often-used strategy entailed bringing the perpetrators into the public spotlight to make their tactics visible as violence. In organizing sessions workers discussed how to resist the inclination to submit to fear by running away or keeping quiet. They learned how to register legal complaints and call press conferences. They practiced what to say and how to say it when speaking on the radio or meeting with the mayor or the bishop. They drew up plans for occupying the plaza.

One dramatic example of the about-face this affective reorientation entailed occurred one night in Río Bravo during the Duro worker's strike. A group of workers was driving around town delivering pamphlets that encouraged their coworkers to vote in the union election. Suddenly, they realized their truck was being forced off the road by thugs from Mexico City who were hired by the company to intimidate the organizers and squelch their campaign. Instead of making a getaway, the organizer driving the truck turned it around and headed straight toward the car of hired thugs, who then backed off and drove away. That this organizer was a woman added to the readjustment in the group's understanding of power. This incident was proudly retold many times, accompanied by smiles or laughter or a delighted "que chingona!" This moment of resistance was not, however, as spontaneous as I have scripted it. In actuality it grew out of an extended period of many meetings and strategy sessions among the workers that entailed coaching and training in tactics for refusing to be ruled by fear.

A rumor that one of the organizers had an affair with one of the hired thugs also featured in the stories about that time. Like the action of the driver who confronted her intimidators, this tale of a woman who slept with the enemy was couched in terms of transgressed gender norms. In this case, though, the transgression was melded to the scandal of a woman's sexual impropriety compounded by betrayal. Unlike the proud story of turning the tables on intimidation, this tale was not shared in meetings or made part of a lesson. Speculation about what it meant, whether it actually happened or was cunningly circulated to divide the group, was swallowed up by the unofficial discourse of gossip, a potentially potent supplement to the ruling emotional regime. So far as I know, the story remained on the margins of the organizing campaign's ability to address gender and sexuality as elements in the politics of fear.

The Other Economy

Since the drug wars erupted in Mexico's eastern border region, a chronic social malaise has settled over border cities and towns, a dis-ease characterized by varying levels of anxiety punctuated by nauseating and eventually numbing shock when shootouts, assassinations, beheadings, and mass killings occur and when the news of disappearances is whispered. The effect has been a qualitative alteration in civic life as the soft weapons of intimidation and corruption are displaced by actual machine guns in the hands of mercenaries for the criminal state. Since Calderón proclaimed his war on drugs, estimates of the rising number of killed and disappeared vary. In 2011 the Mexican government stopped announcing official counts of the dead. As of 2013, unofficial conservative estimates indicate that more than sixty thousand people in the country have been killed or disappeared; many contend, however, that the actual count is much higher. As the drug cartels fight for control of territory and power, they go after members of enemy cartels but also target federal soldiers and local police or pose as federal soldiers and police. Often, innocent people are killed randomly or caught in the cross fire.[42] Against a backdrop of daily shootouts, kidnappings, and murders and the fear they have produced, it might seem that labor and community organizing are impossible, but even in this terrorized situation, some workers are carrying on campaigns for freedom of association and workplace rights, and residents of colonias are moving forward with community projects.

Cuidad Juárez, in the Mexican state of Chihuahua and across the border from El Paso, Texas, was long considered ground zero for narco violence and for community organizing efforts to confront it. By some accounts the most violent city in the world outside declared war zones, Juárez has come to be known as "murder city," as the title of Charles Bowden's 2010 book all too chillingly conveys. In 2010 alone there were over three thousand homicides in Juárez, and in the past two decades, an inordinate number of victims have been young women. Since 1993, somewhere between three hundred and six hundred women have been murdered in Juárez, and thousands are still missing.[43] There have been a few arrests, a revolving door of special investigators, and scores of theories hedged in surmise and melodrama of who and what is responsible. The female victims are mostly young and poor. Many have been sexually violated, and their bodies bear marks of ritualized torture. A considerable number of them were workers in the maquiladoras. What makes these crimes more remarkable than those that occur anywhere else in the world is the seeming pattern that early on defined the government's response to them: few of the perpetrators have been caught, and few preventive measures have been pursued. Indeed, the official handling of the brute evidence of bodies found in pieces in the desert or of women and girls who never return home has been a study in irresponsibility and neglect, a jumble of pretexts, alibis, and contradictions or, worse, inaction and orchestrated silence. Like other marginal subjects, the majority of the murdered and missing women remain shrouded in layers of public invisibility, the traces of their lives etched in the narratives they have generated, testimony to the disparity between the public and the private calculus of their value.

There have been local demonstrations calling for justice and protests in Chihuahua and other Mexican states, in Mexico City, and in cities across the United States. The murders have also gotten a fair amount of press coverage in extended stories in the *El Paso Times, Harper's, La Jornada,* the *L.A Times, Ms Magazine,* the *New York Times,* the *Texas Observer,* and the *Washington Post,* as well as in reports on the BBC, Univision, and CNN. Lourdes Portillo's film *Senorita extraviada* went a long way toward bringing the femicides into public consciousness.[44] A growing body of critical work has circulated in conferences, books, and journal articles on the murdered and missing women, and much of it documents the tentacles of economic and political power to which the violence is tied and the challenges of organizing against it.[45]

The conditions that bred the femicides in Juárez are now part of the fabric of life in other maquiladora communities, and many of the difficulties faced by organizing efforts on behalf of the murdered and missing women and their families are now shared by campaigns for labor rights. As Melissa Wright noted in 2001, groups focused on labor and those focused on women's issues have much in common, yet historically it has been difficult for them to work together. One of the common threads is the contradictory valuation and devaluation of Mexican women as workers who do the socially necessary labor in and outside their homes. Moreover, as many of those who have written on the murders have documented and as I will discuss in the context of labor campaigns in the following chapters, the discourse of sexuality has a gendered inflection that is a key ingredient in the culture of violence deployed in the accumulation of capital and in the exercise of domination by legal and extralegal sovereign actors. As the Juárez example demonstrates, this sex–gender discourse can be a very effective technology for soliciting affectively charged public opinion, structuring the discourses of fear, and dividing organized resistance.[46]

Looking at the spread and intensification of brutal forms of violence and their gendered profile from the vantage point of Juárez offers a window into the consequences of structural adjustment in Mexico's twin economies—the legal one and its extralegal supplement.[47] Take, for example, the fact that before the early 1990s almost no women were murdered in Juárez.[48] Female homicides averaged a scant handful of cases annually—far lower than in U.S. cities of similar size. Then, something happened. This something was less the melodramatic arrival of a serial killer than a convergence of forces that do not easily fit into popular formulas. By the mid-1990s the effects of a national economy held hostage by spiraling external debt and neoliberal structural adjustments were rippling through Mexico. In Juárez and all along the border, the effects of NAFTA were also kicking in, compounded by the narco economy's shift into Mexico.[49] Many border cities were transforming from agricultural economies offering tourist services into manufacturing and assembly-for-export centers that would be major transfer points for drugs.[50] Because Juárez, unlike other cities, did not restrict sex work to a specific zone, it developed—and continues to carry—the stigma of a sexualized and perverse border town, and the weight of that stigma fell on the feminized workforce in the tourist, sex work, and maquiladora sectors.[51] By the mid-1990s the factories were thriving on the advantages of a labor surplus at the same time that the effects of several generations of women in the maquilas were pushing up against the limits of a deeply entrenched patriarchal gender system.[52]

As a sense of weakened masculinity seeped into the pores of everyday life, incidences of domestic violence increased, and institutions that would explain women's and men's changing public roles were sorely lacking.[53]

The contradiction between the economic value of women and their social devaluation has been a key factor in the violence. Although young women were initially considered the ideal workforce for the maquiladora industry, this economic value did not translate into public value, the value that endows a subject with benefits, access to resources, and justice. Moreover, the economic value of women as workers is premised upon the devaluation of their bodies and their designation as members of an unskilled, quick-turnover, disposable workforce.[54] The economic and political devaluation of women workers is compounded by their sexualization, exemplified when officials insinuate that the women who were murdered or disappeared were asking for trouble. The devaluation of women is also reflected in the organization of urban space that discounts the needs of women workers for safe transport. Most of the young women who work in the factories must travel long distances from their homes in the outlying colonias.[55] When they cross the city's public spaces, they become targets not only because they are newcomers to its institutions but also because they are traveling in the dark and on foot through dangerous streets and fields.[56] Public officials have managed the fears provoked by the murders and disappearances of young women not by making improvements in urban space and transport but by blaming the victims for inappropriately gendered behavior as girls who got what they asked for because they were out in the streets, where they did not belong.[57]

Another factor in the violence has been the push–pull between the two political economies. As work opportunities in the legal economy eroded and people's life chances dwindled, the extralegal economy grew. The state's shrinking accountability to the needs of its citizens has been a linchpin in that process and one of the hallmarks of neoliberal structural adjustments. In Juárez, as throughout Mexico, the social fabric was frayed by the state's aggressive pursuit of policies that unleashed foreign investment and the business interests of Mexico's elites. The effect amounted to the abandonment of civil society. Services like education, health care, water, and electricity have been rolled back or privatized, and services for the poor have all but evaporated. The governing political parties in the north, the PRI and the PAN, have both traditionally supported business, and their networks traverse state and private institutions, including the maquilas. In all of the border cities, a group of ruling families controls the economic and political infrastructure, some of whom are also involved in the business of the cartels, although that information circulates mostly as an open secret.[58] Now, wealthy landowners, new corporate and narco businessmen, and politicians (sometimes the same families) vie more openly for control of the trade flowing through the maquiladora transport system, U.S. customs, and large U.S. banks.

In Juárez civic neglect is sewn into labor's devaluation in a declining legal economy. There were once over three hundred factories there. With the economic downturn in 2001, many companies left for China or the south of Mexico, looking for the wider profit margin promised by even lower wage standards. The flight of so many factories pushed people closer to the edge of desperation and generated anxiety and insecurity. In 2003 one labor organizer in Juárez said the precarious labor situation at that time made organizing especially difficult: people who had jobs were afraid to question or do anything that might put their jobs in jeopardy, and those without jobs were overwhelmed by the struggle to survive. By 2009 the latest U.S. recession hit Juárez even harder, and job losses in the formal sector skyrocketed. The state protects the interests of its select propertied core and tends to wall off intervention by organized groups of citizens. This is one face of impunity. The other face is the state's abnegation of responsibility for civilian protection and policing, an abandonment that effectively sanctions the cartels' business and sovereign power. This is not surprising, as the state and the cartels are, in essence, the same actors. If this alliance lifts the mask from a corrupt democratic state, it also installs a more brutal form of governance. As Rita Laura Segato argues, the cartels operate like feudal regimes. Their violence is a ritual that announces their power over life and death. The violence creates fear, and this fear enables impunity, not the reverse.[59]

In May 2003 Rosario Acosta of the Juárez-based grassroots organization Nuestras Hijas de Regresa a Casa (Bring Our Daughters Home) spoke with me about the state's systematic abandonment of the families of the murdered and disappeared. Rosario decided to take action after her ten-year-old niece was abducted and murdered in 1997. She spoke with clarity and deliberation about the events surrounding her niece's disappearance. Occasionally, her eyes moistened when she referred to the broken lives of family members of the missing *jovencitas*. She conjured sleepless nights turned into days of desperate searching for a lost child and for information and help, and as I listened I imagined the panic and numbing feeling of having been transported into a bad dream or into someone else's life. I imagined the guilt. She spoke of that. Even before anyone officially pointed fingers or friends hinted about responsibility, questions haunted her: Why wasn't she there? Why didn't she tell her niece about this or that? Then, she mentioned the body as they found it . . . . Rosario shifted in her chair, adjusted her gaze. The veil closed over. The ghost of her niece settled into the stillness.

At first Rosario hammered away at unresponsive authorities, acting as an individual citizen advocating on behalf of her family. Then, in frustration at the lack of official attention to her niece's case, she quit her job as an accountant and helped found Nuestras Hijas. In her speeches across Mexico and the United States as a representative of the group, Rosario focused on the problems of visibility and reading.

"How one sees the situation depends on statistics, sources of information. One's perception is also conditioned by the lies," she said, "because this did not happen by chance. These events occurred within a context that does not only consist of the history of these murders."

She pointed to the "the giant puzzle of the Mexican government's impunity," the repression that amounts to a general and normalized moral abandonment, to the feeble responses of the maquiladoras, the poverty that blocks access to justice. In the face of this coordinated wall of indifference, she solicited solidarity and collective action.

The conditions of life in Juárez, however, as in many other maquila communities in Mexico, make sustained organizing difficult. Since I spoke with her that day, Rosario has left Nuestras Hijas. Internal discord in the group, like the conflicts that strain many maquila-based organizing efforts, tore at its fragile cohesion. These conflicts could be seen as predictable given the control over public discourse exercised by the government and its allies and the tension on the social fabric from so many directions.

Since the mid-1990s, organizing in support of the victims and their families—some led by the families directly, some by coalitions of allies—has gone through various stages as activists have been forced to invent new approaches in the face of government and media efforts to discredit and blame the victims or their supporters and to divide the coalitions.[60] As local nonprofit organizations rallied in support of the families, charges that some of them were profiting from their work circulated in the press and found willing believers. These allegations are not unique to this organizing effort, but they are one more reminder that conflicts over resources almost invariably feature in organizing campaigns, that resources are affectively loaded and can be manipulated to destructive ends. Internal divisions were so powerful that they have dissolved many of the local groups that once supported the murder victims and their families. By 2010 the few remaining women human rights defenders had become targets of violence. Mariesela Escobedo, a mother who sought her daughter's killer, was herself assassinated on the steps of the state capital. Shortly after her assassination, Susana Chávez, a feminist poet who was very involved in the Juárez women's movement, was found murdered with her left hand sawed off.[61]

In recent years researchers have broadened their assessment of the violence to address the high numbers of murdered men in Juárez, a toll that far exceeds the numbers of murdered women.[62] Cecilia Balli and Rita Laura Segato each read the femicides in Juárez as a hieroglyphic of masculinity in crisis in a situation where men are deeply wounded, betrayed by a city where teenagers are gunned down for no reason and gangs recruit boys as young as ten. They decode the murders and other forms of violence against women not as hate crimes per se but rather as messages sent to other men, as efforts to prove one's life has value as a man. Other important work that targets men holds accountable Mexico's entrenched patriarchal sex–gender system. The psychologist Efraín Rodríguez Ortiz, an instructor at the Autonomous University of Ciudad Juárez, has investigated the numbers of homosexuals among the murder victims, and he traces the reasons for their deaths to the deep roots of homophobia that prop up a widely shared culture of vulnerable and reactive masculinity. In collaboration with grassroots organizations in Juárez and El Paso, Kathleen Staudt has tracked this culture of hypermasculinity through the hidden numbers of domestic abuse cases among the murders, a fact that is related to the high levels of unemployment for young men, some of whom are consequently drawn into the drug business.

The militarization of the border by both the Mexican and the U.S. federal governments has intensified and promoted this culture of hypermasculinity, in which men secure their manhood through violence against women and other men.[63] Countrywide, attacks on women by army and security forces have increased as the militarization accompanying Mexico's drug war has sent the army into the streets. When military practices and weapons produce gender codes that exaggerate the patriarchal sex–gender system, a new normal is inculcated in which violence against women is the standard against which young men measure their worth. This new norm is reinforced by the glorification of hypermasculine military and paramilitary violence in the media. Girls and women suffer under its pressure, as do boys and young men.

The military presence in border cities is intense and palpable. It has been enhanced by U.S. support through the Mérida Initiative, also known as the Regional Security Cooperation Initiative, or Plan Mexico, which was approved by the U.S. Congress in 2008 and designed to send $1.4 billion in direct donations of military and intelligence equipment and training programs for Mexican law enforcement officials over three years. It was supposedly aimed at propelling the offensive against drug traffickers.[64] As U.S. assistance to fight the drug wars poured into Mexico, the numbers of killings rose. Critics of Plan Mexico argue that funding and equipping Mexican security forces in the context of growing corruption and impunity worsens the problems, reduces civil society's role in reform, and inhibits construction of democratic institutions. Certainly, with few legal or social controls, it has fostered the militarization of Mexican society.[65] As support for the war on drugs blurs into the war on terror, increased military aid has become an instrument of direct and indirect repression of political opposition and the criminalization of dissent.[66] Because the cartels are fully integrated into the economy, the state apparatus, and the criminal justice system, arms and training from the U.S. border security program move easily into their hands, making a travesty of state policing and ramping up the state of siege. Paramilitary groups on the streets are found to be using anti-tank rockets and armor-piercing munitions that are the same ones found on the battlefields of Iraq and Afghanistan.[67]

Since the beginning of Calderón's administration, the violence and the government impunity that was once considered a Juárez phenomenon has spread along the border and throughout Mexico as the cartels vie for control over trade routes running north and south, east and west. Government–cartel alliances are now pervasive and blatant. In Tamaulipas, municipal police have been so infiltrated by the cartels that their offices have been officially closed. Many people see President Calderón's installations of federal troops into border towns quite cynically as one more maneuver in the fight between warring cartels. Just as it is difficult to discern the difference between federal soldiers and narco ground troops, the lines between the two economies and governments also blur. As unemployment grows and jobs in the formal economy dry up or become increasingly precarious, people are becoming desperate. Men are unable to sustain *un proyecto de vida,* the Latin American expression for the "way of life" that a man must pursue through steady wage employment or farming. Even for those with jobs, the paltry minimum wage of five dollars a day cannot meet the high price of the basic food basket. More and more men and women are turning to informal and illegal sectors for work. It is no wonder that the cartels, who are also undergoing a transition, can so successfully recruit new members, and they do so openly, advertising on public billboards the promise that working for them will pay more than the army. As the structure of the cartels has shifted in the past ten years, the business has been outsourced on the local level, where ground troops are young men and, increasingly, women eager for dignity and work. In 2011 a resident of Nuevo Laredo reported that the narcos were hiring more and more people as informants. In one instance a young person was earning two hundred dollars a week for that job.

The drug economy has long been entangled in the history of the maquiladoras. As Julian Cardona puts it in this chapter's epigraph, "Maquiladoras-narcos-migration—that's the triangle. If you keep these things separate you'll never understand what's happening in this city."[68] The same is true of other border cities, especially Nuevo Laredo, where 40 percent of all trade between Mexico and the United States crosses the border, along with a large portion of the estimated 70 percent of the Mexican drugs consumed in the United States.[69] Until 2011 some eight thousand U.S. trucks converged daily on Laredo, Texas, to rendezvous with the same number of Mexican trucks in order to transfer payloads in freight yards ten miles inside the United States. Now, Mexican trucks can go deep into the United States without transferring their product to U.S. trucks. Nonetheless, U.S. authorities still inspect only a fraction of them. Wherever there is transport like this, a proportion of the payload will be drugs, which are included with off-the-ledger goods and waved through by officials on both sides who have been bought by the cartels.[70] Besides the containers leaving Mexico, other trucks and cars bring guns south from the United States. Illegal traffic in guns is as lucrative a component of the narco business as are drugs, and it is one of the shadow economy's main contributions to the militarization of the border.

This porous border is the prize in the Mexican cartels' competition over markets and territories. By the mid-1990s long-standing deals between the cartels and Mexico's ruling political party, the PRI, were already shifting at the same time that the new emphasis on the free market was making inroads into the PRI's administration of the corporatist model through its patronage system.[71] Since 1992, the ruling political party in Juárez has been the PAN. In the years following the PAN's national victory, an upsurge in violence was sparked by the opportunistic efforts of the Sinaloa cartel to take control of the city from the Juárez cartel that had long controlled its markets. In 2000 when the PRI was voted out of the presidency and PAN candidate Vicente Fox was voted in, ties that had begun to strain between the PRI and the cartels were broken at national, state, and local levels. Even in these changed conditions, the federal and state governments wanted to control drug traffic not to destroy it, because to destroy it would have been to lose one of the pillars of Mexico's standing in the global economy.[72] There is open conjecture that after Felipe Calderón began his term, his administration's national drug strategy was to eliminate the smaller cartels and control the big ones, and a fair amount of evidence exists of his government's collaboration, especially with the Sinaloa cartel.[73] The election of Enrique Peña Nieto in 2012 brought the PRI back into power, and his plan to overhaul Mexican law enforcement with U.S.-trained paramilitary forces threatened to make conditions actually worse.

Whereas the violence in Juárez has been in the spotlight for over a decade, cities like Reynosa and Nuevo Laredo in the state of Tamaulipas have recently had rising levels of murder and kidnapping but do not have the NGOs, research, or aid to victims and their families that descended on Juárez.[74] Tamaulipas has been governed for eighty years by the PRI, and throughout these years the party has maintained settlements with the Gulf cartel that controlled the plaza. In 2010 agreements between the Gulf cartel and its armed wing, Los Zetas, broke down when a high-ranking Zeta was murdered by the cartel. Since then, the Zetas have been at war with the Gulf and the Sinaloa cartels over control of the territory that stretches across the northern border of Tamaulipas.

Wherever they rule, the cartels now operate more overtly. The degree of control they wield is evident in the fact that many mayors and business owners in Mexican border cities have moved to the U.S. side.[75] The form of sovereignty the cartels enact mimics feudal structures and technologies. Drug lords operate through hierarchies that procure loyalty and impunity, and they do so via atrocities. They enlist *sicarios* (executioners) whose work is usually done at night. Some say many of them take drugs in order to mitigate any emotional reactions while torturing or killing. They bury the dead clandestinely, or they leave their decapitated corpses in the plaza or hang them from bridges to send the message that power operates through fear and a new form of sovereignty, necropolitics. As Valentin Mbembe has argued, necropolitics is a form of power in which the threat of violent death is a technique of governance, and wars over control of the state and its subjects are waged through the capricious determination of who dies and what forms their violent public executions take.[76] As in all rituals of terror, public displays of this power over death are evidence of a dictatorship's need to continually resecure control.

It is hard for those who do not live in border cities to imagine the degree of extreme violence and the extent to which the culture of fear it has created disrupts people's everyday options and routines. For example, the cartels declare curfews, often beginning as early as 7:00 p.m., so that at night the city streets are completely theirs. Often, they are eerily empty. If you go out of your house for any reason after curfew, you risk being shot or taken away. This means that maquila workers on the second or third shift must travel through dangerous narco-controlled streets. Some workers report that when shootouts occur while they are on their way to work, causing them to arrive late, the managers do not consider this a legitimate excuse, and so they dock their pay. People who are not working have had to change their habits. One woman who lives in Nuevo Laredo said that she now goes outside only to get groceries and go to church and that she then quickly returns home. The ruling cartel may also decide that on a particular Sunday there will be an all-day curfew, which means that no businesses can open and there can be no activity in the streets on the appointed day. Only the cartel can conduct its activities— perhaps a shootout with a warring cartel. In Valle Hermoso they may let small businesses know about this planned battle through messages conveyed in person via their networks. In other towns the shootouts occur without warning. Sometimes they hang *mantas* (banners) across the bridges or in other public places announcing the details of the latest violence. As the war between the Gulf cartel, the Zetas, and the Sinaloa cartel heated up in spring 2012, killings and disappearances in eastern Tamaulipas towns increased and convoys of men with covered faces arrived. Some had machine guns; some were in uniforms with official logos and some were not.

The cartels also control people's movements in public spaces through their police and military networks. They have set up *retenes* (checkpoints) on the edges of all the border towns and on the major roads. These are staffed by men and some women who wear uniforms resembling those of the police or federal soldiers but without badges. The federal army also has checkpoints, but they are often on roads not used by the drug traffickers. When confronted by soldiers, it is sometimes difficult or impossible to tell who you are dealing with. Are they local police, *federales,* or narcos? The narco military carry machine guns, and they stop vehicles, including buses, randomly. They get on the buses and ask the passengers to present their IDs. Sometimes, they take people away. One organizer said that when she traveled by bus from Tamaulipas to Durango in 2010, the bus was stopped six times during the trip at these *retenes* as narco soldiers with guns got on and interrogated passengers. One of those times, they removed two men, and the bus drove on without them. Now, night busses that had long been a popular option for long-distance travelers are considered by many to be too unsafe.[77]

Some incidents of violence have been publicized in the media, especially when officials are assassinated, shootouts occur at parties, or mass graves are discovered, as they were in San Fernando, Tamaulipas, where seventy-two bodies were found in 2010.[78] But many violent events in border towns never appear in the newspapers. Some are brutal and horrific, like one that took place in Nuevo Laredo in June 2011 and was reported to me by a high school student in Laredo, Texas. After their senior prom, a young couple from Laredo decided to cross to the Mexican side because recently the restaurants in Laredo had been closing early, one of the effects of the violence spilling over into the U.S. side. Members of one of the cartels came up to them in a restaurant and held a gun to the young man's head, telling him either he could give them his girlfriend to spend the night with their leader or both of them would be killed. He decided to let them take her. They told him she would be returned the next morning to the plaza on the U.S. side. He left distraught and contacted her family, and they all went to the plaza. She was indeed returned, traumatized and beaten after having been gang raped. She died in the hospital two days later. Neither she nor her boyfriend had anything to do with the cartels; their mistake was being in the wrong place at the wrong time.

This story is only one example of the sovereign power that now dominates civic life in border cities. Innocent people are routinely caught in the crossfire or disappear for reasons that are never clear, and women are often used as pawns in the traffic between men whose message is at times indecipherable. In February 2011 four decapitated bodies were dumped in the main plaza of Nuevo Laredo, and a colonel hired by the police department was killed along with his six bodyguards. In August 2010 two officials in charge of investigating the massacre of the Central American migrants in San Fernando, Tamaulipas, were found dead only days after the investigation started. In Juárez that same year, thirteen maquila workers were massacred on a bus that was taking them home after work. In the recent past horrible deeds like these have occurred many times.

The fear these incidents has generated is intensified by the violent muzzling of the media as public watchdog. Mexico has become the most dangerous country in the world for reporters. The Mexican National Human Rights Commission reports that since 2000, seventy-four journalists have been killed.[79] The Mexican media in the most violent border cities have for the most part been terrorized into silence. Several papers have closed down; others self-censor. Some, like the weekly *Zeta* in Tijuana, continue to take a courageous stance against the cartels, even though they paid dearly for it when their cofounder Héctor Miranda was murdered in 1988 and their coeditor Francisco Ortiz was killed in 2004. *El Mañana* in Nuevo Laredo, once known for taking strong positions against the cartels, no longer publishes editorials and news stories on the drug violence, because of the reprisals they have suffered. In 2004 *El Mañana*'s editorial director, Roberto Javier Mora Garcia, was knifed to death in front of his home. In January 2006 reporter Jaime Orozco Tey was critically wounded in a gun and grenade attack on the newspaper's offices. On February 6, 2008, gunmen broke into the newsroom and began firing AK-47 and AR-15 rifles, and on May 14, 2012, gunmen again attacked with gunfire and a grenade.[80]

As newspaper and television coverage has receded and the violence has accelerated, people have turned to social media like Facebook and Twitter to communicate warnings about where violence is taking place. The cartels are, however, using violent means to suppress these outlets, as well. In September 2011 in Nuevo Laredo, the mangled dead bodies of a man and a woman were found hanging from the international bridge right outside the colonia Blanca Navidad. The woman was topless, hog-tied, and disemboweled. Posters found with the bodies contained messages mentioning two blogs and demanding that users of social media stop reporting drug-related crimes. According to CNN reporter Catherine Shoichet, the network "tried unsuccessfully to get information about the grisly murders at the local, state, and federal levels. Officials were either unavailable or unwilling to release any information about the killings."[81] Two weeks later, the body of the editor of a Nuevo Laredo newspaper, *Primera Hora,* was found decapitated at the foot of a monument. It is believed that she was murdered because of her reporting on an anticrime website.[82] She was the eleventh journalist murdered or disappeared in 2011. In Reynosa the previous year, eight journalists were killed within two weeks.[83] Some Mexican newspapers continue to run graphic photos of the violence, and yet many media stories and reports retain a level of abstraction that protects the perpetrators and cultivates a culture of fear.[84] When the violence itself dominates the public narrative, what remains out of sight is the link between the cartels' ability to recruit and control and the corrupt elites at the helm of a transnational political economy that thrives on the ruined lives of so many. Nonetheless, in these impossible conditions some Mexican and U.S.-based journalists have done courageous work in the battle for Mexico's civic life in border cities, among them Adela Navarro Bello, Charles Bowden, Francisco Ortiz Franco (murdered in 2004), Héctor Félix Miranda (murdered in 1988), Sergio González Rodríguez, Sam Quinones, and Diana Washington.

Organizing in the War Zone

Without question, the networks of intercommunity and cross-border collaboration that sprang from the earlier phases of the labor movement in northern Mexico have been affected now that key border cities are in the hands of organized crime. In cities that once had fledgling independent labor movements and small but growing grassroots efforts to address needs for water, health care, and education, the organizing strategies have had to change. The forces that have traditionally deterred labor organizing—the companies, the official unions, and the government—are still in place, but they have been overshadowed by the narcos' power. Where fear itself is an encroaching civic death, some workers refuse to give in or to give up their struggle. They face new challenges, though, and have had to devise new tactics.

Two labor campaigns in Tamaulipas that have continued even during the rise in violence are those of the Key Safety Systems (KSS) workers, who assemble seat belts and airbags in Valle Hermoso, and the TRW auto parts assembly workers in Reynosa. Valle Hermoso is a small town a short distance southwest of the coastal city of Mata-moros. Formerly an agricultural community that produced corn and sorghum, it is now a town in decline. When the factories arrived in the 1980s, people migrated from the rural areas. When the farming communities deteriorated further as credit support for farming dried up, migration increased. In the wake of the economic recession of 2000, the flood of emigrants to the United States from rural areas and the town crested, leaving houses and farms abandoned. With its high unemployment, Valle Hermoso is a fertile recruiting ground for the cartels, and now the city is a nest for narcos. As in many other border cities, huge oversized houses, or "narco mansions," line the main road into town; black SUVs with tinted windows are parked outside them. Their anomaly is an open secret. Although the east–west highway between Matamoros and Reynosa is lined with federal soldiers and their checkpoints, none of them are on the road to Valle Hermoso. Even in this narco stronghold, however, labor organizing by maquiladora workers goes on.

Beginning in 2007, the KSS workers in Valle Hermoso organized to improve their unsafe working conditions and low salaries. Although KSS workers assemble automotive safety equipment for a global supplier, working conditions at the plant have been toxic; workers' babies have been born with birth defects, and women workers have had miscarriages. On one assembly line there was one chair for nine people, and workers have not been given basic safety equipment like goggles and earplugs. So they formed a workers' coalition and mo-bilized to expose the complicity between the company and the labor authorities. KSS has a code of conduct that asserts, "We recognize and respect employee rights to join or not join any lawful organiza-tion of their own choosing," but as invariably happens, those who organized the coalition were fired.[85]

The problem of narco violence is now on the list of topics that the KSS and other workers in the region suggest for organizing workshops, but fear has provoked debate on how to address it. Some workers are reluctant to openly speak about the violence because they are afraid of the narco informants, who are everywhere, and they are concerned that a workshop discussion of the violence might unwittingly endanger themselves and their *compañeros.* Others say it is the most pressing issue in their daily lives and should be a part of their strategizing, but in a way that makes clear that the narcos per se are not the root of the problem.

In the sprawling, dusty city of Reynosa, about forty-five minutes northwest of Valle Hermoso and across the border from McAllen, Texas, the TRW workers have been organizing since 2009 to protest the company's forced relocation of their jobs—its strategy for downsizing the plant without having to pay workers their severance payment and a practice that is in violation of the labor law. In 2010 the workers began to hold their organizing meetings on Sunday mornings, a time when those responsible for the narco violence in Reynosa are sleeping and there is a little opening for public life. Roughly 140 factories are in Reynosa, and like Nuevo Laredo, it has become a war zone in the battle among the Gulf and Sinaloa cartels and the Zetas. Despite the potential danger of occupying public spaces, TRW workers have held demonstrations in the plaza and in front of the labor board, and they have traveled to the state capital to demand justice in their case from the governor. On November 2, 2010, they celebrated the Day of the Dead with a public march in which they carried a coffin representing the symbolic burial of impunity, corruption, and complicity by the government, the TRW corporation, and the CTM. For two years on May 1, International Labor Day, the TRW workers decided to parade, but the CTM said there would be no march, because of the threat of violence. The workers marched anyway, and the CTM was pressured to hold its own parade. On Labor Day 2011, the workers again declared they would hold an independent march, and again the CTM was pressured to hold their march. In August 2011 the TRW workers solicited public support for their case by holding a vigil in the plaza of Reynosa. When a bomb went off, they sought shelter in the church. As the murder toll in Reynosa rises, they continue to mobilize for their rights.

One organizer says that she asked the people of one colonia in Tamaulipas in 2011 what they needed and what mattered most to them. Their answers revealed the degree to which the narco economy and its sovereignty had penetrated people's lives and set their visions of the future. They said that first they needed jobs because many who used to work in the factories had been laid off and now the cartels controlled even the informal economy. People who once sold food or other goods in the streets could no longer do so, or if they did, they had to pay bribes to the cartels and risk being caught up in their violence. Next, they wanted to be safe and to restore their former community life. They saw the education of the next generation as the key to a better future. They recognized that this future was in the hands of their children and that they did not want them to grow up to be *sicários* (killers). Right now, however, this job seems to be the only one on the horizon.

One Saturday in 2010, a labor organizing workshop being held in Reynosa was interrupted by gunshots in the street outside. The children, there with their parents, immediately fell to the floor, a practice they had been taught in school. The ability to react swiftly to the ever-present possibility of a shootout is a new reflex all residents practice. The fear provoked by the violent regime now in power on the border adds layers of terror to other dangers. It compounds the risks, narrows the opportunities for collective strategizing, and potentially silences those who might otherwise speak out. On December 27, 2011, a woman organizer in Valle Hermoso was in front of a funeral home where she was attending services for the mother of a fellow worker. When a group of men jumped out of a truck and began harassing the women gathered there, she confronted them verbally. They grabbed her, pulled her into the truck, and sped away. When her parents pursued information about her whereabouts and followed a tip that led them to another town, they too disappeared.

In the northern arm of the state of Tamaulipas, civic life has been overtaken by the cartels. Some estimate that a third of the population works for the cartels in some way, many as informants. People who have lost loved ones are at a loss for ways to combat this outlaw sovereignty. Many are too afraid to even talk about what might be done. Nonetheless, some women and men are meeting clandestinely and strategizing how to break through the fear and the impunity. Some grassroots groups continue their sustainable food and energy projects. Their resolve echoes the words of the worker quoted in the chapter epigraph.[86] Much has changed since he was interviewed in 1975 in one of the first reports on the abuses of the Mexican factory system. However, the determination to act in the face of fear that propelled worker uprisings in the early days of labor organizing on the border still burns in the hearts and minds of a few who carry on that legacy and for whom "nothing is impossible."

« 2 »

The Materiality of Affect

Affect: The Last Colony

Over the past decade or so, scholarship on affect has proliferated to the point that the trend some call the "affective turn" is already being considered passé.[1] Why all of this attention to affect? One answer is history. In the past fifty years, as capitalism has profoundly invaded the human organism and harnessed the productive powers of life, the human capacity for affect has been raided by the global media, advertising, entertainment, care, and service industries as a lucrative vehicle for profit making. It is fair to say that affects and their expression in cultural scripts are capital's last colony. The affective turn in research is both a symptom and a response to this invasion. Because these historical developments are far from dissipating, we need to have a better critical handle on them. Instead of dismissing affect studies as a passing academic fad, we should pursue a more robust understanding of the investments in affect and their role in organized efforts to devise alternative ways of life. This chapter is a step in that direction.

The most prominent theories of affect have addressed it as a corporeal intensity that confounds the split in Western knowledge between mind and emotion, language and social relations. Nonetheless, as Clare Hemmings contends, I think rightly, some culture theorists have turned to affect because it appears to provide a remedy to the political vacuity that settled over the academy in the late twentieth century. Her point is that in developing a critical vocabulary to better understand this incorporation of affect and resistance to it, what we need is not more attention to affect per se but analyses that do not abstract it from material history.[2]

Decades before the recent affective turn, feminists were contesting the trivializing of feelings and emotion that the empiricist tradition had imprinted upon the disciplining of knowledge. As early as 1973, the sociologist Arlie Russell Hochschild called for a sociology of emotion and feeling, and she went on to theorize emotion work (1979) and to investigate the commodification of feeling in her landmark study *The Managed Heart* (1983), which probes the commercialization of feelings in the rising service industry. During those years other marxist and socialist feminists were also disrupting the separation of mind and emotion in Western knowledge. In her pioneering book *Knowledge and Passion* (1980) and her 1984 path-breaking essay "Toward an Anthropology of Self and Feeling," anthropologist Michelle Rosaldo puts forward affect as corporeal and culturally informed cognition. "Emotions," she argues, "are thoughts somehow 'felt' in flushes, pulses, 'movements' of our livers, minds, hearts, stomachs, skin. They are *embodied* thoughts, thoughts seeped with the apprehension that 'I am involved.' "[3] She affirms that what individuals *can* think and feel is a product of socially organized modes of action and talk. By the 1980s the importance of emotion to the making of knowledge had become a major theme in feminist thought as feminists continued to break open the Western equation of emotion with all things female and dangerous and elaborated lessons gleaned from their struggles in social movements, from the practice of consciousness raising and from women's entry into the professions. Audre Lorde's 1981 groundbreaking essay "The Uses of the Erotic" claims the value of emotions as a critical resource in everyday life. Like Gloria Anzaldúa in *Borderlands/La Frontera* (1987), she tackles the lived intensity of abjection for lesbians and women of color. Lila Abu-Lughod's 1986 study of Bedouin women's use of poetic conventions to manage conflicting emotions discloses the ways emotion is culturally scripted and coded rather than spontaneously expressed. She and Catherine Lutz were among a growing number of feminist anthropologists, including Nancy Scheper-Hughes and Ruth Behar, whose work over the next decade critiqued Western assumptions regarding the naturalness of emotion. Among these feminist innovators, socialist and marxist feminists from Canada, France, Germany, Italy, the United Kingdom, and the United States recognized emotion as vital to social reproduction and theorized its integration into analysis of everyday life under capitalism.[4]

Though I argue that this feminist line of thought provides the least partial approach to affect, there are, in fact, multiple materialist approaches with varied and contesting understandings of what is meant by "affect." Some have ancient roots in European classical and Enlightenment traditions. Others have been more recently generated within anthropology, sociology, psychology, phenomenology, culture theory, and feminist and queer studies. Even to carve out the historical materialist approaches in this archive confronts us with a considerable body of work: from the writings of the great seventeenth-century Portuguese philosopher Baruch Spinoza to those of Karl Marx and Western Marxists, including thinkers like Alexandra Kollontai, Walter Benjamin, Theodor Adorno, Herbert Marcuse, Wilhelm Reich, Klaus Holzkamp and the Free University of Berlin group, as well as many marxist and socialist feminists.

The upsurge of interest in affect has included several approaches that draw upon these materialist traditions. Some of that work devotes considerable attention to Spinoza, whose monumental *Ethics* was also a major touchstone for the French philosophers Michel Foucault and Gilles Deleuze, who adapted Spinoza's interventions into the Enlightenment tradition, as have the Italian philosopher Antonio Negri and his U.S. collaborator Michael Hardt. Foucault and Deleuze broke away from historical materialism, and in some respects Hardt and Negri have as well, as they inserted the body into what might be considered a post-Marxist materialist approach to affect.

Other intellectuals less directly engaged with historical materialism opened important new problematics for theorizing the materiality of affect. Sylvan Tompkins's extensive investigation of affect intervened in the cognitive and behavioral approaches that dominated psychology in the mid-twentieth-century United States. His research profoundly influenced Eve Sedgwick's work on shame, which in turn opened new lines of inquiry on affect for other queer theorists, among them Jasbir Puar and Sara Ahmed, as well as Lauren Berlant and the Public Feelings network she helped organize.[5]

In this chapter I consider some of the contributions to affect theory that elaborate what is meant by its materiality. Ultimately, my aim is to build upon the insights of historical materialist and feminist work in this tradition in order to assess the role of affect in the practice of organizing. The majority of organizers whom I met in Mexico were not familiar with materialist theories or marxist feminism, but I think that this standpoint, which addresses affect as a feature of the struggle for justice and of capitalism's dependence on devalued labor in the market and the home, much of it the labor of women, is a perspective that they would find echoes their own good sense.

Framing the Feeling Body

In general, recent theories of affect identify it as a human capacity that underscores the impossibility of any neat separation of body, mind, and emotion.[6] The neurobiologist Antonio Damasio's widely reviewed and very accessible book *Looking for Spinoza: Joy, Sorrow, and the Feeling Brain* is an instance of this argument. Damasio brings together his background in neurobiology and his fascination with Spinoza's philosophy to trace the regulatory systems that enable organisms to survive and maintain their integrity in a state of well-being. He draws upon Spinoza's radical alternative to the neglect of emotion that came to dominate modernity and furthers his understanding of "the affections of the body by which the body's power of acting is increased or diminished, helped or hindered, and at the same time, the ideas of these affections."[7] What Damasio ultimately calls "affect" refers to the dynamic interaction between what he terms "emotions" and "feelings." Emotions play out in the theater of the body and are part of the basic mechanism of maintaining homeostasis, or the automated regulation of life processes, and of behaviors associated with pain or pleasure that constitute drives like hunger, thirst, exploration, play, and sex (31–35). In Damasio's terms emotions are responses to stimuli that provoke action, and they include joy, sorrow, fear, pride, shame, and sympathy. They occur in the body under the guidance of the brain but without conscious knowledge. When the consequences of emotional reactions are mapped back onto the brain, they become what he calls "feelings." Feelings play out in the theater of the mind; they are involved in life regulation but at a higher level than the drives. Feelings guide deliberate action like choices about self-preservation.

Damasio maintains that emotions and feelings are so intimately related along a continuous process that we think of them as one single thing, but he posits feelings as functionally distinct because their essence consists of the thoughts that represent the body. They translate the body's ongoing life state into the language of the mind (85). They are perceptions supported by the brain's body maps. He stresses that without the brain and its life-regulating mechanism that causes reactions such as emotions and appetites, there would be no feeling (111). A feeling of emotion is an idea of the body when it is perturbed by emotional process. Important to note, alongside these perceptions of the body are perceptions of thoughts with certain themes, or a style of mental processing (85–86).

Elaborating upon Spinoza, Damasio takes as primary the affects of joy or pleasure and sorrow or pain. Joy maps greater ease in the body's capacity to act, whereas sorrow maps a body state cut off from the tendency to self-preservation. Joy is the transition to a state of greater power and freedom to act. An organism's maps of sorrow correspond to disequilibrium or a less than optimal coordination of life functions (138). Feelings can be our sentinels, letting our conscious selves know about the current state of the organism. They are "witnesses to life on the fly . . . mental manifestations of balance and harmony, of disharmony and discord" (139). They testify to our state of life (140).

Damasio acknowledges that Spinoza's view of the human organism is preoccupied with self-preservation, but he also notes that Spinoza recognizes achieving equilibrium is a virtue precisely because "in our inalienable need to maintain ourselves we must of necessity help preserve *other* selves. If we fail to do so we perish" (171). This insight of Spinoza's corresponds to the basic premise of historical materialism—that is, survival depends on social relations to produce what is needed or, in Spinoza's terms, "the reality of a social structure and the presence of other living organisms in a complex system of interdependence."[8] Spinoza understands that humans coexist as social creatures who can procure what they need much more easily by mutual help and that they can avoid the dangers that threaten them everywhere only by joining forces.[9]

Despite his endorsement of Spinoza's recognition that affects are bound to the cooperative maintenance of social life, Damasio does not give much attention to the impact of social relations on the organism. He also does not address the ways social relations are related to the development of certain themes in our thoughts or the transmission of emotion and feeling into cultural practices. His theory of affect does align, however, with approaches that see affect as embodied emotion or feeling in an organism whose existence depends on cooperative activities.

Other recent theories of affect also trouble the body–mind dichotomy, but some emphatically ground affect in corporeal matter or energy that is autonomous from history and social life. The most often-cited example of this approach is the work of Brian Massumi. His essay "The Autonomy of Affect" (1992) calls upon culture theory to return to the body and to do so by attending to affect, an argument that would later become the core of his book *Parables of the Virtual* (2002). Like Gilles Deleuze, Massumi contends that affect is a corporeal intensity "filled with motion, vibratory motion, resonation, a non-conscious, never-to-be-conscious autonomic remainder."[10] When Massumi asserts that affect "is asocial but not presocial," he draws the line that establishes the autonomy of affect. He acknowledges that affect includes social features, but these are mixed with elements belonging to other levels of functioning and combined according to a logic he calls "quantum logic." The quantum logic of affect consists of mutually exclusive pathways of action and expression, or tendencies, that are never completely actualized; they exist only as potentials (92). On the biological level quantum logic signals a margin of undecidability that accompanies both perception and affect as the organism chooses among possible pathways of action and expression. On the human level that undecidability is embedded in the structure of language and ideas. On the political level it appears as resistance, what Massumi identifies as "the specter of crisis haunting capitalist economies" (98). For Massumi this quantum logic is not a metaphor. It is an objective indeterminacy. "The quantum is productive of effective reality," he asserts. Indeed, affect and its quantum logic of indeterminacy are for Massumi the fundamental material of life (98). Even more boldly, he announces, "Affect is the whole world"

(105). When he claims that affect is autonomous, however, Massumi means that much of it remains an unassimilable something that is not actualized by any cultural script. He calls this domain of the unassimilable remainder the "virtual." It is all that remains unactualized, inseparable from but unassimilated into any particular, functional knowledge (96).

Massumi's characterization of affect as bodily sensation that exceeds what is actualized through language has some features that I want to retain. In elaborating on his work in her research on AIDS activism, Deborah Gould pursues this tack. She reminds us that we often experience our feelings as opaque to ourselves, as something we cannot fully grasp or do not quite have language for, a "bodily, sensory inarticulate, nonconscious experience."[11] In figuring out what we feel, "we draw from culturally available labels and meanings and from our habits and experiences through which a gesture or linguistic naming that 'expresses' what we are feeling emerges."[12] In the process a transformation occurs, "a reduction of an unstructured and unrepresented affective state with all of its potential into an emotion or emotions whose qualities are conventionally known and fixed. Language and conventionalized body gestures thus in a sense 'capture' affect or attempt to."[13] Like Massumi, Gould stresses that every capture of affect coincides with an escape. Due to that escape, a certain potential accompanies the processes through which affect takes determinate form within culture.[14]

How can we more fully understand the materiality of this potential? Massumi conceptualizes the materiality of the intriguing *something* that gets lost when affect is translated into representation as the virtual essence of the quantum. We can see the implications of this version of the material if we compare Massumi's quantum logic with Raymond Williams's often cited formulation "structures of feeling," which echoes some of the same vocabulary, but with a difference. Quantum physics does indeed open our understanding of the properties of matter to its subatomic activity, and as a result it throws into question many of the presuppositions underlying modern notions of objective measurement, perception, form, and substance. It is also an ongoing field of debate. Massumi rightly foregrounds the body as one dimension of social life that had been suppressed in modernity, but in claiming that affect in all of its quantum logic is the ur-substance of physical, biological, and human life and in asserting that affect in late capitalism is a "real condition as infrastructural as a factory" (108), he collapses different social systems into one another and eliminates history in the equation. The indeterminacy of quantum physics at the biological level is not the same as indeterminacy at the social and political levels.

Like Massumi, Williams too is interested in that area of culture "at the very edge of semantic availability" that is felt as "an unease, a stress, a displacement, a latency."[15] What distinguishes them is what Williams emphasizes and Massumi does not: in the social and political life that comprises history, the meeting of survival needs takes place through social relations that are structured, contested, and mutable. Modes of production and power regimes are organized to the advantage of some and the disadvantage of many. This unequal and contradictory social relation persists as a fundamental structure of capital and also as a site of struggle within it, and for that reason this social relation is unstable and open to change. The bodily sensations and feelings that are a part of this social relation are indeed indeterminate in that affects follow multiple pathways of sensation—some readily expressed, some only potentials—but the ontology, or existence, of this indeterminacy is grounded in the historical organization of the social relations that support life. These relations set the terms of the ecologies and economies, themes and conventions that define the possibilities for intelligible expression and enable the brain's body maps of sensation. Many of these conventions insist upon closure or the determinacy that supports the maintenance of an established order, even though human systems of interdependence are complex, debated, and resisted and often do not fit within established norms. Affective capacities are socially disciplined to comply with prevailing norms, but they also attach to potentials and expressions that defy regulation. It is in this sense that they are indeterminate.

Although Massumi acknowledges capitalism as a social reality and implies that it has a negative impact on life and well-being, he does not address how its inequitable social relations impact affective potential or how that intensity features in the struggle over resources and meanings. Ultimately, his notion of the virtual splits the pairing of emotion and feeling that Spinoza and Damasio stress is integral. For Massumi, affect operates according to quantum logic, while emotion in his lexicon pertains to a different order, one that is closer to what Damasio calls "feeling"—the conventional, consensual point of intensity's insertion into narrative, function, and meaning.[16] Massumi is not interested, however, in the process of selection that takes place as affective intensity accompanies the collective process of meeting survival needs. His attention is on affect's virtual, asocial character, which in his scheme keeps it always just out of reach. As a shadow that accompanies perception, affect is virtual in that it is un-actualized, unknowable, and resistant to critique. The problem with reducing affect to an autonomous, inchoate force is that it becomes an ethereal abstraction, its historical materiality removed from the grasp of critical assessment. Consequently, although his work re-directs culture theory away from its preoccupation with language to attend to corporeal intensities, Massumi's concept of the virtual forecloses analysis of the very thing we need to better understand: the relation between felt sensations and the limits of their articula-tion. This relation is precisely what constitutes affect-culture as a site of struggle, of capital investment and resistance.[17]

Sylvan Tompkins is another major theorist of affect who insists on its autonomy, but for him this autonomy operates within, not outside, a social-communication loop. Tompkins posits affect as the "primary innate biological motivating mechanism" that works in tandem with other mechanisms in the biosocial system.[18] He argues that affective response is similar to but not the same as other responses (e.g., pain or pleasure), whose duration and impact it amplifies and extends. Affect lends its power to memory, to perception, to thought, and to action no less than to the drives (7). It makes one care by feeling, for without the amplification of affect, nothing matters (70). Tompkins believes there are basic cross-cultural, universal affects: joy, interest, and shame. Only the rules, norms, and habits through which people manage their emotional expressions vary across cultures (15). Tomp-kins borrows his logic of affect from systems theory—namely, the notion that the basic principle of a system is the distinction between an inside (the system) and an outside (environment), as well as the establishment of a feedback loop that takes in the result of an act in order to modify it. The thermostat is an example of a feedback mechanism by which a system modifies itself. Affects function like a thermostat. They reduce information loads, focus attention, and amplify emotional responses—for example, in sensing danger, managing loss, or responding to a smile (15–16).

In his brilliant study of melancholia and modernism, Jonathan Flatley draws upon Tompkins's theory, as well as Freud's insights on the affective relationality of transference, and Walter Benjamin's concept of history in order to formulate an argument for the critical value of assessing the social forces shaping affective responses, a practice he calls "affective mapping." In the following chapter, I discuss the close relationship of affective mapping to the dislocating process of bearing witness.[19] Like Tompkins, Flatley argues that affect has an irreducible systematicity.[20] But unlike Massumi, he emphasizes that affects connect us to the world, traveling along the material specificities of objects until they find a place to dwell. They resist representation, however, and strictly speaking cannot be repressed; they can attach to unconscious ideas, but they will always look for a way out.[21] They operate in their own temporality, as well, meaning they can recur over and over in symptoms or dreams, for example, but each time they can seem to be appearing for the first time. For Flatley emotions are the result of the interaction of affects with thoughts, ideas, beliefs, habits, and instincts. Following Flatley, I preserve this conception of affect's semiautonomy and its adhesion to cultural forms, including emotions, objects, and practices, and it is in this sense that I use the term "affect-culture."

So far I have established that affects are material in that they are corporeal intensities transposed into emotions and feelings that are in turn inflected by the social relations that shape a culture's meaning-making system. But several questions remain. In what sense are these affective intensities and the social forces that shape them part of the collective process of meeting human needs under capitalism? If affective intensities are inserted into cultural forms, are they marshaled by ideology? Always? How can we assess affective intensities that hover on the edges of conventional meaning making or that get inserted into counternarratives going against the grain of convention?

In her provocative study of affect, Teresa Brennan offers the beginning of an answer in recognizing that affects are closely bound to the social forces that enable the human organism's survival. The affects are thickened and the heart sealed, she tells us, when there are real threats to living, such as hunger, homelessness, and grief. These threats give rise to anxieties that undermine peace of mind, as do the related demands of unpurposeful work, which leave the body unrested and prey to passing negative affects. For Brennan, affects are physiological shifts, surges of passion that accompany a judgment.[22] They have an energetic dimension known to us through the drives and rarely simply as energy. Like Damasio, she understands the drives to be automated and conscious processes that regulate the organism and meet its survival needs. Like Massumi, she sees affects as carriers of energy (34). For Brennan, though, they are not autonomous or asocial. Articulated into feelings, affects have a continued bearing on the body's ability to regulate itself and, hence, on survival. Like Damasio and Spinoza, she understands affect to be a significant component of the process of meeting individual and collective human survival needs, and it features as such in what she calls its "transmission."

Brennan maintains that a cultural zone exists in which meaning (Damasio's "feeling" or Massumi's "emotion") emerges from the organism's capacity for bodily intensities and its perception and reception of the bodily intensities of others. The transmission of affect is a process that is social in origin but biological and physical in effect. It underscores that we are not self-contained, that there is no secure distinction between the individual and the environment (6). The notion of the transmission of affect was, she tells us, once common knowledge, but it faded from scientific explanation as the concept of the biologically determined individual came to the fore, severing the knowing subject from her body and the individual from the surrounding environment and other individuals in it (19). The alternative epistemology of affect that she resurrects affirms that affect can be transmitted between bodies, experienced, and then read or articulated as a feeling, though some affects are not readily namable. Music provides an example of how the intense impingement of sensations on the body can mean more to people than they can articulate. Because it is unformed and unstructured, affect is transmittable in ways that feelings and emotions are not, and because it is transmittable between the lines of conventional discourse, it is such a potentially powerful social force.[23]

Brennan argues that affects are experienced as immediate, as a pressure seeking instant release or expression, and this immediacy can feel like a form of possession or energy that is not necessarily a positive guide to action. Negative affects can be redirected through the critical examination of one's passions, a practice that can lead to the gradual overcoming of those passions through intelligent thinking.[24] Brennan's insights regarding the ability to discern negative affects and redirect them toward more life-sustaining energies have significant implications for the role of affect in organizing, and I return to them in the following chapter.

Several other theoretical projects have pursued the social interface of affects from perspectives that acknowledge their relation to material history. Lawrence Grossberg's *We Gotta Get Out of This Place*, published the same year as Massumi's 1992 essay, is concerned with the affective and ideological features of popular culture. He is interested in affect not as matter but rather in relation to what *matters* to so many people. He draws upon Massumi's work and agrees that affect is a prepersonal intensity that is not structured narratively. Affect for Grossberg comes to have form and structure, however, because its energy binds individuals to practices.[25] He contends that affects are articulated and disarticulated according to what he calls "mattering maps," which direct people's investments. They tell people when, where, how, and with what intensities they can become absorbed in the world and in their lives. In other words, mattering maps locate what matters (6).

Grossberg inserts "affect" into cultural studies as the missing term in a more adequate understanding of how and why ideology is sometimes—and only sometimes—effective, always to varying degrees (82). The notion of affective investment punctuates his analysis, and it is a point of contention between Massumi's model and his. For Massumi there can be no investment of affect, because it remains virtually inaccessible. Though Grossberg does at times collapse the distinction between affect (or in Damasio's sense, the emotions of embodied intensity) and feeling (as the conventional representation of this intensity), his work is an important effort to address the ways affects are marshaled in cultural forms and serve as a bonding glue in ideological ones. In his terms, affective investment in particular ideological sites endows them with motivating power. It is this affective component that also enables ideology to be so powerfully internalized and naturalized (83). But while affect "greases the wheels of ideology," it can also gum them up.[26]

Grossberg's use of the metaphor "internalized" suggests a chain of relations that link representations, subjects, and subjectivities to a felt sense of belonging. Indeed, it may be fair to say that the sense of belonging is a crucial component of a mattering map. Moreover, for Grossberg "the sites of people's investments operate as so many languages which construct their identity" (84). Mattering maps connect sites of investment; they define the possibilities for moving from one investment to another and for linking fragments of identity together (84).

Grossberg also emphasizes that daily life always involves the inseparable articulation of ideology and pleasure, and this articulation is a site of struggle within and over the affective plane, "for it is in their affective lives that people constantly struggle to care about something and to find the energy to survive, to find the passion necessary to imagine and enact their own projects and possibilities" (83). Though his analysis inserts affect into history, its focus is primarily on affective investments in ideological narratives and their articulations. Moreover, while he raises the issue of need, the materiality of affect in his analysis is only loosely related to how needs are met.

More recently, feminist theorist Sarah Ahmed has put forward an argument for affect as social and material. Although Ahmed also does not relate the materiality of affect to the meeting of human needs, she is interested in how affects and emotions do things through their circulation. In this respect the material of affect is, for her, exclusively cultural. Unlike Massumi, Ahmed contends that affect is not autonomous from culture but conveyed and even formed through the movement of signs. She argues that affective value accumulates as an effect of the circulation and repetition of certain signs and through the movement between signs. She emphasizes that affect does not reside positively in the sign; rather, it is produced as an effect of its circulation.[27] The more that certain affectively laden signs circulate, the more they appear to contain affect.[28] Ahmed's attention to what she calls "affective economies" does not readily explain the relation between the economy of labor and culture, nor does she distinguish affect from emotion—rather, at times she collapses them into each other. Nonetheless, her work makes several valuable contributions. She attends to affect as social and psychic material that works through signs to align individuals with communities, and she underscores that the accumulation of affective value shapes "the surfaces of bodies and worlds."[29] In this regard her insights extend our understanding of affect as a component of culture and the relational nature of social life. As she writes, affects and emotions work by sticking figures together, and it is their stickiness that binds associations (of signs and individuals) and consolidates identities.

What I am calling "affect-culture" draws upon insights from each of these theories. Affect-culture is the transmission of sensation and cognitive emotion through cultural practices. I would underscore, however, that the materiality of affect-culture is inflected by the social relations through which needs are met and produced. One of the ways this inflection takes place is in the circulation of cultural narratives that are themselves sites of struggle as they encode the mythologies that reproduce dominant power relations and alternative narratives that question or reinvent them. In other words, the signifying chains and narratives of affect-culture are unstable because they include both ideologically sanctioned material and what Alison Jaggar calls "outlaw emotions."[30] As Ahmed reminds us, reiterated affectively laden signs in the circulation of cultural narratives are inscribed on "the surfaces of bodies and worlds," or in Grossberg's more humanist terms, they are internalized in a sense of oneself. In other words, affect-infused narratives produce social subjects, and they do so within and against the structured relations for meeting human needs.

Although William Reddy's *The Navigation of Feeling* also does not explicitly address the interface of needs and emotion, he does offer a conceptual logic that echoes my understanding of affect-culture's role in the disciplining of subjects through normative emotional regimes.[31] Drawing upon research on emotion by cognitive psychologists and anthropologists, Reddy proposes that emotions are a part of a series of cross-modality transfers involved in the process of meaning making that might be characterized as translation between and among sensory modalities, procedural habits, and linguistic structures. As a metaphor, "translation" captures what cognitive psychologists have identified as the links between emotions and goal setting. Deeply integrated goals are sustained by overlearned cognitive habits involving many mappings. Working through intense emotions (grief, shame, anxiety) is a process of changing those deeply integrated goals. Translation consists of what Reddy calls a combination of "activated thought material" and "attention." Any individual is at any one time confronted with an enormous number of translation tasks, each involving sensory input, memory, habits, and codes, many of which are incomplete and indeterminate. In order to achieve a goal, some of these tasks must be carried out while others remain undone or fragmented. Emotion is a "range of loosely connected thought material, formulated in various codes, that has goal-relevant valence and intensity that may constitute a schema (or a set of loosely connected schemas, or fragments of schemas) that when activated exceeds attention's capacity to translate it into action or talk in a short time."[32] Here, in the failure that accompanies emotion, affects feature as interesting and potent components of politics. Though Reddy does not speak to the distinction between affect and emotion, affect can be thought of as a set of transversal intensities accompanying the sensory and cognitive modalities of the thought material that emotional expression navigates and as a part of the excess that escapes attention's ability to capture.

Reddy proposes a way to more fully understand the dynamic interrelation between social norms and individual expression and behavior that situates emotion in the open-ended interplay of the various schemas that comprise thought material. He charts the textual evidence of what he calls "emotives" or speech acts that have an exploratory and self-altering effect on the activated thought material of emotion (unlike performatives like "I declare!" or "I hereby enact" that make things happen or constatative utterances that describe).[33]

He uses "navigate" to convey the process by which individuals and a community set goals and emotional behavior in relation to pre-scribed emotive norms. "Navigate" suggests the potential for move-ment among possibilities in the thought material that can lead toward changed goals. His analysis of the value of emotives and emotional regimes to politics offers a much fuller understanding of what had been referred to as emotional "expression" and "internal-ization," and it discloses the ways navigation of the emotives of a normative regime may entail identifications as well as the irruption of far-reaching life-course changes.

Affect-Culture in Organized Resistance

Though they would not necessarily claim to be working within a historical and materialist framework, a considerable number of social movement scholars have begun to tackle the transmission of affect when individuals mobilize to act collectively. Sociologists of social movement have been taking research on emotion seriously since the 1980s.[34] Some of that research recognizes that attention to emotion was a foundational component of second-wave feminism, especially as it featured in the practice of consciousness raising.[35] Recent work in cultural studies has also addressed affect as a facet of politics and public feelings.[36] Since the 1990s, social movement research has paid attention to the varied ways affect features in sustaining a collec-tive.[37] Notable among this work is the sociologist Deborah Gould's outstanding study of the affective ontology of the AIDS Coalition to Unleash Power (ACT UP). Gould's analysis of a movement in which she was herself deeply engaged and that was thoroughly saturated by ambivalence, anger, shame, grief, and finally despair demonstrates why affect matters. The core concept in her analysis of the changing affective contexts of ACT UP is drawn from Pierre Bourdieu's theory of the habitus. According to Bourdieu, the habitus is the common-sensical understanding that structures individual and group practice. By the "emotional habitus" of a movement, Gould means "a social grouping's collective and only partly conscious emotional disposi-tions" toward certain feelings and ways of emoting.[38] Gould under-scores that the emotional habitus of a group is both acquired (social) and nonconscious. Her detailed narration of the shifting emotional habitus of ACT UP is a rich and informative history.

Though I did not study a single group like ACT UP, I return to the concept of emotional habitus as useful for elaborating the material relations in which affect-culture is entangled when structures of feeling resonate in the identity formations of relations of labor and organized resistance. Jonathan Flatley refers to such a habitus in broader terms as "mood," and likewise, he asserts that any political project must have the "making and using" of mood as part and parcel of its goals, for "no matter how clever and correct the critique or achievable the project, collective action is impossible if people are not, so to speak, *in the mood.*"[39]

Theories of affect as a component of organized resistance have also been influenced by the work of Michael Hardt and Antonio Negri on affective labor and the commons. Hardt and Negri's *Empire* trilogy is a cogent philosophical and political assessment of capital's increasing appropriation of bodies and nature and an argument for recovering them. Their attention to affect is related to the political aim of reclaiming natural and human resources from capitalism's ravaging grasp, and in this regard their books echo grassroots efforts around the world, many of them shaped by women's organizing. In order to come to grips with the place of affect in their argument, we first need to briefly consider some of the concepts on which it is premised. Here are three of them: *biopower,* or the power over life; *biopolitical value,* or the power of life to resist; and *bodies,* or for Hardt and Negri, the constitutive components of social life. They acknowledge that capital's claim on bodies has been neglected in the Marxist tradition, and they maintain that historical materialism has to be reoriented in order to account for it. In pursuing this claim, they turn to Foucault and Spinoza. Specifically, they embrace Foucault's assertion that bodies are constitutive of the biopolitical fabric of being and Spinoza's conception of the body as the basic life force that constitutes the formation of society.[40] These presuppositions underlie their contention that bodies and their drives are the baseline of history.

Hardt and Negri argue that capitalist production increasingly draws upon biopower, in large part through what they call the affective domain of "immaterial labor." Their concept of immaterial labor refers to a change in the valorization process of capitalism, in which a growing service economy gives more weight to the production of information, knowledge, and affects than to the production of commodities. In other words, they maintain that the labors of the head and of the heart now dominate capitalist production. Immaterial labor exercises biopower in that it produces subjects rather than commodities, and it does so, in part, through the affective capabilities of workers.

For Hardt and Negri biopolitics is a political subjectivity articulated in a discourse that links political decision making to bodies in struggle.[41] One of the problems with this formulation of politics is that the notion of bodies in struggle covers such a broad sweep that it could encompass without distinction political groups ranging from the extreme Right to the progressive and radical Left. More important, when resistance is formulated in these terms—as an inchoate life force emerging randomly and anarchically in scattered forms of subversion targeted at identities and norms—the politics of struggle loses any clear reference to material history. What is obscured in their notions of biopower and biopolitical value is that the valorization process of capitalism necessarily produces unmet needs and that these unmet needs are a basis for political agency. This is not to say that bodies are irrelevant to politics but rather that making life the fundamental political subject eclipses the material interface between bodies and the social relations through which needs are met, including the cultures through which demands are articulated. In other words, Hardt and Negri's concept of biopolitical value, like Massumi's virtual materialism, substitutes matter for materiality. In their formulation the value of biopolitical value lies in the struggle for a better way of life, but because they posit this struggle as generated through the assertions of bodies and life, we do not get a clear understanding of the relations that bind bodies, politics, and capitalism's production of value and unmet needs. In other words, Hardt and Negri's biopolitics relies upon a materialism that ultimately cannot explain how political struggle is related to the incorporation of bodies and their affective capacities into the accumulation of surplus value in the labor of commodity production and in social reproduction outside the formal market.

Nonetheless, in recovering the concept of the common as a critical ground for anticapitalist organizing, Hardt and Negri do offer a glimpse of what a materialist approach to affect as a political value might entail. I return to this concept of the common in chapter 8, but for now it is enough to say that their formulation of a common wealth that may be rescued from capitalism's ravages asserts that the affective dimension of political process matters. Unfortunately, however, they offer only a vague explanation of how capitalism's surplus common and its affective resources can become a political force.

This is precisely Ernesto Laclau's critique of their work. Laclau's analysis of what he calls "populist reason" is interested in how the articulation of common political demands takes place and the affective investments it requires. The value of his analysis lies in his attention to the discursive practices that give naming and affect key roles in the formation of political identities. Laclau claims that in Hardt and Negri this dimension of political strategy disappears.[42] For Laclau social demands that begin as isolated complaints become a stable system of signification that constitutes a collective subject like "the people" through their equivalent articulation. He contends that what enables the shift from individual demands to equivalent popular ones is at its root the experience of a gap or lack in the imagined harmonious continuity of social life. The construction of a common identity like "the people" is an attempt to give a name to this absent harmonious continuity. For Laclau affect is a crucial component in the discursive formation of such a collective subjectivity because it is sewn into the very fabric of language. Affect is constituted through what he calls the "differential cathexis of a signifying chain," a concept that draws upon a psychoanalytic version of what it means to be a subject.[43] Here, the body is conceptualized as possessing needs and drives that aim to fulfill these needs. As formulated by the French psychoanalyst Jacques Lacan, the subject comes to be through entry into the symbolic order when the drives elect external objects, including symbolic ones, capable of satisfying something more than need. Radical investment in an object means making that object the embodiment of a mythical fullness. Laclau uses as an example the substitution of the breast for the demand for milk. In this story affect is the essence of radical investment.[44] For Laclau the materiality of affect lies in the loss of wholeness that takes place as a result of entry into the symbolic order and the turn to a substitute for the satisfaction that vanishes in the process. The lack from which affect is born is demand, where demand is always discursive and formulated within the social relations of a situation lived as deficient being.[45]

What is the materiality of this deficiency? Here, Laclau is vague, and his vagueness is tied to the psychoanalytic story of demand and desire that would locate unmet need in an absolute feature of human culture—a lack formed by entry into the symbolic order. From this standpoint affect as investment in a lost mythical fullness is the very premise of social demands, but it is a premise that eclipses the historical and material forces that shape the meeting and not meeting of needs. What disappears in Laclau's symbolic materialism and its accompanying version of politics is the historical and material production of lack as unmet need and its relation to representation and affect. In other words, naming or *cultural* politics has subsumed a politics of need. The value of Laclau's work is that he acknowledges that affect matters in political organizing, and he extends its analysis into the dynamics of the discursive formation of political subjects. One of the casualties of his veer into psychoanalysis is, however, a fuller understanding of the relationship between the material losses capitalism incurs and the affective resonances of those losses in the formation of subjects and political alliances.

A Materialist and Feminist Perspective

In pursuit of a clearer explanation of this relation between affect and those losses—that is, of the place of affect in the meeting of human needs and the role of affect-culture in organizing around the unmet needs capitalism produces—I turn to the work of marxist feminists. Here, I join Clare Hemmings's call for more attention to affect from the vantage point of its insertions into history and as a feature of one's capacity to act in the world and form political judgments.[46] She cites as potential directions for such an effort the earlier work of feminist theorists. My arguments elaborate upon her suggestion.

Marxist feminism embraces the fundamental premise of historical materialism, which is that the meeting of needs constitutes the baseline of history, and it is from this premise, I argue, that we can most productively consider the affective dimension of organized collective politics. Feminist work in the Marxist tradition has rethought Marx, elaborating his claim that the materiality of social life resides in the labor of cooperation to meet needs and reproduce the means to do so, a process that is shaped by historical conditions and always in some relation to nature. The subjects involved in these relations are sensate beings, and the cooperative interactions that reproduce life function through the meaning-making practices and political processes they employ. As physiological capacities that are part of the reproduction of human biological, social, and historical existence, affects are material. Their materiality lies in their integrated transit across biology and social history. The human capacity to experience physiological intensities and make sense of them is enabled by biochemistry and the forms of collaboration and cooperation through which social life is reproduced. In this sense the materiality of affect disassembles the conventional distinction between ontology and epistemology.

I return to this point in chapter 4, "The Value of a Second Skin," but in brief, "ontology" traditionally refers to the nature of existence and "epistemology" to the nature of knowledge. Because human existence is always social, the ontology of affect is radically social, too. It lies in organisms' physiological states and the social relations of labor that sustain them: the energies and sensations that inform attention and interaction in care and the labor that enables group survival. Affects also adhere to the ways we make sense of our existence and how we know and name reality, how we assess truth, belief, and judgment. These affectively laden epistemological assessments inflect, in turn, the social activities through which the reproduction of human *being* takes place. As a component of our social bonds and knowledge production, affect is both ontological and epistemological.[47]

In short, a materialist approach to affect sees it as a human capacity intrinsic to the fabric of biological–social life and articulated through historically variable meanings and practices, many of which adhere to the labor of meeting needs. Needs are corporeal—they involve keeping the body alive—but they are not natural, because meeting them always takes place through social relationships. Basic human needs bind us to nonhuman animals and to the planet. They also adhere to human capacities that are so close to needs that they might be considered needs in themselves, as they enable well-being and life lived beyond the edge of mere survival: the ability to exercise intellect, imagination, invention, and the capacity for communication and affection. Affective capacities are closely tied to basic needs because they permeate the social relations through which these needs are met or denied. Both physiological and psychosocial, affective energies become meaningful only when articulated in the cultural categories or feelings that represent them.

As I use it, the term "feelings" refers to the rhetorical strategies that (re)situate affects in a feedback loop to the cultural systems and social relations of which they are already a part. As a concept "affect-culture" underscores the connection between culture and intensities that the term "feelings" does not conventionally convey. Affect-culture mediates the social interactions through which needs are met and subjects are formed. It propels and tempers action, judgment, identification, and aversion. It can nurture life or abuse or destroy it. Woven into the circuit of nature-labor-bodies-cooperation through which social life is reproduced, affects are a crucial part of capitalism as a mode of life. They are integrated into the physical-psychic-emotional material of labor power that accumulates surplus value. They leaven the cooperation required in the labor of the formal marketplace and outside it in what had been called the labor of social reproduction.[48] Under capitalism the full meeting of human needs is structurally foreclosed for the simple reason that labor is organized so that profit margins grow as workers' needs are reduced to the barest feasible minimum. Affect features in the consequent shrinking of well-being as people feel that pinch. Unmet needs pose a constant threat to capitalist interests, however, and as such they must be reckoned with continually. Affect-culture can activate that threat and fertilize the seedbed of capitalism's monstrous outside, the collective possibility that haunts it.[49]

Feminist work in the historical materialist tradition has built upon and revised the premise that the materiality of social life resides in human activity to meet needs through the labor of cooperation, a process that is always in some relation to nature. It has also rethought how Marx formulated social production and the accumulation of surplus value in capitalism. Marxist feminists like Lourdes Benería, Silvia Federici, Frigga Haug, Maria Mies, Lisa Vogel, and others recognize that capitalist production is tied to social reproduction and always mediated by the incrementally altering circuit of nature-labor-bodies-cooperation. They also acknowledge that neither nature nor labor, the body nor cooperation speaks for itself. These entities are represented in social life through the discourses and practices of culture.[50] Marxist and socialist feminists—among them Pat and Hugh Armstrong, Margaret Benston, Mariarosa Dalla Costa, Nancy Folbre, Leopoldina Fortunati, Selma James, Arlie Hochschild, and, more recently, Encarnación Gutiérrez-Rodríguez—have opened for analysis the value to capital of labor in the domestic sphere and the value of affective labor and affect-culture in both unwaged and wage work. Since the 1980s, the attention that marxist, socialist, and ma-terialist feminists have paid to labor outside the formal market has moved beyond a paradigm that conceives of social life in terms of two separate systems of patriarchal and capitalist relations. More-over, a persistent thread in more recent research recognizes affect-cul-ture as a feature of the social reproduction taking place both in the home and in the market as care work, including dependent care and service work.[51] Indeed, one of the most important contributions of marxist feminists to feminist theory is their redefinition of work and their elaboration of domestic labor as a key source of capital accu-mulation. This paradigm shift has profound implications for how we understand the materiality of affect.

In redefining domestic labor as the labor that reproduces labor power, marxist feminists uncovered a crucial ground of exploita-tion that Marxist theory had largely ignored, and in doing so they reoriented what constitutes the value system under capitalism. In their early efforts marxist feminists conceptualized the labor of so-cial reproduction together with the wage-labor market as the two fundamental sectors of the economy. One of these theorists is the Italian feminist Leopoldina Fortunati. She claims that Marx did not realize that "the wage does not have an immediate use value for the male worker, and that the consumption of the wage's use value presupposes some other work has taken place—either housework or prostitution."[52] This other labor is the care and provision that is incorporated into the use value of the worker's labor power, which gets exchanged for a wage.[53] In other words, domestic labor is surplus labor that hides behind the exchange value of the wage. It is a surplus in that it is consumed by capital without being bought as a part of the calculus of exchange value.[54] That is, the capitalist does not have to calculate domestic labor into the cost of wages. As Sue Ferguson points out:

> Unlike the market . . . households are oriented to fulfilling human needs—a mandate antithetical to capital accumulation. As a result, households are not purely functional units but are themselves the source of a distinct set of dynamics put in motion by the impulse to meet the human needs of social reproduction—that is, the human need to reproduce daily and, in the case of households with children, generationally.[55]

The labor of reproduction takes place in activities that include the transmission of emotion and feeling in the affect-cultures of birthing, teaching, and nurturing the young; feeding, clothing, and caring for those who work in the marketplace; and tending to the sick and the elderly. Much of this labor is done by women for free or for minimal wages thanks to ideologies of motherhood, wifehood, and domesticity that devalue this labor as feminized.

Now, a considerable body of research by feminists exists on the affective components of labor in the marketplace and in the ever-more-integrated domestic and market economies. It goes by various names: "emotional labor" (Hochschild, *Managed Heart*), "intimate labor" (Boris and Parreñas), "attention labor" (Clough), "dependency work" (Kittay), and "global care chains" (Hochschild, "Global Care Chains"). Feminists have long argued that human life is sustained through relations of dependency and that women have been responsible for the bulk of the caring labor this dependency entails. Research on caring labor acknowledges that the care humans require includes a certain level of attention from others, attention leavened with life-enhancing affects. Daniel Engster, for example, defines care as labor that is related to the meeting of needs but that occurs before and after the productive activities that directly satisfy needs.

He further distinguishes care as labor that makes the development and basic well-being of another its direct end.[56] According to Engster, care fulfills three aims necessary for human development. First, it helps satisfy basic survival needs. Among them are the needs of all for food, clothing, and shelter and of infants and children, especially, for human physical contact. Care at this basic level helps to develop capabilities for sensation, emotion, movement, speech, reason, imagination, literacy, and numeracy, and it helps avoid pain and suffering.[57] Second, care involves not just satisfying these basic needs but doing so with attentiveness—that is, noting others' needs and responding appropriately. Attentiveness entails the transmission of affect in empathy and the anticipation of the needs another might have. Caring attentiveness engages with others to determine the precise nature of their needs. Third, care entails respect, treating people in ways that do not degrade them in the eyes of others.[58] Workers in the unpaid and low-paid domestic sector provide this attention in caring service directly to household members.[59]

Services that entail caring attention are also provided by employees in the public and private sectors of the paid economy and in the voluntary sector. Hochschild's research on emotion work was one of the first efforts to understand this underside of service labor by connecting social structures to the management of what she called "feeling rules" and their class inflection across the paid labor force. Drawing upon and extending the earlier research of Émile Durkheim (1961), Clifford Geertz (1964), and Erving Goffman (1974), she opened to investigation the ways women workers in the relatively new service industry had to do "deep acting emotion work" in accordance with emotion rules not of their own making.[60] Though her early research focuses less on affect as sensation and more on the social rules for managing emotions, it remains a groundbreaking contribution to understanding affect as socially regulated and incorporated into the commodification of labor power. She acknowledges that the strategic management of emotions in the service economy helps sustain cooperation and civility, even though it is not generally recognized as labor. Like housework, the emotional work of the service sector of the economy is a form of shadow labor, unacknowledged as labor and undervalued.

Kathleen Lynch and Judy Walsh recognize differences in the affective components of care as they register in various levels of attentiveness across paid, unpaid, and volunteer labor.[61] They identify the most intense attentiveness in primary relations of dependency, which they distinguish from secondary relations that are less immediate, demanding, extended, or frequent. There may also well be affective distinctions in the ways the physiological dimension of affect inheres in care work of different sorts and how its gendered features are felt and lived.[62] What Eileen Boris and Rhacel Salazar Parreñas call "intimate labor" may or may not entail the manipulation of feelings, though it does involve affective interactions in the service of social reproduction.[63] Intimate labor may be of fleeting or long duration, but it invariably involves affective attentiveness to objects and materials that improve the quality of life for someone, among them creating and sustaining emotional ties and providing bodily upkeep, health and hygiene, sexual services, housecleaning, certain forms of therapy, elder care, and child care, including surrogate mothering. Although these sorts of intimate care may not always entail face-to-face emotional discipline, they have an affective dimension. Moreover, when intimate labor is articulated and devalued as feminized through ideologies of gender, ethnicity, and race, it can carry a negative affective charge. As I argue more fully in part 2, regardless of the cultural value it carries or the degree of emotional control it entails, all labor under capitalism has an affective dimension, as affect-culture is integrated in capitalism's value systems across economic sectors.

From the vantage point of this research, the concept of immaterial labor, which has been used to refer to the emotional and intimate labor of care in the domestic and service sectors, is simply wrongheaded. One of the most cited examples of the concept of immaterial labor is Michael Hardt's essay "Affective Labor." Hardt recognizes what Gayatri Spivak had already noted as "the productive relationship between affect and value" and the potential of the production of affects for liberation.[64] His concept of immaterial labor does not acknowledge, however, that affect-culture has a material component as a biocapacity integrated into human communication and cooperative relations and that as such it is a value-producing element in all labor. I am suggesting that "immaterial" as a descriptor for caring and affective labor is a misnomer. Affects have a material force in that they are integral to human social relations. They are historically inflected and harnessed by the organization of life under capitalism to help produce and enhance the labor power that contributes to the accumulation of (surplus) value. Affects enter into exchange value as a component of domestic care that reproduces labor power for the market and does so for low wages or for free. They are also a capacity of the worker's labor power that is purchased and expended in the market. Affective expertise—that is, mastery of affective norms and conventions—is an integral feature of the cultural systems that help to set the value of certain forms of labor. By acknowledging these various affective dimensions to unwaged and waged labor and by distinguishing among them, feminists have advanced our understanding of the materiality of affect-culture and its incorporation into economic relations.

In her research on migrant domestic workers in Europe, Encarnación Gutiérrez-Rodríguez underscores the relational character of living labor as a feature of what she calls "affective value," and she emphasizes that it is informed by what Spivak in her 1985 essay "Scattered Speculations on the Question of Value" calls "the materialist predication of the subject."[65] What Spivak means by this phrase is that the history of capitalism and imperialism has been predetermined by the feminized and racialized codification of the corporeality of labor and its geopolitical locations. Gutiérrez-Rodríguez maintains that the use value of racialized and feminized subjects to capitalism persists in "the trenches of coloniality," of which Mexico's maquiladoras are only one instance.[66] I return to her argument about this feature of labor in chapter 5, but what is noteworthy here is that Gutiérrez-Rodríguez posits affect as a linchpin of the value-producing materiality of labor and the cultural values through which subjects are formed.

As Grossberg and Laclau remind us, the materiality of affect-culture also lies in its insertion into ideology. In her extensive overview and critical analyses of sentimental culture, Lauren Berlant addresses the affective work of ideology, represented in structures of feeling like national sentimentality or state emotionalism, or cruel optimism, as strategies of social bonding in which emotion trumps dissenting counternarratives and works against a collective political stance.[67] In its ideological formulations, Berlant argues, the "traffic in affect" makes feeling "a hardwired truth," or what goes without saying, beyond mediation or contestation, the core material of mythology.[68] As her incisive analyses of public sentiment disclose, feelings that are translated into commonsense emotional rhetoric can reinforce the cultural obvious and the social inequities it reproduces. I agree with and applaud this critical work on affect-infused ideology. It is important to remember, however, that affects mediate culture as a site of struggle, adhering to both dominant and subaltern discourses. At times this affect-culture circulates as ideology, or the common sense, but affect-culture is also articulated in counterdiscourses that interrupt the prevailing sentiments and norms. Sometimes, it operates only obliquely as an intuition of something wrong, the sense that accompanies good sense.

In other words, it is helpful to think about meaning making as taking place through various kinds of *sense,* and I stress "sense" as a salient term that carries with it traces of the body's ties to knowledge. Common sense is knowledge that is widely held to be obvious, often referenced as what feels right or natural or the way things are or ought to be. It has deep roots in the prevailing truths that reproduce existing class relations—that is, ideology. What Antonio Gramsci calls "good sense" is something different, a conglomeration of discourses that can run alongside the common sense but counter its logic. Good sense sees through the abstractions that veil injustice and recognizes unmet need as unwarranted. It is the seedbed of radical critique and revolutionary conviction. Affect-culture is integral to both common sense and good sense. It can legitimate oppressive conventions, lure one into conformity, or spur intuition to pursue a line of thinking toward action that redresses injustice.

What Does Sex Have to Do with It?

Gutiérrez-Rodríguez suggests that because affect is bound epistemologically and ontologically to the predication of the subject, it is incorporated into the processes of abjection and identification through

which the production of identities takes place. It is in this respect that
we can consider the relation of affect-culture to sexual identity. Sexuality is a historical discourse that has a close relation to affect in that
it is a strong attractor of affect's intensities and sensations; it endows
them with meanings and channels them into cultural categories.
Sexual identity is an imaginary (ideological) invention that draws
upon the discourses of sexuality in articulating a psychic, cultural,
and social standpoint. Sexual identity names and organizes corporeal sensations, passionate energies, attachments, projections, and
abjections into a discourse of selfhood. As it is lived, sexual identity
is deeply affective, traversed by mattering maps whose affective investments can direct and also disrupt a gendered symbolic order. The
affective relations of daily life reproduce and interrupt imaginary
formulations of sexuality and sexual identity, both normative and
nonnormative ones. The mattering maps of affect-culture direct and
redirect the processes of abjection that identity formation entails. It
was Eve Sedgwick's genius to name the "paradigm clash" that organizes the maps of sexuality into the distinction between those that
universalize and attend to the labile play of desires and those that mi-
noritize and attend to discrete (hetero- and homosexual) identities.[69]
Addressing the affective dimension of sexuality takes us into territory where both paradigms circulate and collide. I attend to these
competing configurations as they organize affect and sexuality in
more detail in several of the following chapters—in chapter 4 as a
component of the open secret of unstable erotic ties and an identity
coded as gender transgression and in chapter 5 as one of the second
skins of workers. I mark these paradigms here as a structural feature
of the integration of affect-culture in the discourses of sexuality.

My thinking about the affective dimensions of collective organizing and their articulation in the discourses of sexuality and sexual
identity grows out of the alliances I formed with Mexican maquiladora workers and my lived identification as a lesbian, an identification that was almost never mentioned in my relationships with
workers. Perhaps because of this open secret, in listening to organizers and working alongside them in campaigns over the years I began
to discern an element of the unspeakable in their words and actions,

as well, a feature of the risks they were taking and that clung to whatever propelled them to organize themselves and say, "Ya basta!" (Enough!). I also became aware of how often sexuality was an ingredient of the affect-culture of a group, and I began to think about the negative affective charge attached to feminized subjects as a crucial component of the value embedded in the labor power exchanged for a wage. In witnessing workers' interactions, I noticed the transmission of affects binding them to one another and to charismatic leaders. While many affects flow through the culture of organizing, in this book I focus on the affect-culture that found its expression in the discourses of sexuality and sexual identity. In listening to organizers and workers and thinking about what moved them to make courageous decisions, I noticed how often sexuality hovered on the edges of the caring bonds that maintained their collective commitments and at times unraveled them. Sometimes, sexuality defined the turning point in a decision to act, adhered to good sense, or drove the commonsense plot of banal melodramas that undermined collective endeavor. At other times it evaporated into erotic charges that defied easy naming. Though in the following chapters I focus on the ways sexuality circulated in organizing culture, in fact I often struggled to formulate in familiar categories many of the passions I witnessed or that swept me up, the energy infusing workers' convictions and their care and affection for each other. This mobile and elusive erotic force most captured my attention, perhaps in part because of the unwieldy passionate investments I was also living and managing.

In Sum

The turn to affect in culture theory is testimony to the fact that reclaiming a facet of our history and human capacity that has been trivialized and made invisible is itself a site of struggle. In arguing for a historical and materialist understanding of affect-culture, I am claiming that affect matters for three key reasons. First, because it is a feature of our complex humanity that permeates the circuit of nature-bodies-labor through which needs are met and social life is reproduced. To fully understand the mediating role of affect-culture, we need an analytic that explains the relationship of affect-infused culture to capitalism as the prevailing global regime for meeting human needs. Analysis that draws upon the insights of historical materialism and feminism enables us to understand how affect-culture is integral to labor and care and how it weighs in the relations through which value is extracted in the marketplace and produced at home. This problematic enables us to consider affect as a component of culture that accompanies the legitimation of exploitation and domination and infuses feelings of identity and belonging.

The second reason affect-culture matters is that it is so integral to an element of social life that capital both harvests and fails to capture completely: the human capacity for collaboration and cooperation, for attachment and living attention. It is its role in these relations that makes affect-culture a crucial component of political resistance. Affect is recruited into the ideological management of social relations, but it also "animates the sensation that something is not right or fair, the insight that shakes up deep-seated patterns of thinking and feeling and advances new imaginings."[70] These intuitions are not asocial or virtual or autonomous from reason. They are elemental to the good sense that recognizes the collective, social basis of survival. As Gutiérrez-Rodríguez reminds us, echoing a long line of feminist theorists, among them Gloria Anzaldúa, Audre Lorde, and Chela Sandoval, affects are fundamental to our social being in that they "make us aware that we are interconnected, related to each other, that we do not exist as singular, sealed monads. Our bodies, our skins, are porous, and open to somebody else's feelings, to the energies of the environment haunted by our past and energized by our present."[71]

Finally, affect-culture matters because it is a key component of the knowledge base for social movement. Wherever it occurs, organizing is a pedagogic site, and it can provide a more robust critical vocabulary by attending to the affect-culture people bring with them.[72] Feminists have long recognized this fact. As Deborah Gould has argued, social movements, like organizations and political regimes, establish emotional imperatives and normative emotional orders, and therefore we need to explore the affective pedagogies they offer.[73]

Much organizing is not critically reflective, however, regarding the affect-infused culture that lingers as an open secret in its activities, a largely unconscious influence on the success and the failure of many campaigns. We ignore it at the risk of losing the ground for collective struggle and the shared horizon of our goals, for it is the glue and the solvent of social movement.

Bearing Witness

The Charge and the Chain of Witness

To be an organizer or an ally in an organizing campaign is to bear witness. Both the *bearing* and the *witnessing* open you to a new position in history as you assume responsibility to others and carry their message to the wider community. The "bearing" part of the phrase "bearing witness" suggests layers of meaning that are aptly conveyed in the Spanish word *cargo*, loosely translated as "charge" or "responsibility." Taking up the *cargo* of involvement in organizing entails assuming responsibility in the sense of providing for others, and it also carries the sense of taking on duties that are accountable to a broader public. Not incidentally, the word *cargo* has an emotional association, as it can connote an unspecified affective weight, as in the phrase *me da cargo de conscientia*, or "I feel badly," in the emotional-affective sense. To assume the *cargo* of involvement in an organizing effort situates you, in all of these respects, on new ground, dislocated from familiar social relations and thrust into a public role in which new attachments and their accompanying emotions, one's own and those of others, are a part of the substance and the weight of your charge.

Organizing campaigns like those I write about here include a wide-ranging network of actors and allies, stretching from the workers on the front lines to those who lend support on their behalf from elsewhere. They may be workers in other cities in Mexico, across the border in the United States, in other countries in Latin America, or in Europe; they may be journalists, teachers, researchers, or activists who support maquiladora workers' struggles. Because of the accidents of birth and life circumstance, many of these witnesses are less brutally impacted by the structural violence they bring into public view. In this chapter I am interested in the different social locations of witnessing and, especially, the position of those who offer support from elsewhere, who may enter the front lines occasionally but are for the most part separated by several degrees from a campaign's principal actors. What are the responsibilities of these witnesses? What are the traps in bearing witness from here? What subjects do we speak for? What history and what future?

The act of witnessing has been a compelling philosophical and political concern because it poses fundamental questions about the obligations of representing on behalf of a collective and of acting to redress social injustice. In the first half of this chapter, I consider the genres of testimony and ethnography for what they tell us about the passionate politics of bearing witness and the often vexed position of the witness-ally. In the chapter's second half, I shift to stories that capture some of the complicated affective relations that bearing witness entailed for me in my encounters with organizers in maquiladora communities. As a supplement to the first part, these stories flesh out some of the affective dynamics that shape relations along the chain of bearing witness. Told from my outsider-witness stance, they convey my own and others' dislocation by practices that bind affects to collective action. They indicate that the ability to bear the *cargo* of representing a collective endeavor for justice is bolstered by affirmation, a form of affective transmission that is sometimes enacted through rituals and rationalities that stretch beyond recognition. They also confirm that bearing witness is a process of learning to navigate the affective accompaniments of failure. Anecdotal and particular, these stories nonetheless offer evidence that I hope is portable in its implications, evidence, that is, of the profoundly affective material that binds actors in the chain of witness across the far-flung locations of organizing.

The Affective Epistemology of Witnessing

In the labor organizing campaigns in the maquilas, the chain of witnessing brings together multiple knowledges. In the best scenario, workers' good sense is a fundamental ground for strategizing, but it is also a site of struggle. That is to say, it is knowledge that is at times undervalued by outside actors or by the workers themselves. It is open to history and never coherent in any simple way. Moreover, it is not the only knowledge base. The standpoints that an organizing effort articulates draw upon a rich legacy of proletarian knowledge circulating in the local community, as well as upon the national and transnational legacies of both social movements and neoliberal discourses that shape desires and analysis. Blended into this mix are many discourses of feeling. What is their relation to this knowledge base of bearing witness?

Now, an extensive archive of research exists on the emotional component of witnessing, much of it produced by feminist scholars in anthropology and philosophy. Like the arguments of 1970s feminists on the relation of emotion to knowledge, this work has sparked considerable controversy. One notable example is Ruth Behar's 1996 book *The Vulnerable Observer.* In these essays Behar calls upon anthropologists to take seriously as knowledge the "intermediate space we can't quite define yet, a borderland between passion and intellect" that constitutes the "rigorous but not disinterested" witnessing of ethnography.[1] Over a decade later, we are still struggling with that definition. If interested knowledge is a "borderland between passion and reason," it is a stance that—to use a term that the philosopher Kelly Oliver proposes—"vigilantly" draws upon both.[2] This vigilance is a crucial feature of the epistemology of witness. It echoes Teresa Brennan's insights regarding the critical examination of one's passions and distinguishes the transmission of affect in witnessing from the "sanctifying respect for sentiment" that Lauren Berlant brilliantly critiques in her work on the circulation of public feelings.[3] Sanctified feeling is "interested," but it has become sentimentality, or feeling that conforms to hard-wired truths. Sentimentality is fetishized feeling. It dispels critical thought and preserves the status quo. Understanding sentimentality and other ideological formulations of affect-culture is a crucial component of radical intellectual work, but the ideological formulations of public and private feeling do not fully account for the affective charge that motivates and sustains organized resistance. In other words, although in an organizing campaign affect-culture does get mobilized into forms of feeling that reiterate the commonsense, this does not mean that it always has this effect.

The genre of testimony understands witnessing as both an emotional and a critical practice. One strong line of testimonial research has arisen from work with survivors of the Holocaust, for whom testimony has been a therapeutic representation of unspeakable trauma. Research on these testimonies has highlighted the complex negotiations between memory and history, feeling and truth, and the problematic lapses in the chain of witnessing that carry both a cognitive and an affective charge.[4] In *Homo Sacer* and *Remnants of Auschwitz,* Giorgio Agamben addresses these lapses through his reading of the figure of the Muselmann, the victim of atrocity in the Holocaust who is so destroyed that he occupies a place between life and death.[5] The Muselmann is the impossible witness for whom the language of testimony is unavailable.[6] As such, he represents the failure of adequate representation that Agamben finds encrypted in all testimonial witnessing. Agamben recognizes the inability of representation to adequately convey a lived experience of suffering so physically and emotionally extreme that it crosses the boundary between the human and the no-longer-human, but not all witnessing navigates these limits. Countering Agamben, Anne Cubilé argues for a broader understanding of testimony as a performative act. As such, it takes place in a relationship that can recognize its own compromises and failures, including the disparity between the political aspirations and historical limits of representing the other.[7] This understanding of failure as integral to testimony inserts into the emotive chain of witnessing the affective charge of humility. I return to its importance in the stories that follow.

Testimony's long-standing tradition in the Americas acknowledges this performative and relational feature of assuming responsibility for the impossibility of witnessing the violence legitimized by slavery and other forms of state violence. The nineteenth-century narratives of ex-slaves and the writings of twentieth-century scholars of African American culture draw upon marginalized discourses and symbolic lexicons to bear witness to the lost archives of unspeakable violence.[8] In Latin America testimony has been a way for people to come to terms with the psychic and social effects of state repression and to bring this knowledge into public circulation.[9]

In her writings about the testimonies of survivors of twentieth-century state-orchestrated atrocity, Anne Cubilé marks a useful distinction between testimony and the Latin American tradition of *testimonio*. Although testimony sometimes falls within the genre of testimonio, it is not synonymous with it. As it has been elaborated by critics such as George Yúdice, John Beverly, and Doris Somer, testimonio has an added political and collective edge because it aims to set right official history by denouncing the exploitation and oppression of a group the speaker represents.[10] As such, testimonio has developed into a powerful form for consciousness raising among indigenous women leaders and in transnational political education.[11] Grounded in the history of organized resistance in grassroots and indigenous communities, the narrative framework of testimonio weaves a chain of relations to incite affective and cognitive connections among speakers, listeners, and a collective. As Doris Somer comments, in testimonio "the map of possible identifications through the text spreads out laterally."[12] Not least of all, in the testimonio tradition the chain of witnessing springs from and generates an outside stance through a critical purchase on the history of the criminal capitalist state. This stance is outside in that it aspires to the transformation of a violent political economy from the standpoint of the social majority most affected by it, and for that reason it offers a less partial, less narrow, and less mystified way of seeing and knowing.

Maquiladora workers enact testimonio when they solicit fellow workers and members of far-flung communities to ally with them and with a common cause. In so doing, they recruit epistemic outsiders— that is, those who have a critical perspective on the way things are and entertain the possibility of an alternative. Not all workers who give their testimonies nor all of their interlocutors embrace this outsider stance, but it is a strategic and utopian horizon that circulates in the discourses of political education and is reiterated by many of the frontline actors. Some of the allies who accompany organizing from afar also claim this outsider epistemic stance, but the chain of witnessing in support of workers' campaigns actually traverses a range of perspectives. The mix of social locations and subjectivities along that chain is the object of critical vigilance, and it is enacted at times in heated debates. Unlike the familiarity of sentimentalism, the affective charge that accompanies this vigilance is often discomforting. It can call into question familiar bonds and imaginary communities even while offering new possibilities of affiliation.[13]

Scholarship on the genre of testimony has addressed the role of affect-culture in the politics of witnessing, principally as it features in empathy. Empathy bridges the distance between the social locations of speaker and audience. As a component of testimonial witnessing, it modulates the relation of witnesses to one another by soliciting identification with a common cause and fostering collective action. In this regard it is quite distinct from compassion, although the two are often thought of as synonymous.[14] Compassion denotes an affective response to the suffering of an abject other by a subject in a privileged social position. Unlike the empathic solicitation of witnessing, the affective responses and social relations it elicits are private and sentimentalized. In contrast, the affective register of witnessing aims to interrupt compassion through its emphasis on collective action against structural injustice and its humble recognition of the failures that effort can entail.

Testimony given by the principal actors in a struggle also pursues more pragmatic empathic responses from audiences in the form of donations, letter writing, participation in public protests, and other concrete activities to support a campaign. Organizers from grassroots organizations on the border have used empathic rhetorical strategies for these practical ends on their tours in the United States and Canada. At the same time, their speeches are pitched to move audiences to contest the violent conditions that Mexican workers experience and to recognize the social relations that bind them to workers elsewhere. Audiences are moved by these testimonies because they identify as workers or as fellow organizers and as consumers of the products the workers assemble. As Melissa Wright points out, establishing familiarity between the testifier and her public is a risky business. The danger is that the circle of familiarity can reinforce stereotypes and close out critical perspectives. It can also mitigate the appearance of contradictions within an organizing movement, especially one that crosses national borders.[15]

It can be a pedagogic challenge for a witness to move audiences, to dislocate them from compassionate platitudes without so alienating them that they cannot respond with critical solidarity. The trick is to maneuver around the seductive pull of familiar emotional categories toward a radical elsewhere. "Who is empathy for," Nancy Saporta Sternbach asks, "when it is solicited from an audience to testimony? For the intermediary/narrator? For the collective she comes from?"[16] Or, I would add, for the cause and hoped-for alternative the witness represents? Indeed, the answer may be that the empathy solicited in bearing witness touches all of these referents.[17] In this respect the empathic transmission of affect along the chain of witnessing shares features of caring labor in that here, too, the affective transmission that is enacted involves care-full living attention. In witnessing, that attention slides from speaker to audience and invites the navigation, in William Reddy's sense, of losses and aspirations that enable alternative possibilities for identification.

Witnessing sets out to span social and epistemological distances, but sometimes they may not be bridgeable. Traversing epistemic distance is especially challenging for the witness from the overdeveloped sectors who represents people in the two-thirds world. George Yúdice refers to the imaginary geographies that structure the flow of affect in these situations and the chasm that can be created across which empathic bonds simply do not cross.[18] He cites Joan Didion's 1983 *Salvador* as an example of a form of testimony in which such a chasm appears, in this case in her characterization of the ineffable untranslatableness of the horrific events she witnessed in the reign of terror during the civil war in El Salvador. Her narrator's aesthetic distance may have been unsettled and overcome, he claims, had Didion conducted interviews with mass organizations of peasants, workers, students, and women or visited the guerrilla zones of control.[19] I am interested in the affective consequences of risking what he claims Didion did not.

Anthropologists have been most concerned with this dimension of witnessing, and many have avidly critiqued the presumed epistemic privilege of the disengaged outside observer. Disciplinary self-reflection in anthropology began simmering in the late 1970s, and now, wrestling with the politics of witnessing is a fundamental feature of the ethnographer's ethical responsibility. Much of this critical reflection highlights the relentless subjectivity of observation that is played out in the field and in writing and that puts pressure on the accountability of researchers to the people whose lives they represent.[20]

The affective dimensions of the ethnographer's witnessing have been broached most often by feminists. As I mentioned, Ruth Behar stirred up a fair amount of controversy on the propriety of revealing the emotional side of ethnographic research. Her 1993 ethnography *Translated Woman* tells the story of Esperanza Hernández, a sixty-year-old Mexican single mother, peddler, and possible *bruja* (witch) living outside San Luis Potosí, but the book is also the story of the contradictory and conflicted relationship between Esperanza and her biographer, Ruth, who is regarded as a *gringa* from the United States but who knows herself to be also a Cuban immigrant perched in her life on the border between nations and in her storytelling between history and fiction. In her proposals for an "anthropology that breaks your heart," Behar honors the insights of her teachers, Michelle and Renato Rosaldo, whose pioneering research disclosed the field worker's emotional investments. For Behar "vulnerability doesn't mean that anything goes," because "the exposure of the self who is also a spectator has to take us somewhere we couldn't otherwise go."[21] In the empathic connection that triggers dislocation to this "somewhere," she sees a potential Pandora's box. Opening it raises many vexing questions about the researcher's responsibility to disciplinary boundaries and to the truth of what she sees. It brings into the zone of critical vigilance the desires and longings that punctuate the first-world researcher's place in the chain of witness, including those she leaves in her wake at the doorsteps of the people she encounters in her fieldwork.

The researcher's responsibility to the communities on whose behalf she writes and whose struggles she joins has also been addressed as "activist scholarship" and sometimes referred to as "action research," "participatory research," "engaged research," or "public intellectual work." These approaches advocate for a fully integrated relationship between the researcher and the community and emphasize the practical steps that can be taken toward that end. Activist scholarship promotes a research practice that is collaborative and reciprocal, where community actors share in framing the questions to be addressed and in evaluating the results. This approach maintains that knowledge produced out of such a collaborative relationship has the potential to yield insights and analysis that otherwise would be impossible to achieve.[22] As the title of Charles Hale's collection *Engaging Contradictions* acknowledges, however, contradictions circumscribe even a project that involves the community in its design, implementation, and evaluation.[23] Nonetheless, it is a distinguishing feature of activist research to foreground and probe the inequalities in research, including the tensions that punctuate the collaborative process. These tensions can include discrepancies between the scholar's understanding of a community's struggle and its reality as seen by the protagonists themselves, between the outcomes of the research for the scholar and its impact on subjects' lives, or between the researcher's ability to be accountable to the communities with whom she works and the material limits on that relationship. In practicing and conceptualizing research that is collaborative and reciprocal, activist scholars extend the work of witnessing into what Ruth Gilmore calls "organic praxis," while recognizing that not all research can pursue this path.[24] Indeed, my own involvement with the organizing campaigns on the border was never the fully engaged practice of the activist scholar. I was, however, keenly aware that I was able to approach workers and organizers and establish a limited trust with them because of my support for their struggles from vantage points at times in their local communities and more often from afar.

The philosopher Kelly Oliver shifts attention from witnessing as a research practice to witnessing as "the essential dynamic of all subjectivity, its constitutive event and process."[25] She makes a case for witnessing as an epistemology and a political stance that can reorient justice claims "beyond recognition." Oliver contends that social justice struggles for recognition presume a petition to the dominant group, and by virtue of that petition, they assume that what can be recognized is familiar within the terms of the ruling regime. She suggests that this sort of recognition is a "symptom of the pathology of oppression"(9). Victims of oppression are not only seeking something to be conferred upon them by those in power; they are also seeking witnesses to horrors beyond recognition. Calling for justice that is beyond recognition, Oliver contends, puts forward a political practice generated from the standpoint of the other. She asks what it means to testify from here, to listen for what is beyond recognition, for what we don't know. Her answer explores witnessing as a politics of responsibility.

Human dependence on the natural world and each other carries with it an obligation to conserve nature and to insure the justice of the social relations that sustain life. Oliver instructively delineates that responsibility as also involving the conscious experience of ourselves as subjects, a stance that is maintained in the tension between one's subject position and one's subjectivity. She clarifies the distinction. Subject positions are determined by history and politics, by one's situation within a social world and culture, whereas subjectivity is a sense of agency as it is constituted through encounters with others. In experience both are interconnected and often in tension (17). Oliver clarifies that bearing witness calls upon the attachments to others through which subjectivity is sustained and that inflect one's subject position in a society and culture. When testimony solicits listeners to enter a chain of witnesses, it invites audience members from diverse social locations to draw upon their good sense and identify with a collective cause. Its empathic charge directs identification toward an uncharted future beyond recognition. Such unsettling imagination is sparked by witnessing that breaks through the narrow confines of individualism. I return to this topic and a more detailed discussion of common aspirations in chapter 8, although some examples also appear in the following stories.

Jonathan Flatley's description of what he calls "affective mapping" suggests a practice of self-distancing that the critical vigilance of bearing witness beyond recognition also entails. Affective mapping is like the mattering maps that Lawrence Grossberg tells us constitute the pathways by which affects come to get invested in what matters, but with a critical difference.[26] An affective map "establishes a territory for the representation to oneself of one's own historically conditioned and changing affective life."[27] In other words, affective mapping provokes a defamiliarizing epistemological stance. It "allows one to see oneself as if from the outside . . . making one's emotional life, including moods and attachments, appear weird, unusual, and thus capable of a new kind of recognition, interest, analysis"

(80). Affective mapping enacts critical vigilance. It traces the paths, resting places, dead ends, and detours we share with others, including those who came before us (7). Through the mapping process, we learn that the logic of the world we live in is not compulsory.

The popular education workshops that are a crucial component of the political education of organizing on the border could incorporate this learning exercise more than they do, but it does take place in some of them. In chapter 6, I discuss one example from a labor legal advocates workshop. As some of the following stories demonstrate, affective mapping also occurs in the rituals that sustain an organizing effort. Here, as in the aesthetic experience of literature and other art forms, dislocating affective encounters throw into relief subjectivities and subject positions so that their histories, limits, and potential can be seen as if from the outside. Mapping them fosters a witnessing practice more fully able to act in the world.

The Stories

In his wise assessment of the affective power of narrative, both literary and therapeutic, Flatley reminds us that stories are valuable and powerful not for the knowledge one finds in them but "because of the affections they allow to be transferred and the relationships they thereby create."[28] The stories that follow offer, I hope, such transfer points. They are constellations rather than tales—that is, the ideas they contain are underelaborated, evocative rather than analytical, and a little vague around the edges. Some touch upon triangulated intimacies. Others tell of mundane events that evolve into rituals. All speak to the power of affirmation that filters the education and care that sustain the critical work of witness. They are also snapshots of my own efforts to get a handle on the emotional ties that became my purchase on witnessing. They offer glimpses of affective mapping and of affect-culture's radical potential. Mostly, they are invitations to consider its leavening power in the practice of bearing witness.

The stories include workers' testimonies, but they are also, indeed principally, accounts of my own affectively charged encounters in the organizing campaigns I became a part of on the border. Some display the ideological traps I fell into; some enthrall me still. Rereading

Joan Didion's *Salvador,* I am struck by some of the similarities I would rather disown between her narrative and mine, characteristics our tales both share with well-worn ethnographic and journalistic conventions, like the outsider's arrival to the field (mine by car, hers by plane) or the detailed description of the hotel in a foreign place. These conventions invite the reader to identify with the narrator's newcomer perspective and offer this subject position as a vantage point from which to know. It is a perspective that can seductively naturalize the knowledge it offers and unwittingly reiterate a long history of colonial relations that shape what is seeable. I have not excised these conventions from my narratives, because they in fact shaped my notes and reveal my subject position, despite my desire to tell another story, to telescope in where Didion pulls out.

Conducting one's own affective mapping is not a simple process. If it is guided by an openness to history, it is also enacted through a pedagogy of failure.[29] In other words, it is a practice that folds recognition of limits into a refusal to give up on dreams. It acknowledges that you can never entirely shed your subject positions; the best you can do is enact a vigilant relation to them. A pedagogy of failure also implies that witnessing's critical purchase has its roots in a humble willingness to be vulnerable and receptive to the other. Admitting mistakes is difficult, but it is essential to the vigilance of bearing witness. For that reason it too punctuates these stories.

Finding Carmen Julia

On September 20, 2001, when the president of the United States was about to declare a war on terror, I drove from Tucson to San Antonio to the U.S.–Mexico border to live for a while with a worker and her family. When I could, I listened to NPR as I drove, which meant not often, as it was not broadcast in much of west and south Texas, where country music and Christian stations were my window on the world. By the time I crossed the border and entered the hotel lobby in Río Bravo, the TV was broadcasting George Bush's address to the U.S. Congress, with Tony Blair sitting in the audience and a hundred fighter jets on their way to the Middle East. These momentous events seemed oddly unreal. The broadcaster's voice had a heightened affective pitch that I could not parse as I tried to get my bearings in this border town, where I had come for a few weeks to listen to the stories of organizers who led a historic strike at the Duro paper bag assembly plant.

Like many small cities', Río Bravo's commercial district consisted of a few main streets lined with small businesses huddled around a plaza, where invariably a noonday group of people scattered on the benches in the sparse shade. The shopping area stretched in two directions, two strips of stores selling everything from shoes to CDs. To the east on Calle Francisco I. Madero, not quite on the edge of town, lay an area where many chapters of the Duro workers' struggle unfolded. Here, the principal hotel, La Mansion, with its spare, institutional tile floors, Spartan atmosphere, and modest though not inexpensive accommodations, was strategically situated. Directly across the street from the hotel and visible through the side entrance was the police station; around the corner were the offices of *El Río*, the local newspaper; and a block away was the *refaccionaria* Almaráz, the auto repair shop now managed by the son of Señor Almaráz, a young lawyer and up-and-coming progressive politician whom everyone referred to simply as Almaráz. Almaráz supported the Duro workers throughout their strike and had earned the allegiance of many of them by providing legal support, a meeting place, and at times transportation. They in turn had worked on his campaign for mayor under the banner of the relatively progressive Party of the Democratic Revolution (PRD) during the summer of 2001. After losing in what his supporters claimed was a blatantly fraudulent election, with the predictable stealing of ballots by the PRI candidate, he went on to run for office as a representative in the state legislature.

Given the hotel's location, its restaurant served as a clearinghouse for many of the town's dramas, as the principal actors from the police station, newspaper, radio station, and the *refaccionaria* crossed paths daily. Organizers with resources to stay in the hotel used its facilities from time to time, and its meeting rooms had occasionally served as the location for workshops for workers and organizers. In the week before the Duro union election that previous March, the culminating event in the workers' strike and campaign for an independent union, a delegation of teachers from New York state had stayed there, as had the hired thugs the Duro company brought in from Mexico City. I had also stayed at the hotel that week, working to support the Duro workers' election. The bizarre contradictions of this shared space had been most palpable during breakfasts in the restaurant, when the workers, organizers, reporters, and police, along with the hired thugs, passed through or huddled over their coffee at adjoining tables. But that is another story.

That night, as before, the hotel managers and their staff were a crew of supporting actors, their faces fixed in the guarded expressions of the uninvolved who nonetheless surveyed every detail. They seemed almost smug if not for a slight nervousness around their eyes. Clearly, they had a cozy relationship with the police, and despite their detached professional pose and occasional sidelong glances, I found myself projecting onto them some degree of solidarity with the Duro campaign. Then, however, the guy behind the desk glanced at me with an "I know who you are, lady," expression, and I wondered if he had already alerted the police that one of the *gringas* from last March was back. There was little other activity in the lobby that night. The TV and me were about it.

Begin Again

It was Friday September 21, 2001, in Río Bravo, and the voice on the phone was saying, "She asked me to tell you to meet her by the hotel on the other side of the railroad tracks, near the road to the factory. The hotel where people go to make sex. You know the place."

"OK, OK," I said, hoping this organizer in San Antonio who had helped arrange my visit to Río Bravo would not think I was incompetent.

But I asked myself, "What hotel?" because the only hotel I knew was La Mansion. "Is there a hotel near the road to the maquila?" I wondered.

I had just been to the place where I thought I was supposed to meet Carmen Julia, but I left never having seen her or any hotel and figuring either I was in the wrong spot or maybe I had missed her. I hung up the phone and returned to the road near the factory and asked a guy who seemed to live in a converted train station if he had seen a woman with kids.

He said, "Sí, they were here but left a little while ago."

I phoned San Antonio, again, and confessed that I didn't know my way around and had missed Carmen Julia once more.

"She is coming back," the voice announced. "She will wait by the hotel."

I returned to look for the elusive hotel but saw no evidence of any building resembling a place "where they go to make sex." After about a half hour of waiting, eventually in the darkness, I realized that buried in the trees beside the one-time railroad station, almost on top of where my car was parked, was a rusted sign for a hotel—one of my first mistakes in looking for sexuality in Mexico.

At Carmen Julia's house she told me she was very worried before I came. Her house was so small, she said, without bathrooms and so on. But it seemed I didn't mind.

"It must be hard for you?" she asked.

"No," I told her, "I don't have much, and when I raised my children, we didn't have much, either."

I thought, though, about what "much" meant for me and weighed the ethics of comparative truth. I flashed on a story my daughter Molly tells about when we lived in Syracuse and I was a graduate student. She was four or five years old, and one afternoon she found me on the front porch, where I was fighting back tears, lamenting some financial crisis. As she tells the story, this was the day she learned "we were poor," which was of course an exaggeration of our precarious middle-class life, but she embraced this epiphany, went into the backyard, and also cried. Carmen Julia's repeated apologies and explanations drew me back to listening.

"For me it is an accomplishment that you are here," she said. "It is a really big event for me because . . . I don't know. I am really demanding. When I learned you were coming, I said to myself, 'Well, I have to buy new furniture, and I have to make the house presentable.' I'm not kidding you. These sheets—I bought them because my sheets were really old. This chair—*chin*!—how I washed it! Yes, this was a new experience for me. And I asked myself, 'How is Rosemary going to react when she sees my house? Will she like it or not? Maybe it is going to give her allergies with all this dust!'"

As we each gradually revealed more of ourselves in the days that followed and during late-night chats, Carmen Julia spoke about her experience in the strike and her first year as an organizer. I gradually learned that her accomplishment was about much more than hosting me, for a transformation had taken place in her life, the result of forces that moved her to become one of the workers in the front lines of a campaign for an independent union. This story would take some time to be revealed.

Meanwhile, during this September visit, I was becoming more intimate with Carmen Julia's neighborhood, Colonia de las Américas. The air in the colonia has a texture that is only Mexico, a distinctive smell and taste and feel. It enters your nose and eyes and creeps into your skin. Gritty like dusty roads and palpable as the scent of sewage, smoke, and sunbaked earth, it rides on the wind and within seconds is a part of your skin, a thin film that doesn't leave. It insists upon your flesh the breath of insects and animals, the cells of others. The matter of life and death floats in the air and fills your pores. Music from distant radios travels across the yards, and *gallos* strut and call through the window, "Wake up! Wake up! Mexico summons you to another day."

When I awoke my first morning in Carmen Julia's house, the TV was already on and "psychosis" was flashing across the screen as reporters interviewed people in New York City about how they were affected by the attack on the twin towers, how their everyday lives had been transformed, and what it meant to live with uncertainty and fear. Against this virtual backdrop of the first days post-9/11, the small acts of keeping life on track in the colonia made me consider psychosis as a disorder characterized by false beliefs about what was real. Here, in another corner of the Americas, daily routines held uncertainty at bay, as well as knowledge of horrors that no more qualified as news than did the psychosis of consumer culture or the international disaster of land and water contaminated with chemical effluent, unborn babies made toxic from parents' unhealthy workplaces, and bodies ground down from overwork. Against the hum of shock and blame and grief across the United States, morning in Río

Bravo slowly unfolded as Carmen Julia fetched water from the faucet by the road and returned to wake her boys and warm the tortillas.

Carmen is a solid, strong woman, thoughtful and patient. Much to my surprise, she told me she was twenty-seven years old, and I realized that she was not much older than my oldest daughter, who was much less settled into family responsibility. The home Carmen held together was devoted to the husband she adored, Lúcio Elías, then somewhere near South Bend, Indiana, picking squash, she thought, and their sons, Lúcio (seven) and Luis José (soon to be four). When we talked that morning, she described the customs of her domestic space and its gender politics. She told me her mother was active and smart but always deferred to her husband and silently put up with his behavior. This was the way for men and women, and they defended it, she said. She disagreed, however, and felt that a woman's ideas should matter in the home. The husband was the head of the household, yes, but the wife's ideas should be taken into account.

"For example," she said, "if he is painting the inside of the house, he should ask if she likes this color or another. Outside the house her ideas are her own."

I asked her why she maintained this difference between what a woman could claim inside and outside her home.

"I chose Lúcio," she said, "because he is not *macho*, because he is respectful of me as a woman. Still, many of his ideas and ways now are only the result of lots of discussion."

Carmen emphasized that men would not change without a lot of discussion, but even that had its limits. She did not tell Lúcio when she was chosen as one of the workers who would go inside the Duro plant to monitor the election, a monumental event in her life and a dangerous one. She kept it secret from this man who was so dear and important to her because, she said, if he had known, he would not have let her do it. She added that afterward her brothers and sisters joked about giving her a mask like Subcomandante Marcos's, but her grandfather genuinely cheered her on and called her a revolutionary.

As more days with Carmen Julia unfolded, it was clear that she enjoyed talking with me and revealing herself, something she said was a new experience. She was, she stressed, a woman who didn't gossip. In fact, as she mentioned several times, she rarely talked. Even her husband had to encourage her to talk. She told me that as a young girl she did not have many friends, and until last year in the Duro struggle, she really had no women friends. This past year was therefore immensely important for her, in part because of the friendships she had developed. As Carmen talked about these experiences in the strike, she began to cry. She referred to the many difficulties that she and the others had experienced over the course of the year, and she spoke of the organizer based in San Antonio who supported them as a very special person.

"I feel for her like she is my . . . mother," she said. Once more, tears welled in her eyes, and she stated, "She believes in me in ways even my mother doesn't."

Although I think that psychoanalysis has many shortcomings, I respect its insights into the process of concealment and attachment, which are the very texture of consciousness—that is, the work of the unconscious. So I found myself turning to the concept of transference for help in understanding some of the affective dynamics in these conversations with Carmen Julia. Avery Gordon reminds us that in the relationship between analyst and analysand, a story is the affective consequence of the dynamics of speaking and listening. The repetition that takes place in its telling is always repetition-as-displacement. The transference that prompts and accompanies the story creates a "complete change of scene," a memory of the present.[30] What is transference, she asks, but the

> giving over to what one loves a recognition of the complicated love
> relation between oneself and another. This love is not mystical or
> a mystification; it is the intimacy of a contact with another, often
> asymmetrical, usually fragile and fraught with strains of mastery.
> It is a prerequisite to sensuous knowledge.[31]

If trust developed between Carmen Julia and me, it now seems to me that this description of transference captures some of what made it possible. Her story comes to you through the nets of triangulation and mastery in our conversations. Old losses and buried desires, childhood pains and longings were among the ghosts that haunted our exchanges, filtered through the fact of her being a Mexican worker-organizer and my being *una profesora de los Estados Unidos.* This last fact made me doubly an outsider, and perhaps for that reason I was an ideal interlocutor for Carmen, even though in my awkwardness and halting Spanish I did not feel like a professional anyone. It is my fantasy that from time to time she did forget my strangeness as the transference that took place between us—if "transference" is, indeed, the right word—weaved a charged web of complicated affects. I now think of its material as the eros of passionate politics, born in Carmen's initiation into organizing and my own into Mexico. What allowed the stories we exchanged was the *salto mortal*—the "fatal leap"—we each had taken: hers into a fragile new identity as an organizer and my own from teaching and writing culture theory in a university in Upstate New York to being this outsider-ally to labor organizers on the border. Transported by these enormous life choices, each of us arrived at events where we met intermittently over four years, our interactions always warm and somewhat formal and shy. The residue of the times we had shared up until this day in September 2001 and the mark they left on each of us made possible our exchanges. Most especially, it was a particular woman, that organizer in San Antonio—a legend of sorts on the border—who provided the medium through which Carmen and I came to know one another. She was present even when Carmen Julia and I were alone, though the meaning of her presence was enshrouded in the rhetoric of the public secret.

"I didn't receive affection as a young person," Carmen said, "except for Lúcio, who was my boyfriend, so I was very cold, very hard."

I told Carmen this was difficult to believe, and she protested, "Believe it. Believe it because it is the truth about me. Like I told you, I want a lot, and for that reason I think that I hurt a lot when anyone betrays me, because I surrender and entrust so much. I surrender my heart in each friendship, and then, when someone betrays you, it simply breaks your heart, and that is what happened to me. My hard and cold being was like a defense mechanism before the bad things of the world. And then that one and that one and those crazy women and this woman, the witch, yes, this astrologer from San Antonio, made me let it all out. Yes. These crazy women who left their children in their homes and their husbands to be in a strike for almost a year—they taught me to live. And that is why I am now talking to you. If you had come two years ago, we wouldn't have had this conversation."

The Haircut

Saturday dawned in Colonia de las Américas, plunging us into wetness. It was raining, and all outdoors had become a sea of mud. A planning meeting was set to be held at Carmen Julia's house. Several of the workers involved in the organizing at the Duro plant were coming to prepare for a big meeting the next day, and Martha was coming from San Antonio to facilitate it. Margarita, Elvira, Luisa, Sylbia, Eric (Margarita's six-year-old son), and Luisa's daughter joined Carmen Julia and her two boys while I went to get Martha and supplies for Sunday's meeting. Once we were assembled at Carmen's, I kept one eye on the discussion and the other on the TV that kept delivering news from New York.

During the meeting at Carmen's, the three boys, like all children of a certain age on a rainy day, were being good, but only to a point. Eric was a high-energy kid, and he and Lúcio and Luis were wiggling on the bed and devising games that involved crawling under the chairs or between the beds in the tiny room then filled with nine women. When they got even a little loud, though, it was impossible to hear. Martha told them to be quiet more than once in a somewhat stern voice, and then she announced, "Either you are quiet or I cut your hair!" Later, she told me this was a custom in Mexico and that everyone knew that. When I ask Carmen Julia about this custom the next day, however, she said that she had never heard of such a thing.

Well, the boys did not quiet down, and so Martha said, "OK. Too bad. I said be quiet or I will cut your hair, and now I will." So she reached for the nearest child, who happened to be Lúcio, and taking a pair of scissors clipped a tiny bit of hair from near his ear and showed it to him. We all sat with our mouths open. "Now see," she said.

Lúcio was stunned and fell to the floor in a fetal position, his head in his hands, sobbing. He stayed like this for a long time, maybe fifteen minutes or more. We women smiled and rolled our eyes at each other. Martha put down the scissors and resumed talking. The other children were, needless to say, quiet. Later, when Lúcio finally came out of his fetal pose and found Eric under the table, I thought I could discern them plotting some imaginary or real revenge against Martha. When I told Martha the next day that I was not sure what I thought of this method of discipline, she said, "Well, it didn't really hurt him. In fact, I only cut a piece that was uneven and needed cutting anyway."

After the meeting on Saturday, Martha explained to a lingering group of women who attended that this was a special day of the year, a day of passage—the autumnal equinox—and she proposed we perform a ritual. It was a day for cleansing negative feelings and for healing, she said. Luisa offered her house, and the group agreed that it sounded just right. When we arrived in her neighborhood, the streets were completely flooded. Water was knee high at every corner and filled some streets. It was a surreal scene. We parked the two cars, removed our shoes, and began wading through the water. This impromptu parade of women made a bit of a spectacle as we passed small groups of neighbors gathered on the street corner or chatting under the streetlights. Luisa suggested we gather in the back of her house. Under the huge *platano* trees, we would be shielded from the neighbors. Her husband and several other family members mingled inside.

Here, we began what would be a moving and strange experience. We stood in a circle. Martha was inside it, and she asked for a helper. Nellie came forward, and the ritual commenced. Martha instructed us to extend one arm, hand open, to close our eyes, and to breathe deeply. She explained that this was not a religious ceremony; rather, it spoke to our place on the earth and to the natural forces with which we lived. She went around the circle and put what we later learned was a small bit of tobacco in each of our hands. She then asked us to feel forgiveness for any of the ways we may have offended our sisters and to give thanks for what we had been given. Women began to speak aloud, asking forgiveness for how they may have wronged a *compañera*. Several spoke their thanks. With Nellie's help Martha took a bunch of burning sage and passed it over each of us. She poured water in our other hand and once more passed the burning herbs over us. The children were in the circle, too, instructed that they could be there only if they were silent. They were. Around the circle and without speaking, each woman shared an expression of what each other person meant to her. Some extended hands and touched; others embraced. The children were solemn, watching expressionless, except for little Jessica, whose face was wet with tears. Before the ritual ended, Martha asked Lúcio to forgive her for cutting his hair.

Ritual, Renato Rosaldo tells us, is a fragmented performance of a storehouse of collective wisdom, a busy intersection of multiple co-existing social processes extending before and after its enactment.[32] It can reiterate cultural platitudes or open doorways onto affective material that enacts a potent social unconscious. It can be a chink through which to glimpse reconciliation and perform a lost relation to nature and each other. Ritual has a profound affective charge, in part because it opens a space outside the realm of necessity and distanced from the alienated experience of everyday life and its sufferings.[33] If it enacts remnants of a common memory, it may also voice desires for a life with dignity and connection to one another and to the earth. It can be a window on utopian longing.

The Disturbance Zone

Freud never developed a theory of the affects, but it is clear that his discovery of the unconscious and his analysis of its role in the therapeutic process touch the profound bearing that affective relationships have on becoming responsibly aware of one's subjectivity. The unconscious draws us to a region where things stand gaping, there and yet hidden, and the question of how we know a world, our own or another's, becomes a question of the limits of representation. We enter a kind of disturbance zone where things are not always what they seem.[34] Freud extends his discovery into a therapeutic practice enacted through a process of identification with others, an identification that was formerly extended to animals, to plants, to inanimate matter, and to the world at large.[35] As Avery Gordon points out, he comes very close to saying that the unconscious is inconceivable outside the worldly relations that structure the encounter between one self and another. Gordon traces the path Freud pursues in inventing the unconscious as something "of which its own possessor knows nothing."[36] He cannot get away, however, from its role as the place where all others in the world and their lives come inside us and unhinge our sense of self as they make us what we are, as they live within us. Here, the specter of a social unconscious raises its head along with the affective attachments that adhere to it. The Freudian unconscious is not a social unconscious, but Freud's early conceptualization of it is haunted by this possibility. Here is Gordon again:

> Freud's Science will try once and for all to rid itself of all vestiges of animism by making the spirits or hauntings come from the unconscious, from inside the troubled individual, an individual, we might note, who had become increasingly taken with the animation of the commodity world. . . . . Freud will try to demystify our holdover beliefs in the power of the world at large, hoping to convince us that everything that seems to be coming at us from the outside is really coming from this now shrunken inside . . . but it is not enough.[37]

The concept of the unconscious and the affective attachments enacted in therapeutic work on it replaced the magic of premodern civilizations, bringing in its revolutionary wake an emphatically individual subject whose relationship to the natural world is housed in the psyche rather than in the magical movement of spirit, of seasons and stars, of the cycles of life and death.[38]

A dimension of the organizing I witnessed spills out of this narrow case for the modern self. It accompanies the official story like a dream that clings to our waking hours. Is it a secret? A charm that works only if concealed from strangers? Or is it urgent knowledge for the present, a vestige of the affect-culture that modern enlightenment dispelled, perhaps not entirely for the better, a memory that can and must erupt in revolutionary times? It surfaces in exchanges during organizing campaigns in Mexico, outside the law and beside the fact of critical judgment. It is too easy for me to dismiss this knowledge as popular superstition, nonsense, so I entertain the possibility that effective organizing relies on melancholic knowledge that speaks to the losses of contemporary life through images and practices that conjure beliefs and hopes from another time and that touch a chord beyond cognition. In the organizing on the border, this knowledge sometimes gathers around iconic figures and images like the Zapatistas and their relation to Emiliano Zapata, whose army of the south inserted the struggle over common lands into the Mexican revolution. It also appears, however, in stories of the seasons and the stars, in rituals preserved through the alchemy of migrations, conquests, and generations: the talismans and traces of *curanderas* and *nagual* shapeshifters. As they become part of affective mapping, they too serve the needs of organizing in ways I am only beginning to absorb. I dance around them, trying to find some ground between respect and cynicism that avoids, if possible, the traps of fetishizing and exoticizing that history has set for me, the outsider.

Rituals impact a group's emotional habitus, or mood. They satisfy the need for affirmation and respect that makes existence bearable. The danger in embracing them is that you can forfeit the defamiliarizing vigilance of witnessing. Walking that tightrope is the challenge of political education.

Saturday Night in Coahuila

Only toward the end of the interview, as I saw the signs of exhaustion on their faces, was I able to get to the heart of what brought me to Frontera, a small city in Coahuila, one October to talk with two seasoned women organizers. I watched for signs of whether my questions registered, and through the weariness, I saw their eyes light up.

"Ah, yes, this," they said. "Yes, it is so important. And no, there is little space to address it. It is so difficult to get to these issues."

So after hours of talk, there we were. Both women had been involved in organizing for over twenty years—Gloria in Mexico City, Bety in Frontera and Juárez. Each had told many stories of working with women in grassroots labor organizing, but then each shook her head, searching for better answers to my question about these nameless affective attachments and their role in what was to be done. Silence settled on us. The plot of history broke down. The tape recorder was turned off; the official story, closed. But then the conversation took a turn. Around the circle tales from elsewhere surged up—of *curas,* planetary alignments, ancient healing arts. What value could I assign to these hushed exchanges in the calculus of a weekend of workshops and discussions about organizing in the shadow of neoliberalism?

Earlier that day in the workers' center in Frontera, I watched an extraordinary exchange. A group of women promoters from a garment assembly plant for Sara Lee talked with one of the organizers who had come from out of town to learn about their struggle and offer support. María Luisa, Julia, Rosario, Laura, Claudia—all leaned forward on their chairs and described their work in the factory. The visiting organizer asked them questions filtered through her expertise in Mexican law and the knowledge of what it meant to be a worker who sewed thousands of sleeves herself in the maquilas—questions about quotas and salaries, *bonos,* accidents, and health problems. All of it. Their faces were animated. Everyone took a turn. They could not keep quiet. They had more and more to say. She took notes as they detailed their work lives. This was an inquest and a lesson, and the lesson was that in the short term, knowledge of the law could be a weapon, but one must know it in order to use it. A copy of the Mexican federal labor law sat on the desk.

The session ended, but the young women lingered as another lesson began, this one about one's capacity, and the visiting organizer taught it through the filter of the planets and the stars. She held up a mirror to each woman in turn and talked with each in hushed tones about her strengths and who she could be.

María Luisa told her, "When you come here, you really want to get to know us, each of us."

Indeed, this seemed so. I left the meeting with the others, impressed by this ritual of affirmation, and I wondered how much it might enable each woman to step up and make use of the law. The law could be a weapon in labor organizing, surely, but it was not all. There was also this sensuous knowledge that affirmed confidence, propelled action, and bound a group. It announced that we were not just subjects of modernity's laws and violence. We were fighting together for our lives, and in that fight we touched one another elsewhere, in places that were nameless but certain, lodged within the facts of our labor, our stories, and our desires for a life with dignity.

They flashed in this teacher's every gesture, announcing, "Yes, on this *onda* you are strong, and we are together, and all is of a piece."

Limited Trust

When need is great, the arrival of an outsider with resources can complicate solidarity. A resource can be anything—something quite tangible like money or less tangible like a skill. In my visits to the organizing groups on the border, I was aware that my presence and who I spent time with was calculated in terms of the things I brought and gave as gifts and the intangible benefit of being connected to me for access to opportunities. Material resources are a part of the affect-culture that filters bearing witness for someone coming to Mexico from the United States. Words like "trust" and "transparency" that circulate among NGOs working on the border do not cover all of the contradictory relations involved. Among the U.S. groups there can be competition for an in on the Mexican side, for connections, credibility, and legitimacy. These desires are driven by the political economy of NGOs, which not only offer workers support but also need the workers for their organization's programming and funding. In other words, the dynamic of bearing witness as someone from the United States is complicated by the affect-laden vestiges of a long history of imperial power relations. It can register explicitly in heated debates over money or motives or be played out in manipulations or gestures of awkwardness or condescension that whisper the open secret of mutual interest.

During my stay with Carmen Julia, I attended a *lotería* (bingo) at Margarita's house one Sunday afternoon, and in this gathering of a dozen neighbors raising money for the Duro strike, I felt the self-consciousness and isolation of being the outsider from the United States, welcomed perhaps for the resources she provided but definitely alien: too tall, too blonde, possibly suspect. I read the question, "Who is this *gringa,* and why is she here?" in the glances of the children and the women, some of whom I had already met. I sat near Ana and her son Miguel and shared friendly exchanges with Felipe and his wife and kids. My outsiderness eased as the bingo began. Eventually, both seven-year-old Miguel and Felipe's teenaged son simply put stones on my card when I didn't see the figures fast enough. Trust is a practice of letting go.

I have often thought about the ways my own sexual identity was evident or known or featured in my evolving relationships with workers during visits like this one. In some of the conversations I had with organizers about their experiences as lesbian, gay, or homosexual, it was an empathic bridge between us—but not always.

In the middle of my interview with one organizer who was openly homosexual, he turned to me and said, "OK. You were married, and now you are lesbian, but you were never with a gay friend willing to listen and open your life like I am doing to you." I was taken aback and stumbled to better explain my history. He then made a speech that was confusing, and so I asked for help with the sense of it. He continued talking, saying, "Let me tell you, since you aren't someone who has had a gay friend or who has talked like this with a gay man, openly like I am talking with you."

In the moment I struggled to grasp what Andrés was driving at. Was this total projection? Blame? Critique? I tried to check my urge to be defensive, thinking, "How can I legitimize myself as someone who is not that? But what is it he thinks I am? What is he leading up to?"

Meanwhile, he kept talking, saying, "And let me tell you, for a lesbian here in Mexico to be in a relationship with a gay man is to be a real shit."

The interview had been focused on gender roles within gay life and how that was or was not related to the *machista* he had spoken about earlier. Now, though, it had taken an amazing turn.

"Well, let me tell you," he said, "I was in love with a lesbian."

What followed was the story of the love of his life, a woman he fell in love with when he was working in a maquiladora in Nuevo Laredo. This story was a part of Andrés's narrative of an organizing effort in Fábricas de Calidad, one of the only times homosexual rights were a part of the workers' demands, a campaign I discuss in chapter 5. This charged confrontation in the middle of our interview amplified my growing zone of uncertainty about how I was seen and how my reasons for being in Mexico were understood in the complex dynamics of projection and transference that occurred in the intimacies that opened in conversations. It was a key element in the pedagogy of failure that I was coming to recognize as central to witnessing.

During my visit with Carmen Julia that September, I urged one of the organizers from out of town to come to Río Bravo for a meeting at the workers' center—a man who was openly gay and who joined the Duro workers' permanent demonstration when they were on strike but who left because of the homophobia directed at him. I assumed his bad experience was a thing of the past because the homophobic perpetrator had left town. So Iván came to the meeting along with his partner, Juan. I imagined there would be lots of smiles and warm conversation. I was wrong. Their reception was cool though polite. Iván, Juan, and I ended up on one side of the room and the women workers on the other, huddled in conversation among themselves. The food we had brought sat untouched in the other room. When a few other men arrived, they formed a small circle outside, and Iván eventually found a place among them. Juan seemed to float on the fringe of this gathering, not part of any group. Later, when I drove them home, Juan admitted—or Iván admitted for him—that he was dying of boredom, tired of being ignored or of simply not having anything to say. I told them I found the cold reception they received very strange because the women had seemed so enthusiastic about the prospect of a visit.

Iván replied, "Rosemary, you have to learn that in Mexico people will say what they think you want to hear when in reality they think something very different."

I wondered how true this might be of Iván, as well, and pondered my own foolish ineptness. Was I also being shunned at the meeting, recognized as the lesbian friend of Iván, but my abjection was tempered by the potential resources I bore? Did I just not see what was going on? As events like this one remind us, vigilance can mean learning from being caught in nets of desire and ignorance as we navigate our relations to others.

I have no neat conclusion to these stories, in part because the work of bearing witness is unfinished and messier than anyone would like. It continues in part 2 where specific organizing campaigns disclose the *ambiente* and the affections of organizing on the border.

II

Sex, Labor, Movement

« 4 »

Open Secrets

The open secret is a familiar figure in gay culture and sexuality studies, conjuring an epistemology in which knowing becomes not knowing.[1] For the French philosopher Michel Foucault, the open secret is a silence that permeates and gives shape to the requirement to speak about some things, a discretion that accompanies a preoccupation.[2] It refers to a cultural environment in which much is known but unrecognized. In her book *Ghostly Matters,* the sociologist Avery Gordon points to another manifestation of open secrets: the failures of established knowledge to convey the dense site "where history and subjectivity make social life."[3] The evidence of these losses abides as "that which appears not there" and yet is "a seething presence, acting on, and . . . meddling with the taken for granted realities."[4] It "draws us affectively, sometimes against our will and always a bit magically, into the structure of feeling of a reality we (may) come to experience, not as cold knowledge, but as transformative recognition."[5] Each sort of spectral knowledge has a different relation to power. Together, they define the two faces of the open secret: one a disciplinary technology aimed at conserving existing norms and power relations, the other a subversive and expansive counterdiscourse. In each, desire and need mingle; fact and fiction overlap.

The affect-culture of organizing is saturated with both sorts of open secrets, at times mixed up with each other. They are parts of the undercurrent that maintains a campaign's cohesion and direction or pulls it off course. In any organizing effort, bonds of loyalty, camaraderie, and friendship and of competition, jealousy, and betrayal are seething presences. If we know little about them, we are even more challenged to understand sexuality as their dense transfer point. As I mention in chapter 2, sexuality is a historical discourse that has a close relation to affect and emotion. It names and organizes corporeal sensations and intensities, attachments, and abjections. Like race and gender, it is a strong attractor, which means that affectively loaded cultural values adhere to it, and for this reason sexuality is a powerful ideological vehicle. This affective dimension makes sexual discourses so readily naturalized and internalized.

Sexual identity is an imaginary formulation, a discursive, psychic, and ideological effect that directs the human capacity for sensation and affect by way of categories that uphold or disrupt a gendered symbolic order. Normative sexual identities (hetero- and homonormativity), as well as their abjected others (sexual perversions), are historical constructs. They emerged in industrializing countries, and their changing contours are related to adjustments taking place in relations of labor.[6] As Judith Butler elaborated over two decades ago, normative sexual identities are insecure. But their insecurity is not only because the languages that represent them are slippery. The crises and failures of prescribed sexual identities are more properly understood as sites of social struggle. Sexual identities are open to question and have to be continually resecured because although their configurations are arbitrary, relations of labor and power are invested in their normative configurations. This struggle over meanings is rife with feelings, especially when identities fray ("Oh, I always thought you were gay!") and imaginaries get mended ("Me—no way!").

Foucault recognizes that sexuality is an effective terminal for connecting networks of power. In historical materialist terms, it mediates the relation between people's affective capacities and their survival needs. This does not mean that the discourses of sexuality necessarily serve capitalist interests, though as strong attractors they are a potent conduit for them. The narrow options that normative formulations of sexuality offer have made them efficient agents of capitalism's squeeze on human needs and capacities. These unmet needs must be continually reckoned with, and the open secret of homosexual identity is a powerful medium for this reckoning. For this reason it is important to track its circulation in organizing efforts and to better understand the other open secret that haunts them: collective action's capacious and unspeakable passionate attachments.

Homosexual Identity in the Maquilas

Much has been written about the gendered division of labor and its impact on women workers in the maquiladoras, but no research has been done on women's affective and sexual attachments to other women in this massive female workforce. The topic has been enshrouded in the epistemology of the open secret. Are the maquilas, where sometimes thousands of women work together day after day, a breeding ground for lesbians? In this concentrated all-female work environment, do women develop new or different affective and sexual relationships with one another, whether or not they call themselves "lesbian"? How do these relationships feature in the dynamics of organizing? What about gay men? At what point did they enter the maquila workforce? And how? Are gay men and lesbians out at work? And what are the consequences if they are? How does sexual identity, no matter how unstable or imaginary a category, feature in the affective cultures of collective organizing in the maquilas? Why has it taken so long for these questions to be raised?

Many of the organizers I met were lesbian or gay identified. Their stories reveal that this identification—what it means, how it is lived, and how it is received—can be a catalyst for leadership, but it is also material for gossip, secrecy, sabotage, and betrayal. In Mexico, homosexuality is an open secret with particular connotations.[7] It is conditioned by a Napoleonic legal tradition that considers private, consensual sexual activity to be beyond the scope of the law and a Catholic religious tradition that teaches homosexuality is a sin.[8] Attitudes about homosexuality also vary and are inflected by local custom. Practices that may be commonplace in northern border towns do not necessarily apply in Mexico City or the Yucatán, and cultural variations between mestizo and indigenous groups are considerable.[9] The reification of sexuality that was one of the conditions for the emergence of homo- and heterosexual identities around the turn of the twentieth century in Europe and the United States also took hold in the cosmopolitan center of Mexico City and played a part in state regulation of the national body. In Mexican law homosexual relations between adults over eighteen have not been criminalized since the mid-nineteenth century. Moreover, in the past few years a series of reforms have extended civil rights protections for sexual minorities.[10] In 2006 in Mexico City, civil unions were legalized for same-sex and different-sex couples, and in 2007 the northern border state of Coahuila reformed its civil code, allowing same-sex and different-sex couples to legally unite under a civil union. In 2010 the Mexican Supreme Court recognized marriage between partners of the same sex.

Despite these reforms, constitutional civil rights are overwritten by civil codes and moral norms codified in criminal and labor law and entrenched in patriarchal gender schemes. Article 201 of the federal penal code, entitled "Transgressions against Morality and Public Decency," provides a broad, vague legal category that when reinforced by ordinances at the federal, state, and municipal levels, can be used to penalize gender and sexual dissidents. Moreover, the Mexican federal labor law contains a clause that allows workers to be fired for committing "faltas de probidad u honradez" (unethical acts). While this clause connotes dishonest behavior, a later clause prohibits *actos immorales* (immoral acts).[11] These moral codes leave employers lots of room for interpretation and manipulation in order to discriminate against gay and lesbian workers. Moreover, beyond the letter of the law, stigma and discrimination are common.[12]

In the cities and towns along the northern border, as in the rest of the country, sexual cultures are volatile, and networks that draw on shared histories and vocabularies rapidly absorb new ones as people migrate internally and cross back and forth between Mexico and the United States. Although civic life is expanding in faraway Mexico City and a few other urban areas and popular *telenovelas* and some films increasingly portray gay characters in a positive light, many northern border cities and towns remain hostile and potentially dangerous places for those who do not publicly conform to heterosexual gender norms or abide by the code of the open secret.[13]

Because sexual identity is gendered, though never simply or coherently, no discussion of the open secret of homosexuality can avoid addressing its relation to gender. In northern Mexico's border towns, gender norms are changing, in part because increasing numbers of women have joined the urban workforce. The opportunities for

mobility and relationships outside the family that wage work provides strain long-standing patriarchal values and provoke considerable backlash. Several important studies of masculinity at the
Mexican border have addressed the ways these tensions have registered in conflicting performances of masculinity in the workplace
culture of the maquiladoras and in men's insecurities outside work.[14]

In the prevailing patriarchal gender culture in Mexico, as in the
United States, masculinity and femininity are still considered to be
discrete and opposite characteristics that apply to men and women,
respectively, with masculinity valued over femininity. These gender
codes are both reiterated and transgressed in homosexual culture. Recent scholarship on gender in Mexico has critiqued the representation
of this gender scheme as *machista,* arguing that doing so replicates a
neocolonial perspective by separating the cultural history of gender
from the political and economic forces of which it is a part.[15] For
this reason some U.S. scholars refuse to use the terms *machista* or
machismo,[16] seeing them as an oversimplified and even stereotypical
representation of Mexican and Latino masculinity to which a host
of social problems has been attributed.[17] Many Mexican scholars do
use these terms, however, as apt ones for the cultural codes of a patriarchal masculinity that overcompensates for men's vulnerabilities in
a neocolonial situation. When Mexican machismo is represented as
traditional and positioned against an enlightened and more modern
gender culture in the United States, the implication is that more U.S.
influence would modernize Mexico and save the country from itself.[18]
As Lionel Cantú, Eithne Luibhéid, and others have shown, however,
some professional gay Mexicans prefer to stay in Mexico because they
see the United States as racist and intolerant. Indeed, working-class
Mexican gay immigrants to the United States are often subjected to
intense homophobia, as well as racism and economic exploitation.[19]
The most effective analyses of Mexican homosexuality do not focus
solely on the culture of machismo but situate Mexican sex–gender
codes within the country's cultural, political, and economic history.
In addition, recent work on sexuality in Mexico, including research
on homosexuality, increasingly stresses the importance of taking into
account regional and local differences in gender schemes and the
influence on them of transnational migration, tourism, and media

culture.[20] I use the words *macho* and *machismo* as terms for a hypermasculine identification that is itself a historical effect.

Within the cultural formations of the border, as elsewhere in Mexico, the sex–gender codes of same-sex practices are affectively charged. Among men who have sex with men, sex roles can defy or conform to the gendered distinctions of the normative cultural system. Not all men who have sex with men are considered homosexual, nor do they all consider themselves to be homosexual. In the prevailing cultural discourse on the border, "homosexual" generally refers to a man who adopts the feminine role in sex, and it carries the affective charge of a devalued, abjected cultural category. While the word "gay" is now used to refer to both men and women who have same-sex relationships, derogatory words like *joto* or *maricón* are also commonly directed toward male homosexuals, and they too are gendered feminine.[21] As Lionel Cantú explains, though, they are associated with a form of abjection that is not readily equated with normative femininity:

> Being *joto* is not to be a man. Neither a man nor a woman, it is an abomination, a curse. . . . Thus, the relationship of homosexuality to femininity is more complex than a synonymous equation implies. Homosexuality is not the opposite of masculinity, it is a corruption of it, an unnatural form that by virtue of its transgression of the binary male/female order poses a threat that must be contained or controlled.[22]

Héctor Domínguez-Ruvalcaba revises earlier accounts of homosexuality in Mexico by many pioneering scholars—among them Tomás Almaguer, Joseph Carrier, Roger Lancaster, and Carter Wilson—who represent Mexican and Latino homosexual roles in terms of an equation between active/passive and masculine/feminine. Domínguez-Ruvalcaba clarifies that the homosexual is a transgressive subject who lives queer and complex relations that undo simple equations among desire, activity, gender, and object choice. He argues that some feminized men who have sex with men (jotos) are active in that they take the role of seducer, whereas others (identified by the jotos as *mayates*) identify as heterosexual but choose the joto as the target (not the object) of their desire. The mayate's self-image is macho, and his erotic practice is wishing to be desired as a virile body. The joto's active role as seducer and the mayate's lack of attraction to the joto as an object of desire are what differentiate this version of homosexuality from the gendering of desire in traditional understandings of heterosexuality.[23]

From the perspective of the *gente de ambiente* (members of the gay community) of Sonora that Guillermo Núñez Noriega interviewed, various subject positions exist in addition to mayates and jotos. The bisexual enjoys contact with women and men and presents himself as such or as someone who may be experimenting with gay sex. The *jalador,* like the mayate, has sex with men but presents himself as heterosexual, and the *normal* may occasionally have sex with men but unlike the jalador is not accustomed to doing so routinely.[24]

The patriarchal gender scheme that inflects homosexual identity means that feminized gay men are most at risk of humiliation and violence. In their research on transgender sex workers in Tijuana, Debra Castillo, María Gudelia, Rangel Gómez, and Armando Rosas Solís argue that the city's virulent antigay violence is downplayed and that those who live the most dangerous lives are transgendered/transvestite/transsexual sex workers. They emphasize that very little accurate research has been published that would help in understanding the real issues of violence facing the transvestite individual along the border.[25] In his research in Hermosillo, Núñez Noriega also finds that "the cross-dressers tend to be used like a depository for the frustrations and ills besetting the community."[26] Mariana, a former maquiladora worker who grew up in Nuevo Laredo and who was in her late fifties when I interviewed her, recounted one of her memories of the price feminized gay men can pay: "There was an openly gay man who from time to time worked for my cousin. We knew him well," she said. "We called him La Morena. He wore women's clothes and was very open. But people would call him names when he walked down the street—*joto* or *maricón.* They killed him one night. They raped him with a broom and threw him in the street." Life and work for an openly gay man means a series of daily curtailed possibilities that range from the extreme experience of La Morena to less extreme negotiated and imposed forms of violence.

Women who are lesbian identified or who have women sexual partners tend to be less visible, unless they transgress prescribed gender norms. Some say they have less social prestige because they remain women—that is, they are still second-class citizens with fewer liberties than men regarding their sexuality. Others assert there is a growing, if ambivalent, tolerance for lesbians.[27] In her research on sexual culture in Veracruz, Patricia Ponce asserts that most of the city's lesbians are more discreet in their public language and dress than gay men.[28] Here, as on the border, the majority of lesbians live with their families, who may accept them but never discuss their sexual identity. In border towns women identified as lesbians can still be stigmatized as *marimachas, machorras,* or *tortilleras.* Like homosexual men, gender-variant women who have sexual relationships with other women risk the most public stigma, whereas their more feminine partners can escape scrutiny.

In 2002 I asked a group of workers from Sara Lee, makers of Hanes garments, in the town of Frontera, Coahuila, how many workers were in the plant. They replied, "40 percent men, 50 percent women, and 10 percent gays." I was surprised by this unprompted naming of gays. I asked Horacio, one of the workers, how they knew 10 percent of the workers were gay, and he said it was obvious: "The gays are men who look and act feminine." He said there were lesbians, too, and one knew them "because they looked and acted masculine." The women in the group nodded. We went on to talk about the possible intricacies of this gendered division, but the nonchalance with which gays were included in the population of workers and the ready equation of gay men and lesbians with gender variance were notable. Horacio said that although gays were accepted at work, there was no politics around their presence, neither in the organizing in the factory nor in the community.

An organizer in Matamoros agreed that many workers in the city's factories were gay and lesbian but they were not open at work. In 2003 he told me he had recently met with an electronics worker who wanted to talk about his sexual identity. "He felt so alone, like he was a failure and that he didn't belong in this world," he said. "It moved me so much." He said that in Matamoros many of the workers were migrants from the center of the country. Two or more newly migrated men might rent an apartment together, but their sexual identity would not be questioned. Only if they did not eventually take up the expected life of heterosexuals would people begin to suspect. "Homosexuality is spoken about little and understood less," he added. "There is no space for *formación* [political education]."²⁹

Nelly Benítez, an out lesbian in her early twenties and an organizer in Nuevo Laredo, reported that many gays and lesbians lived in that city. When interviewed, she said, "It is a really big community, but they have a social, not a political, presence." Nelly worked at several maquilas—Sony, Alambrados de Mexico, and Barry—before getting fired for organizing. She was blacklisted and unable to be hired in the other factories, so she went to school and volunteered as an organizer with the grassroots workers' center CETRAC. She said that in the 1990s when she worked in the maquilas, a group of lesbians would hang out on their breaks. Everyone knew they were gay, and sometimes they were harassed. She said that lesbian culture outside work revolved around the bars but also around softball and parties. She was in a group for a while that met every Sunday for a barbecue (*carne asada*). Some of the gay workers talked about not having the same rights as married workers—health insurance for their partners, for example. Although the politics of sexuality had featured in workshops Nelly helped organize with CETRAC, the focus was on sexual harassment and women's reproductive rights, not these concerns.

In an interview published in the U.S. gay magazine the *Advocate,* Nelly detailed some of her personal challenges with discrimination while she and her six-year-old daughter lived with her partner, Linda. She said that when she and Linda were out in public, they endured silent stares. When it came to her family, even though her grandmother loved Linda, her aunts disapproved of her relationship, her cousins made jokes about it, and initially her mother so condemned their life together that she threatened to take Nellie's daughter away.³⁰

Women who worked in the maquilas in the 1970s and the 1980s told a slightly different story. One organizer who worked in various factories between 1973 and 1995 said that, yes, many of the women working in the maquilas developed sexual relationships with other women, but no groups of lesbians hung out at work. Although she identified as lesbian, she was not officially out at work, even though she dressed very butch and had many lovers among her coworkers. For her, being a lesbian meant falling in love with a woman who saw their relationship as a way station before a heterosexual marriage and who ultimately discontinued the sexual relationship once she got pregnant or found the right man.

She also knew about a thriving lesbian subculture outside the factory, though, and the following is one of her stories:

> When I was around seventeen years old, I worked in a maquila where my mother also worked. My mother had a friend who was the nurse in the factory, and she needed help. So my mother sent me to be her helper because the work there was easier. There was a woman named Mari Carmen who came to the nurse almost every day, and she would always end up crying. The nurse would give her some pills and listen to her stories. One day, the nurse was not there, and I was tending the infirmary alone when Mari Carmen came in. Like always, she started crying, and she said, "Do you want to hear my story?" I said yes. So Mari Carmen told me how she was in love with a woman named Iris but that Iris was now in love with someone else, a woman named Carla Martínez. She asked me to take her home, and there she showed me a picture of Iris. Another day, Mari Carmen asked me to drive her to the softball game, and Carla Martínez was there. Iris was there, too. Carla Martínez came over, and Mari Carmen introduced her to me. Carla Martínez said, "Well, as long as you are here with her, then you are welcome." It was obvious this was her turf. Then, Iris came over. Maybe she is coming to claim her old girlfriend, I thought. But no. Iris said to Mari Carmen, "Are you with her?" meaning me, and she said yes. I realized then that Mari Carmen only wanted to make Iris jealous. Mari Carmen turned to me and said, "Let's go to the other game." So we went across town where the other softball game was happening. This was the turf of Teresa Chung, who ruled the other team. When the game ended, we went to a party at Teresa's house. There, each woman had her partner, and there was lots of flirting and drinking.

This tale of initiation into lesbian culture begins with a disclosure of unrequited love delivered in the margins of the workplace, a space where unspeakable feelings can be aired, attended to, and medicated. This story harbors many silences—what Mari Carmen would tell the nurse, why she feels she has a sympathetic listener in the nurse's young replacement, and why she recognizes her as someone interested in women. Mari Carmen's melodrama leads her interlocutor outside the factory, where spaces of lesbian culture are revealed from her now somewhat disenchanted retrospective. When I mentioned Nelly's profile of lesbian life in Nuevo Laredo to this older woman, she wryly commented that in the city Nelly described, Carla Martínez and Teresa Chung probably still ruled, one on each side of town—or if not them, then their replacements.

As elsewhere, lesbian and gay networks on the border shift and change with the times, but they remain under the radar of a public culture that is for the most part unapologetically homophobic. In October 2011 Yessy, a gay man in his twenties who had worked at two garment assembly plants in Valle Hermoso, Tamaulipas, talked about the difficulties of living openly in his small town. He stressed the amount of fear. Initially, he said he would have liked to live where he could be more open in public, but by the end of the interview he asked himself, "Why should I run away if I have made my life here? I have to keep going here whether they accept me or not." He spoke about the process of coming out to his parents when he was twenty-two, even though he knew he was gay from when he was nine. He recounted how afraid he was to tell them and how much their acceptance of him had boosted his confidence. "Every New Year's Day now," he said, "they hug me and tell me again, 'Usted es mi hijo, sea como sea' [You are my son, no matter what]." Family anchored Yessy's values and sense of manhood. "For me," he emphasized, "a gay man is manlier than someone they say is a man because many gays help their families get ahead while many men abandon them. We are strong because we endure so many criticisms, offenses, threats, and insults." He said he respected the limits to being open in extended family gatherings because he would not want the homophobic comments of others to embarrass his family. He spoke of the disparity between the realities for gay people in Mexico City or the United States and in Mexico's northern provinces. "They are really *machista,* and if you are gay, they do not recognize you as a human being, much less let you marry. Gay rights is like a cloud," he sagely added, "that came from the north and passed us by to arrive in Mexico City." Although he thought that in a bigger city, like nearby Matamoros, homosexuality might be more accepted, he also knew that some gay men had been murdered there and in the neighboring cities of Reynosa and Nuevo Laredo. He added, however, "Their deaths are not considered to be hate crimes. Each was just one more death, and like so many others in this country now, they went unpunished."

One indicator of the level of public sanctioning of homophobia in the northern provinces is that some newspapers in border cities still publish photos of "homosexual" male suspects arrested on morals charges.[31] Unsurprisingly, legal threats and cultural prejudices attached to homosexuality are convenient and potent weapons for discrediting labor organizers. One woman said that when she was organizing in the factories and confronting the union and company officials, who were all men, the stakes were very high: "The threat of exposure as a lesbian was real, and they would use it, but I was really strong. I wore a tie. Only once did someone threaten me, and I said, 'Show me the evidence, prove it,' and they backed down." In this climate the medium of existence is the open secret.

The Structures of Feeling Homosexual: Masks, Tricks, Balance

Homosexuality haunts organizing on the border, encrypted in innuendos that morph into threats, marking the limits between private and public knowledge, recorded and recordable history, tolerance and belonging. Organizing may be propelled by workplace injustices, yet once under way it is a minefield of open secrets, one of which is homosexuality, a mask and a danger zone. In *Defacement: Public Secrecy and the Labor of the Negative,* Michael Taussig defines the public or open secret as "that which is generally known, but cannot be articulated."[32] Open secrets simmer beneath the surface of official discourse, unacknowledged yet widely shared. As Taussig demonstrates, the open secret covers a broad range of material. He looks at the law of silence in northern Colombia, where peasants are massacred daily and their mutilated bodies appear on the streets, where people know the para-military commits these murders but this knowledge cannot be articu-lated. The smoke screen of "long known-ness" that he details now permeates narco-dominated daily life on the Mexican border and is interlaced with older secrets. Open secrets form an intricate part of knowing what not to know, so that even in trying to extricate our-selves from their traps, we fall into traps of our own making. This process is what Taussig calls the "labor of the negative," "as when it is pointed out that something may be obvious, but needs stating in order to be obvious."[33] These sorts of open secrets are mobile and dif-fuse channels for corporate and state impunity and for the common sense. Whispered in kitchens, on street corners, and in the hallways of workshops and strategy sessions, they can protect the powerful and the powerless. As part of the culture of class relations, open secrets are sites of struggle. They can circulate as soft weapons or as subversive knowledge that surfaces pressure points for social change.

The Zapatistas have made the politics of secrecy their talisman and signature. "Why is there such commotion about ski masks?" Sub-comandante Marcos asks. "Isn't Mexican political culture itself a 'culture of *tapados*'?" (*Tapados* refers to a political process character-ized by cover-ups and behind-the-scenes deals.) "I am ready to take off the mask," he adds, "when Mexican society takes off the foreign mask it so anxiously put on years ago!"[34] The Zapatistas' ski masks conjure the millions of *sin rostros* (faceless ones) who are unrepre-sented in the state. By wearing the ski mask, the indigenous thrust into the public sphere the open secret of coloniality. When Marcos sent a message of solidarity on behalf of the EZLN to the lesbian and gay pride march in Mexico City in 1999, expressing "admira-tion for [their] courage and audacity to make [themselves] seen and heard, for [their] proud, dignified and legitimate 'Ya Basta!' [Enough Already!]," he was not endorsing identity politics as generally under-stood.[35] The Zapatistas' understanding of visibility does not simply affirm recognition as a remedy to exclusion from social belonging. Rather, the masked assertion of indigenous existence aims to reori-ent the political and epistemic foundations of modern democracy in order to expose its colonial underside and to instead *mandar obedeci-endo* (lead by obeying).[36]

Taussig has suggested that the Zapatistas' masks echo the power of disguise and transformation in Mexico and Central America associated with the *nagual,* or *nahual,* a shapeshifter sometimes related to the god Tezcatlipoca (Smoking Mirror), the protector of the distribution of wealth and the god of the night sky, ancestral memory, and change through conflict.[37] Like the Zapatistas, who are their heroes and *compañeros,* organizers in the maquilas are enmeshed in a culture of shapeshifters and secrets, and likewise, their efforts to unmask power are not cynical. They insist there is a difference between truth and lies, and they believe that capitalism's exploitation is not hopelessly with us but can be exposed and transformed. They see through many of its masks. For example, in a workshop on the concept of the wage, several workers spoke about wages as a kind of open secret. They recognized that their workdays included hours of labor that were not compensated for in their paychecks, because they were harvested as profit. They acknowledged that this fact was obvious but rarely stated, and yet it needed stating in order to be seen and known.

When labor organizing lifts that veil in a very public way, sexuality often is the medium of the intimidation it provokes. One August in Río Bravo, during a lunch break at a forum where workers fighting for their right to free association were making their case public, I drove with a prominent Mexican labor organizer and one of the group's main supporters to the radio station in Reynosa, where Roberto wanted to interview her on his show. Roberto was the local reporter and might also have been working for Gobernación.[38] After the show he suggested lunch and insisted that I come along. As they lobbed stories back and forth across the table, I realized the two of them were a lot alike, just working for different sides. Both were expert storytellers, their stories fascinating, funny, and calculated. Their stories also often carried another message at times opaque to me. Roberto told a story about a woman who was then running for office. She was a manager at one of the maquilas, and she was "like Selena," he said—meaning, I learned later, that she was lesbian.

"How do you know?" I asked.

"Well," he said, "there was a suicide, actually five suicides, of young girls."

Because Roberto was a reporter in this small town and his job was to cover all of the news, he said, he went to the sites of a lot of the police calls to get the story. He went to the scene of one of these suicides, and at the scene was a note from this manager reading that she would love so-and-so forever, as well as a pair of panties with her name on them. Roberto's point was that he had the evidence on this woman and could use it at any time. That was not, however, the real message.

The labor organizer retorted, "Well, everyone knows the governor is gay."

"Ah, yeah," Roberto replied.

There was a pause.

"I have always been open about who I am," she said.

End of set—score one for her. As we left the radio station, Roberto joked that Gobernación might be waiting for her outside.

"Aren't you afraid?" he taunted.

"Tell them I am not alone," she answered, laughing. "They know where I am, and I am not alone."

This story is saturated with exchanges of open secrets, and homosexuality is their currency. The narrative fabric is made of false confidences aimed to signal tacit warnings. Roberto's tale of evidence that could be used to slander and expose this maquiladora manager turned politician is a masquerade. The other story, the implicit one, is the class struggle that occasioned his meeting with the organizer. What she offers in response to his shared secret is another veiled message cannily sent through the discourse of sexuality and a command of politics that announces she knows the game and can outwit him. "I have always been open about who I am," she tells him, dispelling the threat of disclosure and bringing the exchange back to the point. Homosexual identity will not stigmatize or isolate her. It will not erode her confidence in the collective effort she is a part of. Like the *nahual* and the Zapatistas, from behind her mask she speaks truth to power: "They know where I am, and I am not alone."[39]

You may be wondering who this woman is. The most I can tell you is that the actors I write about wear many masks, and my effort to tell their stories is a minefield of secrets. Secrets are enmeshed in the events I witnessed, in the narratives reported to me, and in the official records. Unanswered questions leave their traces not only in the fabric of public discourse but also in my own choices about what can be recorded and what can only be hinted at or implied—about what is credible, what serves those I love, and what betrays my fiercest commitments. The identities of some of the organizers I spoke with or came to know well find their way into my narrative only obliquely. Sometimes, this occurs because their words fall into the cracks between the official and the unofficial record and I have made a decision to protect them from the unforeseen consequences of disclosure. Sometimes, they are masked because their personalities or intimacies are not the point and highlighting them would detract from the message of the collective force they represent, a message conveyed in the fearless assertion "I am not alone." The problem for feminist, historical materialist, and any other engaged research—a problem of methodology and concepts—lies in discerning and rendering the labor of the negative in the layers of what is masked and what is lost in the official story, in good sense, and in the work of bearing witness.

Athena McLean and Annette Leibling address these methodological dilemmas as they are spawned in "situations where the borders of personal life and formal ethnography begin to blur and the research field loses its boundedness." They call this problematic site "the shadow side of fieldwork."[40] Like many of the anthropologists in their edited collection, I have found that intimacies with the people I get to know are inevitably folded into my position as researcher and witness. No more easily dissected than ghosts, they cast long shadows across my narrative. In the glare of the southwest sun, sometimes you can see more clearly by stepping into the shade, but the shadowy open secrets of sexual intimacy may also cloud the truth.

For organizers in the maquilas, these open secrets complicate the class politics of collective struggle. One woman who worked in several factories told a story of the perverse ways sexuality filtered her efforts to advocate for her coworkers:

> I remember a time when one of the workers was fired; they said she was always late or whatever. I was the union delegate, and I went to the supervisor and spoke on her behalf, saying, "No, she has to keep

her job," and so on. They said, "Why are you defending her when
she reported you?" "What do you mean?" I asked, and they told
me she had said that I was pursuing her and that I put my hand on
her ass. So I asked her about this, and she said it was true. She did
report this lie because she was interested in me but I never paid attention to her, and this made her mad, so she wanted to get back at
me and did this.

"But you know," she added, "for us the issues had to do with class.
Sexual identity was not a priority."

Although sexual identity may not have been a priority in labor
organizing campaigns in the maquilas, this story confirms that it
inheres nonetheless in the affective cultures of class struggle. The distinction is crucial. Ian Lumsden's important study of homosexuality
and the state in Mexico underscores that sexuality is a class issue,
as does the research of Andrew Reding, Lionel Cantú, and Eithne
Luibhéid, who stress that poverty exacerbates the vulnerability of
gender-variant homosexuals. Crowded households limit the options
for same-sex relations and a fulfilling same-sex-affective life. Discussing this situation in the early 1990s, Lumsden contends, however,
that only a small minority of homosexuals in Mexico placed their
sexual orientation as the main priority in organizing their lives because the range and depth of problems that beset everyday life overwhelmed the issue of homosexual oppression.[41]

There are two points to emphasize here. One is that politics cen-
tered on gay rights requires certain material conditions. Whether
gay-identified communities can thrive has depended historically
on minimal survival needs being met. Only recently and in certain
parts of the world have public spaces that support a gay way of life
emerged.[42] The Mexican gay liberation movement that began in the
1970s in Mexico City and spread to Guadalajara, Tijuana, and other
large urban areas was waning by the early 1990s, when Mexico was
submerged in an economic crisis. Incomes had been slashed, and
people were much more insecure about alternative job prospects. In
this economic climate gays and lesbians were less likely to come out
or to put their jobs in jeopardy as a result of their activism. When
they did, AIDS support and education were the main concerns, not

identity-based gay liberation per se.[43] The second point is that even in situations where gay rights politics and gay community have been curtailed by the pressures of survival, the discourses of sexuality still punctuate the struggle for a better life with fears that target gender and sexual transgression.

Pablo, the organizer from Matamoros, said he thought there were a lot of gay men and lesbians among the labor organizers on the border precisely for this reason. As he put it:

> We have lived a situation of exclusion from when we were little when we had a way of being [*una forma de vida*] imposed on us, and there is a lot of rebellion. I cannot go out to struggle for that openly when it is something that is not even talked about. What follows is that you get involved in the struggle for justice, for better conditions and wages, and for health. And at the same time, you are thinking about the process of discovering and building your personal identity and sexual activity with ties to the labor struggle. It is very difficult.

For Pablo sexual identity was something assigned to one by God. He explained his belief as follows:

> When God was creating the heavens and the stars and us, he was thinking about the gays, and he made us like stars with six points. That one extra point means more fullness and heightened sensitivity. But unfortunately, we are very small, and we don't have the courage to shine and tell them, "Here we are." But that doesn't mean they don't discover my identity. I discover it myself like this: it is a whim [*un capricho*] of God's. I am the product of God's whimsy, a whim of the love of God. And I think that sustains me.

He went on to say that one needed to go through a personal process in order to accept and exercise their identity, but the border had no spaces for this work. When I asked if the customs were changing in Matamoros with the new generation, he said:

> Here, on the border as elsewhere, there is tremendous permissiveness. Sexual practices are much more open now for sure, and there

are changes in gender expectations. Men can be more sensitive, for example, but it is a surface permissiveness. There is no permission to live and dress openly as gay. On the contrary, there is still major condemnation.

There are gay discos and clandestine bars, Pablo added, but these are not the community spaces he wanted. He mentioned conversations he had had with gay workers who struggled with depression in the maquilas, and he lamented that the workshops the NGOs held for workers had no discussion of sexuality.

The need for more political education on the topic of sexual oppression was born out by Eliud, one of the leaders in the campaign for an independent union at a factory in Río Bravo. One night, he told me a story about the previous summer when Olga, an organizer from a nearby Mexican city, came to help. He mentioned how great she was and what a good job she did. She and Iván, who came from Reynosa to also aid the workers striking in the plaza, were a good team. Everything was fine until another organizer started gossiping: she said Olga and Iván always wanted to be with their lovers. Eliud said he did not care about Olga's being lesbian and Iván's being gay. The two did leave, however, because of these tensions. When I asked Iván about it, he said:

> They weren't ready to see, or there was only a narrow opening for them to see. But that is not a reason for me to say to them, "I'm not going to talk to you." It just wasn't the right moment. So because of that, I didn't carry on with them. If you are going to try to pursue a struggle with erroneous criteria, it is going to fall apart in the field. Why? Because you are pursuing something without a balance. There is a saying that goes, "Don't ask for something that you are not capable of giving." Do you understand?

Iván's canny handling of the moment the open secret of his sexual identity was no longer a protective mask speaks to his understanding that effective organizing involves one in a complex politics of visibility. Implicit in his critique of the "narrow opening" available for the group to see him is a deep understanding of a democratic principle he calls "balance." He touches the crippling blind spot of this and many other struggles when he asserts that those who seek justice must also be able to give it, and to give it requires forfeiting narrow ways of seeing.

For Iván, carrying out the balancing act with the striking workers in Río Bravo entailed a vigilant, embodied gender adjustment. "At first, one really has to struggle for a place, not only for acceptance, and a little for that," he said. "In my experience I had to, or felt I needed to, fight with ideas about personal demeanor. I had to change my vocabulary, my way of speaking, my customs." He said his approach to organizing was to try to facilitate the workers' own development as leaders, to pass from the front lines to a position in the back, directing and orienting. "But," he added, "if you have a mistaken demeanor, this process cannot work. So what to do?"

After some of the workers and other organizers began making derisive comments about his being gay, Iván felt his credibility was so undermined that he had to leave. What was the impact of these events on the group? Did talk about Iván's sexuality provoke divisions? Alleviate other fears? Solidify a sense of belonging? Or simply reinforce an available common sense that eluded the political education this group of striking workers had so painstakingly undertaken? I do not know the answers. Iván's own surmise was that organizing was like navigating the waves of the sea. "One has to walk like this" he said, extending his arms, "in order not to fall. If you want to go against the current, you are going to drown. But there is always the possibility that a wave is going to break and you might catch it."

The Very Blood and Tissue of Community Life

That summer, Iván was supporting the workers' strike at the Duro Bag Manufacturing Company (which I describe in chapter 3). Workers at the Duro factory cut, fold, glue, and pack gift bags for Hallmark, Gap, Banana Republic, and other multinational companies. In 2000 they were earning 320 pesos (US$32) for a forty-eight-hour work week. In April of that year, when the official union, the CTM, initiated negotiations for a new collective contract, the workers decided to choose their own representatives and call for higher wages and better working conditions. By June they resolved to go on strike, fighting for their right to form an independent union. Their struggle became a national test case for union democracy. For those on the front lines, affective ties were the binding agent of collective action. In the end they were also the corrosive that dissolved it.

The workers who went on strike made huge sacrifices. Once they lost their jobs and the meager measure of economic security their wages supplied, they had to scramble to provide for their families—to pay for food, rent, gas, electricity, medicine, and clothes. They were blacklisted and therefore unable to get work in other factories in the area. Some lost support from friends and family. They also developed new perspectives on their lives, however, and they met other maquiladora workers from the region and formed networks of allies that stretched all along the border and as far south as Mexico City and Chiapas. They came to see their work in an international context and themselves as players on a global stage with transnational corporations and labor and human rights organizations. For some the experience transformed their lives and gave them visions of alternative ways to live with and care for one another. At some point many of them were no longer workers; they had become organizers. Along the way, relations of friendship, trust, love, envy, resentment, and betrayal were the medium in which every day's events were lived. These relationships are so much a part of the story that the facts cannot ring true without mentioning them, and yet they are invariably absent from public accounts of what took place. Sexuality is a significant thread in this part of their story, as is an inchoate passion that aroused courage and collective action.

Ana, who worked at Duro for seven years before being fired for participating in the strike, said that the day she walked out of the factory to join the group of three hundred striking workers gathered in front of the plant, she was not afraid:

> How can I tell you? I felt—*we* felt—powerless that we could do nothing against these people. But we never showed them fear. Never. And that is why I am going forward.
>
> My husband said to me, "Aren't you afraid?"
> Well no, I wasn't afraid.
> Even if he was troubled and said, "Where are you going?"

"Well," I said, "I am going there to the strike."

"Don't you know that I am here worrying about you?" he said.

"Don't worry, nothing is going to happen to me," I told him.

"Nothing. And if it does you are going to know."

Embedded in Ana's story and in the testimonies of other Duro women who were on the front lines is a growing consciousness of one's place in something big, a discernment that displaces fear. Ana's comments suggest that she measured her own fearlessness against her husband's worry, a stance that subtly hints at the enormous transgression her decision to join the strike represented. Ana was then pregnant with her third child, and as the months of the strike wore on, she was among the striking workers assembled every day in the town plaza. Significant in her narrative is her halting transition from "I" to "we," an acknowledgment that in "going there to the strike," she too was not alone.

In January 2001, almost a year into their daily demonstrations, the Duro organizers held a meeting at which they decided, "We are all leaders." It was a major turning point in the group's dynamic because until then the recognized leaders were, formally and informally, the few men. The decision to have the female majority claim leadership emerged from a veiled discussion of gender politics. These women were especially courageous in taking this stance because the consequences of their leap into organizing were becoming acutely painful. The missing Duro paycheck hurt every household, and the women's involvement in the strike had dramatically altered their roles at home, a change that threw many families into crisis. Some moved away. One of the youngest organizers abandoned the group for a while under pressure from her boyfriend, an organizer from a neighboring town whom she met during the strike. Another woman's husband left her and claimed custody of their seven-year-old son.

After they lost the election, many of the former workers vowed to continue the struggle, and they set up a workers' center that pursued political education in the community. The consequences of the long strike's strain had already registered in their lives severely, however, and as the pressing need for jobs combined with the powerful cultural defaults of competition and family obligation, the women's commitment to collective leadership and to the group eventually dissolved.

Like many other organizing efforts, the Duro campaign took place on ground that was prepared by local and global agents and harrowed by human frailty. In this case, as in so many others, forces converged to deploy the age-old strategy of divide and conquer. Need, friendship, and secrecy were its ready instruments. When people make the choice to go without wages in order to accomplish a collective goal, need is a powerful lever for coercion and compromise, for competition over scarce resources, and for blackmail. In this climate friendship folds into secrecy. Michael Taussig reminds us that in the world of politics friendship is part of the game: "Friendship cements the social process and lies at the heart of what we call 'corruption.' . . . It becomes the locus for sharing secrets just as it is the locus for sharing gifts."[44] Organizing takes place in a hyperpoliticized situation that relies upon existing and new friendships. Herein also lies the importance of gossip. As anthropologists have long recognized, gossip is "the very blood and tissue" of a community life that shelters the open secret that a collective bond is being undermined.[45] In the negative labor of gossip, everyone knows the ideal of friendship is being betrayed, but the fiction of friendship is upheld. In Río Bravo, as in many small towns, gossip is the medium in which open secrets circulate.

Perhaps not surprisingly, sexuality was the conduit for much of the gossip that unraveled the Duro women organizers' once-fervent sense of shared purpose. One early split occurred because the wife of one of the core leaders was rumored to be having an affair. Another division revolved around rumors that one woman in the group had betrayed the others by having sex with one of the hired thugs the company had brought in to intimidate the workers the week of their union election. The disappearance of Olga and Iván was little spoken of after they left, but negative comments about homosexuality punctuated competition over material and emotional support from allies. If one of these supporters was rumored to be lesbian or gay, then the open secret of their identity became the premise for gossip about sexual liaisons. After losing the union election, the number of workers committed to continued organizing dwindled, but a small group of women formed a workers' center and civil association. Within a short time conflicts arose over participation in decision making and control of potential and real resources. Trust within the group was further eroded by homophobic gossip about suspected favorites.

As an example of the challenges labor organizing faces, the Duro workers' case is not unusual. All grassroots organizations have internal tensions, and sexuality is often a medium for conflicts over scarce resources.[46] What is uncommon is a critical understanding of the ways old and new attachments and the discourses of sexuality mediate the raveling and unraveling of solidarity. More knowledge of the ways sexuality features in the emotional habitus of an organizing effort would seem to be crucial to advancing social movement on the border and elsewhere.

In northern Mexico, labor organizing is inseparable from the struggle to stay alive, to meet families' needs for food and shelter, and to withstand violence and even death from the toxic daily grind in the factories or from the criminal state and the narcos. Many who commit to the task bring to it emotional attachments forged by convention and the media. What is remarkable is that against steep odds, handfuls of workers—some gay identified and some not—at times haltingly are catching waves and converting injustice into pockets of collective action. Although the fine points of political economy and culture in northern Mexico's border region differ from those of the cities and towns on the other side, certain cultural logics span social realities here and there. Gender variance as the mark of transgression is one. Both north and south of the border, it continues to secure the boundaries of belonging and human value. In both regions affect-culture, often articulated through the discourses of sexuality, is a medium through which collective consciousness and class struggle are lived and also the lens for narrow ways of seeing that circulate in gossip. Though they may be formulated differently here and there, collective efforts to redress unmet needs in both countries often founder on this covert fact.

Even less recognized is an aspect of the affective culture integral to organizing: those passions and attachments that sexuality's narrow formulations do not and perhaps cannot name. They too are a seething presence that clings to collective action. In the words of Avery Gordon's moving diagnosis, this underside of history "draws us affectively, sometimes against our will and always a bit magically, into the structure of feeling of a reality we come to experience, not as cold knowledge, but as transformative recognition."[47] In this dense shadow where passionate attachments leaven reason and action, another open secret's incendiary potential smolders.

« 5 »

The Value of a Second Skin

If there is a relationship between socialism and homosexual
liberation, perhaps this is it: an irritation of the skin. . . .
Socialism, as an alternative to individualism politically and
capitalism economically, must surely have as its ultimate
objective the restitution of the joy of living we may have lost
when we first picked up a tool. Toward what other objective is
it worthy to strive? Perhaps the far horizon of lesbian and gay
politics is a socialism of the skin.

Tony Kushner, "A Socialism of the Skin"

The principal marker of the untrainable subject is femininity.

Melissa Wright, *Disposable Women and
Other Myths of Global Capitalism*

Thinking Identity as a Second Skin

This chapter discusses the problem of value or, more specifically, the
ways surplus value depends upon cultural value. I consider what it
means to think of the cultural value adhering to social identities as a
second skin that gets folded into the labor power workers exchange
for a wage and is reproduced at home. Throughout this analysis the
narratives of homosexual maquiladora workers who were leaders in
campaigns for better wages and working conditions offer insights
that flesh out an understanding of the process of abjection that identity formation entails. They shed light on the lived and contested
value of gender and sexual identity as affect-laden culture that enhances the fundamental logic of capitalism, a logic that requires taking on and giving over a second skin.

In chapter 2, I explain that embodied sensations are made meaningful and come to have value through affect-culture. The ideological articulation of these values is a powerful component of the cultural material I call a subject's "second skin," a lucrative site where culture and economy meet. As a bodily organ, skin feels not only neurologically but also in the sense of feeling as thought that conveys the mind's perceptions of the body. As the material surface of the body, skin mediates the interface between the corporeal and the psychic, the self and others.[1] Skin is a sense organ that registers how we see and know the world affectively—for example, in shivers and sweat, goose bumps, tingles, blushes, or rashy outbreaks. Skin is also a vehicle for metaphors that connote well-being or distress, as in the expressions "feeling comfortable in your own skin" or "feeling like you want to jump out of your skin." What the skin feels may also hover on the edge of intelligibility, as the meaning of a sensation registered in the skin can be unspeakable, an irritation for which you do not have a name.

As I use the phrase "second skin," it is a metonymy for identity understood as inseparable from the mattering maps of this body wrap of affect-culture. Neither the same as one's physical skin nor ever lived entirely outside it, the second skin is a tissue of values that organizes sensations and affective intensities and integrates them into the representations and lived experience of who we are. These values circulate in signs that plot normative body maps along a differential grid of negative and positive categories that often conform to ideological norms. They are the fabric of meaning making and experience and are laden with affect, conveyed through discourse, image, gesture, tone, and touch. Second skins are also open to history, which means they are sites of struggle. The values inscribed in them are contested and therefore can change and be adjusted, even though they may be represented in the common sense as natural and universal.

I borrow the phrase "second skin" from *Second Skins,* the title of a book by Jay Prosser on the body narratives of transsexuals. Prosser critiques the social constructionist paradigm that overtook theories of gender more than twenty years ago, a paradigm spurred on by the 1990 publication and reception of Judith Butler's *Gender Trouble.* He contends that what is lost in this account of gender as a discursive practice is the relation between psyche and body in shaping gender identity.[2] I agree with Prosser's contention that identity formation is always embodied and that a crucial component of the corporeal dimension of identity is the felt experience of who one is. This feeling is the effect of corporeal sensations and affective intensities, which are themselves the effects of cultural scripts that give sensations meaning and value. All of these coefficients operate in a feedback loop that is not always coherent. Cultural values impact what the body senses; sensations are made meaningful in imagination. The embodied identity one senses and imagines, the body one perceives, and its cultural representation may be radically disjointed, however. The standpoint of the transsexual allows us to see that lived identities incoherently shuttle sensation, perception, imagination, and identification between a sense of body boundaries and cultural values that map what is proper, pretty, ugly, odd, and so forth. This incoherence is not solely the experience of transsexuals. We may even say it is typical of most people. Moreover, it is a space that capital has already invaded. Before discussing this invasion further, I want to underscore that both the corporeal and the cultural sides of this Möbius strip of identity are affectively charged. Affects are churned up and flood what you sense to be the contours and boundaries of your body; your sense of self, which may not always feel embodied; what you see represented as "you"; and your culture's ideals, ideals you know and recognize and measure yourself against.

Several culture theorists have advanced a materialist analysis of the ways embodiment features in the calculus of value under capitalism. In her 1985 essay "A Cyborg Manifesto," Donna Haraway suggests that the body is an accumulation strategy in the deepest sense.[3] Elaborating on her insight, David Harvey reminds us that Marx is aware of this interplay between cultural and economic value, that signs like gender and race as measures of what a worker is capable of are a powerful constitutive force inserted into the circulation of variable capital. These cultural values assist in the mobilization of affects and the creative powers of labor to a given purpose.[4]

More recently, work in queer theory has begun articulating a critical rapprochement between Marxism and queer studies by attending to the value form and capital's investment in particular bodies. Some key arguments have been formulated by way of renewed attention to Gayatri Spivak's 1985 essay "Scattered Speculations on the Question of Value."[5] Although they do not use the phrase "second skin," Janet Jakobsen and Miranda Joseph, each in separate publications, call for an analysis of the structure of embodied domination that inheres in capital accumulation, and they suggest that such an analysis might begin by returning to Spivak.[6] Like Jakobsen and Joseph, I am interested in Spivak's thinking about the mechanisms of domination that are integral to exploitation. Joseph and Jakobsen each extend this relationship between cultural domination and economic exploitation into their investigations of the ways diverse but specific bodies are produced for capital.

In her essay, one of Spivak's concerns is what she calls "the materialist predication of the subject."[7] The moment when capital is fully developed arises when the subject as labor power is freed to produce surplus labor—that is, when the subject is predicated as superadequate to itself. This is the subject who desires to sell her labor power for a wage and in so doing becomes a worker who can produce surplus value.[8] It is here in the use value of a subject superadequate to itself that cultural value plays a crucial role. In opening up labor to cultural domination, Spivak "leads to the question of embodiment, of how bodies that labor are themselves produced in relation to the differential production of value."[9] Jakobsen and Joseph underscore the structure of embodied domination that inheres in this process. As Jakobsen reminds us, embodiment is always itself a double discourse articulated in domination as abjection, "a splitting that abstracts the subject from that which it excludes (the abject) even as the abject is inscribed within the subject."[10]

As Julia Kristeva argues in *Powers of Horror,* "the abject" designates what has been expelled from the (social) body, discharged as excrement, literally rendered Other. Through this expulsion the alien body is effectively established as a not me, a not me that sets up the boundaries of the body proper, which are the first contours of the subject.[11] Abjection is accompanied by the negative charge of repulsion (for example, disgust or shame) upon which socially favored categories and identities rest. In short, abjection refers to processes at work in establishing the subject's embodied sense of self. It is also the scaffolding of a cultural value system that marks certain embodied subjects as shameful, disposable, ideal, or proper. The particularities of abjection's repudiation, like those of propriety, vary historically. Their representation in modern Western cultures has tended, however, to be inflected by gender and race and, more recently, by sexuality. Moreover, gender, race, and sexual differences are not just categories we use to make sense of the world but signs through which we communicate a whole range of emotions.[12] The late nineteenth century ushered in a cultural grid on which all bodies and subjects were situated according to a homo–hetero binary model. These second skins were constituted through discourses of law, medicine, and education and a structure of feeling driven by the will to know, whose central technology was the confession.[13] The labor organizer in chapter 4 who refuses to confess her sexual identity to the baiting journalist enacts a canny refusal of this second skin and its valence. Her dodge shifts the cognitive and affective ground of the encounter and flips the individualized and disciplined subject being elicited into another, collective one.

The mechanism of abjection is inscribed within the social mandate that all workers sell a part of their human capacities, a mandate I suggest we consider analogous to selling a second skin. It also inheres, however, in the normative devaluation of reproductive labor—that is, the both paid and unpaid care work of feeding, child care, elder care, and housework that enables the predication of the wage worker. As a social relation, capital requires workers exchange for a wage (or devote to unpaid care work) their physical, mental, and creative abilities, as well as their living personalities, all of which are worn down during the working day. Through the social processes of abjection, cultural value produces subjects that can be exploited not only because they are able to sell their capacities as labor power (i.e., become superadequate to themselves) but also because they bear second skins that command a low price. In other words, "cultural value is complicit with exploitation because exploitation depends on values carried by the normatively inscribed, dominated, body."[14] Capitalism would not work—that is, capital would not be accumulated—if the disciplining of the body to enter the market and the devaluing of the second skin of labor power there and at home were not under way.

One of the principal cultural vehicles for the recruitment of bodies and capacities into a cheap and disposable labor force is the differential gender scheme in which the valued term is "masculine" and the devalued term is "feminine." In prevailing Western norms, all subjects who transgress this prescribed distribution of gendered bodies are feminized, whether they are men or women. In other words, gender transgression itself bears the mark of abjected devaluation. The abjecting of feminized bodies and subjects has been a very effective mechanism for securing ideologies of respectability that seal hostile divisions within the working class.[15] David Valentine's ethnography of several communities through which the discourse of transgender circulates in New York City bears out this point. He finds a significant link between an emergent homonormative middle-class class sector that values urban chic and professional respectability and its abject, feminized, gender-dissident other. Valentine argues that the association of gender variance (principally feminized men), overtness, and the street with all that the homonormative gay community is not confers stability on the respectable class identifications of (especially white and professional) gay men and lesbians. Stressing the otherness of gender nonconformists as a group separate from gay and lesbian homosexuals seals the normative similarity of homo- and heteronormative models of personhood and citizenship.[16] Gender nonconformists who are marginalized from this mainstream of gay tolerance are mostly poor, black, and Latino men and women who are struggling to survive, many through sex work. Similar findings are illustrated in the National Transgender Survey of over six thousand transgender or gender-nonconforming individuals from all fifty U.S. states. Respondents report twice the rate of unemployment and near universal harassment on the job; 15 percent live in dire poverty, nearly four times the rate for the general population; and 19 percent report direct discrimination in seeking housing and medical care.[17]

Shifting attention to Mexico, it is fair to say that in most regions of the country gender nonconformists are abjected, as well, even in gay male circles, where they are marginalized and referred to as *los obvios* (the obvious ones), as opposed to those homosexuals who pursue some measure of middle-class respectability by exercising more discretion and not defying gender norms in public.[18] In her research on Mexican factory workers, Melissa Wright refers to femininity as the principal mark of the devalued, untrainable worker.[19] The untrainable worker is one whose capacities will be used until they are depleted, and when she is completely drained, she is discarded. The equation of "untrainable" with "femininity" is not a practice specific only to Mexican factory workers, of course. The disposable, feminized worker is the one capital pursues across the globe and continually reinvents because she above all others gives away more of herself for free. As Wright delineates in *Disposable Women and Other Myths of Global Capitalism,* to be feminized means that the value of your labor power lies in the value of your devaluation. This seeming paradox is actually a long-standing capitalist strategy that discloses the intimate relation between cultural value and surplus value. To be feminized is to bear on your embodied second skin the mark of (de)valuation, which is indeed quite valuable to capital. It legitimates your potential disposability, the low limit on the wages you can command, and the excessive value-added charge your labor will produce. Given the degree of superadequation commanded of feminized workers, they not only are the subjects of surplus labor but also are, more accurately, the hyperexploited.

As I use it, the phrase "second skin" captures critical insights at the intersection of feminism, Marxism, and queer theory. It directs us toward a conception of subjectivity as a felt relation to the body, "felt" in Damasio's sense that feeling draws upon the mind's sense of the body's state, a sense that is also shaped by structures of abjection encoded in cultural values. These values and the affective charge that accompanies the abjection or recognition of embodied subjects of different sorts are embedded in the capacities that produce surplus value during the working day. In devaluing some bodies, abjection helps to produce subjects who are worth less—that is, subjects who forfeit more of themselves in the labor relations that produce capital. I turn to accounts of the value attached to the embodied identities through which labor and organizing are lived in some localities in northern Mexico, because they amplify my concept of second skins.

The Mistake, or Not Mistake, of Being Gay

By the time we crossed the bridge into Mexico, Fela had been waiting for hours. She looked tired when we picked her up and continued
driving to the beauty shop in Colonia Peru on the far side of Nuevo
Laredo. Carmen's *estetica* (beauty shop) was huddled in a row of
stores along the railroad. On one side was a small food stand, and on
the other, a taco place. When we pulled up, it looked like no one was
there, but in a few seconds, sure enough, a short, dark man peeked
out and, after a moment's hesitation, gave us a shy welcome before
slipping away to summon Carmen. She arrived in a flourish, a wave
of energy swooshing into the room with warm embraces all around.
Fela laughed and commented on the new name, but Carmen dis-
missed it as she summoned her *esposo*—"Mi Amor, ven!"—proudly
announcing that she was pregnant and stretching her shirt across her
belly to reveal a slightly plump *panza* as evidence of this miraculous
conception. She beckoned me, "Sit here, *hija*," motioning to the spot
next to her, and began to tell about the years she worked with Fela
at a garment factory in Nuevo Laredo that was a major supplier for
Walmart. Her job was sewing waistbands, pockets, and zippers on
pants and sleeping bags, sometimes made of camouflage material.

"I was a worker at Fabricas de Calidad," she began, "and I always
introduced myself with my real name." She continued:

> I said my name is Andrés Rosales Martínez, at your service. I am a
> homosexual, and a homosexual is like any person. I am one person
> who says we are workers and we have to accomplish something. If
> we are going to do that—all the people—we'll have to put nerves
> aside. A person who is homosexual does not have to be humiliated,
> and I was humiliated in all my rights physically and morally.

Carmen reported that workers in production at Fabricas de Calidad
were paid 350 pesos a week (US$35) and a 50-peso (US$5) bonus for
meeting the quotas. "In one night you had to finish 1,000 shirts; if
not, they disciplined you. Do you think a salary of 350 pesos and a
bono of 50 pesos was enough?" she asked, her voice rising. "With fifty
miserable pesos I can't clean my ass!" She continued:

They gave you pills that were vitamins. They made us work at 100 percent capacity with these vitamins. Things worked out to perfection! We were two or three days without sleep. It was pure work, and they fucked us until something happened to Ofelia. With the women it was too much because they were giving them a pill supposedly to sleep, and with that pill they didn't get their periods. Or when they did get their periods, they were bleeding so much it was like they were having a miscarriage. But the only thing they were telling them was, "Espérame afuera" [Wait for me outside], while they were bleeding with big spots of blood all over their clothes.

So my friend Ofelia was working two days *a puro trabajo y pura pastilla* [of sheer work and pills] without sleep, and she was shaking and shaking, and then half of her body was paralyzed. But instead of taking her to the hospital, the union delegate took her to the kitchen. He was saying to her, "Don't be a clown! Don't be faking!" Ofelia was Pati's partner. She was lesbian. It was something where you were saying, Why did this happen to her? Why was she paralyzed? Why were they making her work more with the pills? Why? It was something that you cannot accept.

Carmen's testimony underscores the brutal violation of bodies that capital enacts in an effort to speed up production. The fact that Ofelia is lesbian may be overshadowed by her paralysis, but her cultural devaluation as a feminized and disposable subject made her body the target of a work speed-up aimed at getting more value from the assembly line. For Carmen this event was a watershed. It marked her refusal to incorporate this mistreatment into any acceptable logic, a refusal that registers in her reiterated question, "Why? . . . Why? . . . Why?"

When the workers at Fabricas de Calidad went on strike in 1999, Carmen was one of the leaders.[20] Events came to a head when the owners sold the company and would not give the workers their legally mandated severance pay. When it seemed the owners were simply moving the company to another plant and giving it a new name, the workers united and said, "Either give us our severance pay or hire us in this new plant!" They drew up a list of grievances and a criminal complaint against the manager for the amphetamines that paralyzed Ofelia and gave her coworker Gloria a miscarriage. When they mobilized for forty-three days, Carmen was among them and in the front, one of the women. Then, though, he was Andrés. He and Caretino were the only gays, the only men involved in the movement. Carmen recounted:

> When we went to the bosses with a lawyer, the bosses said, "Why do you have so much anger, Andrés? Why did you stir up all the workers?"
>
> The lawyer replied for me, "Remember how you humiliated him when you told him, 'You are a homosexual, a shit'?"
>
> The humiliation for being openly gay was continuous. They would say that I pooped my pants. They were telling me I was a normal shit or diarrhea and that I had gonorrhea. If I was putting up with all that, it was because I had to. But then I said, "No one is going to humiliate me anymore. No one is going to step on my rights anymore. I am a person, a citizen. You can say my mistake or not mistake was to be gay. But that's up to me to decide."

In the end the workers got the embargo, and the company had to give everyone 100 percent of their severance pay. What was remarkable about the Fabricas de Calidad mobilization was that the rights of homosexual workers were on the list of demands and that two openly homosexual men were respected leaders. As Carmen said, "We were in the front, and we showed them that as homosexuals we are here in Laredo, Mexico. Many people supported us, and many were saying, 'Keep going! Ser adelante, mi hija!'"

Carmen's story makes visible the fact of homosexual workers in the maquilas and also highlights the ways a feminized second skin is folded into the conditions of exploitation. The bosses humiliated Carmen by representing her to herself and to her coworkers not simply as feminine but as feminized, as that which had been expelled from the body (a shit) and from the civic body, the alien who "stirred up" the workers. This abjection was not, however, a novel representation; it was already in place in the cultural values circulating outside the factory. In *Purity and Danger,* Mary Douglas suggests that the limit and surface of the body, the skin, is systematically signified by taboos and anticipated transgressions.[21] Douglas proposes that the body is a synecdoche for all social systems and that all social systems are vulnerable at their boundaries. In this cultural logic bodily margins are specifically invested with power and danger.[22] Any kind of unregulated permeability can constitute a site of pollution. Moreover, bodily orifices are mapped in terms that engender heterosexual exchange. The boss's abjection of Carmen pursues this cultural logic when he refers to her as "shit" and equates this repulsive other with being homosexual. It is an expulsion that Carmen both avows and rejects. Her exclamation, "I am a human being, a citizen," in relation to the "mistake or not mistake" of being gay underscores her disidentification from this abjection, a disidentification that she enacts when she refuses to "put up with this" and recasts the devalued second skin that she bears as a feminized homosexual worker into the proud mantel of an organizer in the front lines of collective resistance.

The New Women of the Maquilas

Carmen's testimony bears witness to an expanded definition of maquiladora labor as feminized that was under way by the late 1990s. As Donna Haraway points out, feminized labor can be performed by either men or women:

> To be feminized means to be made extremely vulnerable; able to be disassembled, reassembled, exploited as a reserve labor force; seen less as workers than as servers; subjected to time arrangements on and off the paid job that make a mockery of a limited work day; leading an existence that always borders on being obscene, out of place, and reducible to sex.[23]

From the inception of the Border Industrialization Program in 1965 through the next decade, the overwhelming majority of feminized unskilled operators on the assembly lines were women. The few men among the labor force moved the materials, handled warehousing, and ran heavy presses. Women were construed as more docile toward authority and as an ideal turnover workforce whose primary interests lay in family and home. At the same time, the femininity that was recruited had to do with a set of meanings that were dislodging feminine labor from family production in the home and reconstituting it as a set of characteristics that could ostensibly apply to men or women: dexterous, docile, tolerant, and cheap.[24] As the example of women workers in the factories of Nuevo Laredo in the 1970s demonstrates, however, from the early years of the program, women workers had proved to be less compliant than expected. Over the next two decades, women were the leaders in strikes and work stoppages all along the border. At the same time, though, the standard profile of the maquiladora worker had been set. Men were being hired, but the profile of feminized expectations continued to define the preferred worker. As the maquila sector expanded, men became the preferred labor force in some plants—for example, those assembling transportation equipment, leather and synthetic goods, wood and metal furniture, and photographic, sporting, and paper goods.[25] In those sectors where labor was the major portion of manufacturing costs, however, women workers still predominated. As the boom years arrived, the proportions changed. The majority of maquiladora workers remained women, but eventually, almost half were men. The gradual changeover began in the mid-1980s when the demand for assembly workers increased but the market of women willing to work in the factories was saturated. Ultimately, the demand for cheap labor made adjustments in the gender demographics of the workforce inevitable and expanded the criteria for those bodies that would qualify as feminized, value-producing labor power.[26]

Based on the changes she saw in the maquila workforce over the several generations she worked there, one worker explained:

> By the '90s the culture inside was changing. There was the biggest invasion of maquilas to the border cities during this decade, and they really needed a workforce. It was then that the informal filters that kept gays out started to relax. Of course, there had been no official policy against hiring gays, but informally this was the practice. They would even write it in the comments on the application. But by the '90s the maquilas needed all the workers they could get, and gay men started appearing as operators on the line along with the women. By then the lesbians were more open, too.

What is significant in this comment is the changing value of sexual identity in relation to capital's need for cheap labor. Excluded as too transgressive by the heterosexual norms for feminized labor in the employment filters of the early years, homosexuals were absorbed into the general calculus of appropriately devalued labor when capital was desperate to take whomever it could get.[27] Carmen/Andrés testified to the cost of this admission for men whose bodies were marked as gender nonconformists. The devaluation that adheres to their second skins continues to be a powerful lever in maintaining their suitability for hyperexploitation and their hypervulnerability as a disposable workforce.

Iván, who also worked in the factories of Nuevo Laredo, theorized that in the 1990s gay men were becoming the "new women" of the maquilas. "Homosexual men who are 'open' typically have few options for work," he said. "But during these years they entered the maquilas and were welcomed." As he put it, "The more dependent you are on the work, the more you are going to be here, and gay men cannot rely on having work outside. So they inverted the role and exchanged women for gays." Iván's reference to "new women" is a reminder of capital's modernizing impulse.[28] In the persistent pursuit of cheap labor, capital will invent and use up any feminized second skins that can command lower wages. Calling homosexuals the "new women of the maquilas" also tacitly acknowledges that variation in the subjects attached to a feminized cheap labor force is historically set within the international division of labor, as is the variable appearance of the abjected second skin itself.

Those whose second skins transgress prescribed gender norms are by their very existence social irritants. Fabián, a cross-dressing man from Hermosillo, in the western state of Sonora, who was interviewed by Guillermo Núñez Noriega, said as much when he recounted events from his life:

> "Like so many other homosexuals, I have been persecuted: in
> the street, with looks, taunts, shouts, insults like *puto* [whore],
> *sidoso* [person with AIDS]. But that has made me grow up. I was
> cross-dressing from when I was seventeen years old, and that

irritated a lot of people. It was like I egged them on to insult me, right?" he says sarcastically.[29]

As Carmen's example testifies, this irritation can propel some workers into collective action and leadership. It is significant that she and Caretino had the positive support of *compañerismo,* an emotional habitus that was fostered by the women workers at Fabricas de Calidad. For others like Fabián, the irritation can provoke small acts of defiance and resistance.

Yessy, a young homosexual worker involved in an organizing effort on the eastern edge of the border, occasionally dressed in drag. He said he didn't have many troubles in the factories where he had worked, but his sanguine attitude belied, perhaps even to himself, the harassment he had dealt with. Upon reflection, he recounted the maltreatment he faced when he worked at a factory ironically named Liberty, where he assembled sportswear for Nike. Whenever someone was needed to perform the job of *inspectadora* (inspector of the machines), a task normally done by a woman, the men would say, "Yessy should do it because he is gay." One day when the men once more insisted he do it, he shot back at them, "You don't need to lose something hanging between your legs in order to inspect a machine." When he refused to submit to their humiliation, he was fired. He finally conceded that this event was an example of the "subtle harassment" of homosexuals he had experienced or witnessed in the factories, his understatement indicative, perhaps, of how much abjection he had absorbed or denied.

For Yessy the process of coming out at work was gradual. At first, he said, his coworkers and bosses did not know he was gay. Then, he started coming to work in tight clothes and women's pants, and finally he wore makeup. He said:

> There was one time when I was talking with this guy and another guy who always criticized me came up to him and said, "Get away from him—you'll be cursed because he is gay."[30] In the end the guy who criticized me became a really good friend. He says hi now when he sees me and accepts me for who I am.

Whereas Yessy managed to navigate his way between insults and new friends to embrace a good-enough life in a town where, as he said in emphatic terms, "¡No hay libertad de orientación sexual!" (There is no freedom of sexual orientation!), others were not so lucky. At Liberty were two other homosexual workers, one who came to work dressed in women's clothes. He was later killed in Tampico. Silence has engulfed the facts of his murder, and no one has found his killer.

Iván, said that when he was in the maquilas in the early 1990s, gay men were being recruited into management positions. When I asked him how he understood this development, he responded that it was, of course, a matter of class. "There is a saying," he added, "that goes, 'They treat you as they see you.' This has a lot to do with class, but it also has to do with the question of identity. One thing can't be separated from the other. It would be like eating cheese without cheese. Without the flavor of cheese, it tastes like milk."

Iván's astute comment points to the ways in which cultural domination divides class sectors and rests upon a distinction between what is visible and what is seeable, a distinction that registers both epistemologically and ontologically in one's relation to capital. Like Marx, Iván knows that capital is first and foremost a social relation between those who own property and those who labor. In that relation Iván stands firmly on the side of labor. He suggests that sexual identity is a palpable part of that stance because "one thing cannot be separated from the other." Sexual identity is factored into how you are seen and known. It impacts how you are treated by others, both those who share your class position and those who do not. It can be used to expel you and exploit you, to divide and divert your coworkers, and to mystify collective interests. Iván's pronouncement that "they treat you as they see you" also cannily implies an epistemological distinction between the visible and the seeable. That is, the visible never speaks for itself; it is seeable only through available ways of knowing. Although the visible may be presented in commonsense culture as what is obvious, reality is seeable only by virtue of the ways of seeing that make the world meaningful. Cultures of domination, or ideology, offer narrow ways of seeing. To see in the more ample and politicized sense Iván indicates is to understand the other you confront from your situation within capital's social relations, where cultural domination is complicit with exploitation. That he formulates this complicity through the metaphor of cheese that has lost its taste adds a corporeal, sensuous dimension to this ample conception of identity.

How we see ourselves and others sets the terms for how we act. A second skin can blind us to our historical position and paralyze our ability to enact its material transformation. It can neutralize the potential, the savor, of who we are and can be. Cheese can become not cheese or cheese that "tastes like milk." Iván's insight that "they treat you as they see you" also echoes David Valentine's conclusions about sexual identity and class. The visibility of middle-class gay workers or managers in the streets of New York or Nuevo Laredo does not simply turn on the epistemology of the closet, for the substance that converts a potentially irritating second skin into a progressive political force is its stance—whether on the side of labor or property.

Loose Bodies

Though Marx does not address sexuality per se, what he writes about the "queer commodity" of labor power is pertinent to the concept of cultural value as a second skin that gets incorporated into the accumulation of surplus labor as profit. First and foremost, as Marx tells us in volume one of *Capital,* commodities are things. They cannot go to market themselves but "must have recourse to their guardians, who are the possessors of commodities. Because commodities are things, they therefore lack the power to resist man. If they are unwilling, he can use force; in other words, he can take possession of them." At this point, Marx adds the following footnote: "In the twelfth century, so renowned for its piety, very delicate things often appear among these commodities. Thus a French poet of the period enumerates among the commodities to be found in the fair of Lendit, alongside clothing, shoes, leather, implements of cultivation, skins, etc also 'femmes folles de leur corps' [wanton women]."[31]

What is to be made of these women wedged obliquely into Marx's explanation of commodities? Their bodies are in the market fair, but they are outside the body of the text, exiled to the bottom of the page, beside the point, their place in a revolutionary theory of the commodity left to trail off, an afterthought, unthought. Perhaps, they are an embarrassment, masked in a French euphemism for prostitutes—literally, "women who are crazy with their bodies." I can imagine Marx stumbling upon the text of this anonymous twelfth-century French poet one day in the British Museum, in a moment when he needed a break from Ricardo and Smith, and finding them—in the far-away time and space of a medieval poet's rendering—a distraction, a curiosity, even a delight. Nonetheless, these market women find a place in the margins of his text. As delicate things among the rough wares, their femininity is encoded in the *corps* that is inseparable from their labor and their persons, but the *folles* (madness) of their trade makes the attachment of *femmes* to *corps* a particularly improper one, marking them as loose women. Loose, too, is their connection to the commodity, as they are like and yet different from the clothing, leather, tools, and skins that are being traded. Had one of them centuries later worked in a factory, the imprint of "delicate thing" and this loose relation to her body would have differentiated her as a preferred and disposable worker. Her value would have been in the very cell structure of this feminized second skin, the commodity labor power she exchanged for a wage. It would have marked her as only loosely in possession of herself and therefore both valuable and worth less.

Within the marketplaces of capitalism where commodities are traded, the commodity the worker brings to exchange for a wage is her power to labor. In chapter 6 of *Capital,* volume 1, "The Sale and Purchase of Labor-Power," Marx explains, "We mean by labour-power, or labour-capacity, the aggregate of those mental and physical capabilities existing in *the physical form, the living personality* of a human being, capabilities which he sets in motion whenever he produces a use value of any kind" (emphasis mine).[32] Marx understands labor power to include both a physical dimension and this other part, which he calls "the living personality." In order for the worker to sell his labor power, Marx says, "He must have it at his disposal, he must be the *free proprietor of his own labour-capacity, hence of his person*" (emphasis mine).[33] For Marx, when the worker and the capitalist meet in the market, they enter into relations with each other supposedly on an equal footing, but this relationship is not between equals.

Free-market exchange relies on and takes advantage of the political and cultural dispossession of certain subjects, a dispossession that registers in the body.

This dispossession is the effect of the process of abjection/ domination, which is accompanied by a negative emotive charge. William Reddy's concept of emotives conveys this link between affect-culture and labels like "homosexual," "lesbian," and "gay," which have a performative dimension in that they channel affective capacities and shape them in narrow ways that we might consider to be ideological, so long as "ideological" carries with it this embodied/ affective dimension.[34] As Spivak's argument on the predication of the subject reminds us, the subject who enters the marketplace to sell his or her labor power already is acculturated, his or her body variously disposed and dispossessed. Moreover, as Carmen/Andrés recognizes, some citizens are more abjected from the social body than others, maligned or considered a mistake in their very being. The individuality of our living personalities that accompanies labor power is supplemental in precisely this sense: it is both an extra and a requisite. Seemingly irrelevant to the ability to assemble wiring, sew sleeves, wait tables, teach, or tend the sick, this second skin is sutured to the cultural value of a particular body's configuration and the emotives it carries. If you are culturally marked as abject or potentially worth less, this second skin will justify a lower price—or none at all—for your labor power.

When a feminized second skin accompanies the exchange of labor power for a wage, it offers a tacit promise to the buyer that the supervision of the physical life and living personality of the bearer of this commodity is more thoroughly out of her hands. To bear a feminized second skin is to be dominated by cultural categories that allow a very narrow exercise of one's capacities and affects. In other words, the capacities of this subject are more fully loosed from her possession than is the case for a worker who is not feminized.

In the context of her research on the murdered women of Juárez, Julia Monárrez Fragoso acknowledges that this interface between culture and political economy regulates the price of labor power in each region of Mexico and leads to a substantial corporate advantage: "These partial standards under which humanity is classified impose generalizations that are inadequate but useful in the purchase of the capacity to labor available in each region, which has a price on the labor market according to its group value and is regulated on the basis of its alterity."[35] From the beginning of the Border Industrialization Program, the value of the female maquiladora worker was articulated in terms of her gender and sexuality. In early newspaper accounts of the program, anxieties about women's sexuality were a constant companion to the topic of women's factory work. Interviews with women maquila workers from the early years bolstered these fears with accounts of their newfound independence from fathers and husbands.[36] By the 1980s media coverage of the maquilas warned of the dangers of "liberated women" in the plants carrying venereal disease to an unsuspecting public, and officials worried about the effects of the dissolute lifestyles of maquila mothers on their children.[37] During the wave of strikes in the 1980s, media accounts of worker resistance were imbued with sexual innuendos.[38]

Spivak's argument on the predication of the subject might also be extended to include the feminized subject who gives over her capacities to caring labor in the informal market and at home. This was the case for Carmen/Andrés. She recounted:

> My mother said, "I prefer to see you dead rather than a homosexual," and my brother said, "If I see you dressed like a woman, I will kill you." But in the *zona roja* this is what I wore. I never asked for a taco from them. I was the one who was giving to them. When my twin sister was in the hospital, I went and she said, "What you are doing here in the hospital if you are a *pinche joto*? I am ashamed. You are a piece of shit." And I said, "I was the one who was paying the bills." And then she cried and cried and said, "I didn't know." I told them I was in the red zone working as a prostitute and all of them were able to eat from my fucking in the Papagayo and the Siete Negro.

Sex and sexual identity were for Carmen inseparable from her labor as maquiladora worker, as sex worker, and as son. She was the only son who cared for her father, and he was dying. "At Christmas time every night, he would wake up crying and shaking me like this," she said, and she shook the arm of the *esposo* who was still sitting there, eyes wide. "He begs to die. When I ask my brothers or sister to come and care for him, they say, 'No, es bien feo!' [No, he is really disgusting!]. I bathe him and wash his ass and clean up the excrement. I am the only son who does this. I am the homosexual, and I am the only son who cares for him."

Attention to the bodily needs of others also defined Carmen's sex work, the labor that paid for her sister's hospital care. In the long haul of life, keeping the night watch with the old, wiping asses, providing for the sick, and fucking, too, all are a part of the affective labor of social reproduction. That Carmen performed these activities in a caring way, not only satisfying her father's basic needs but doing so with attentiveness and empathy, is evident both explicitly and implicitly in her story, as is that fact that this caring labor is marked with the devalued term in a patriarchal gender scheme. The homosexual, the son whose nights were given over to caring for her dying father and who sold her body to pay her sister's hospital bills, declared that it was not fair, and of course she was right. Carmen's cry of protest and her actions recast the devaluation of caring labor and echoed the sense of responsibility to others that swept her into becoming one of the women in the front lines of organizing.

Insofar as I can tell, the Fabricas de Calidad campaign, where gay rights were on the agenda and two open homosexuals were in the front, was an extraordinary event. Carmen's narrative, which so eloquently joins her labor in the factory to her labor in the streets and at home, demonstrates and interrupts what Melissa Wright refers to as "the dialectic of still life," capital's ambivalent positioning of feminized workers in the tension between their value as cheap or unpaid labor and their worthlessness as value producers becoming waste.[39] Workers in the factories and at home who refuse to put up with the injustice of humiliation and the dispossession of their dignity transpose still life into movement. They bear on their second skins the tattoo of capital's monstrous possibility and can incite coworkers into a chain of witnessing that over time reorients basic assumptions, affects, feelings, and goals. Like Carmen, Iván, and Yessy, they put in motion predications of the subject that renarrate the scripts of abjection and the negative affect-culture they carry.

Toward a Sensible Queer Materialism, or a Socialism of the Skin

As human beings we have needs and desires, but modern critical knowledge has been shaped by paradigms that separate them. Over the course of capitalism's development, need and desire have been isolated from one another in the prevailing ways of making sense of social and psychic relations. This segregation is neither accidental nor simply philosophical. It is best understood as a historical effect consolidated sometime in the nineteenth century and, not coincidentally, at the dawning of consumer capitalism. It has registered in the irreconcilability of the two great Western analytics of need and desire, Marxism and psychoanalysis, and in the divergent agendas of social movements that give priority to labor or sexual identity.

Marx situates the laboring subject at the center of capitalism's social relations and relegates sexuality and gender to the footnotes of his analysis, where their bearing on market exchange is noted but not theorized. With few exceptions, most Marxist thought throughout the twentieth century all but ignored sexuality. Marxist and socialist feminism intervened to the extent that they made visible the gendered division of labor, the sex–gender system it relied upon, and their combined value in disciplining women's bodies, controlling property, and enhancing capital accumulation. When the waves of feminism and gay liberation swelled in the late 1960s and early 1970s, many of their pioneers drew upon a foundation in Marxist thought, but the voices that confronted heterosexuality as an institution whose deep roots in capitalism required better understanding were few and far between.[40]

In the last decade of the twentieth century, a new line of inquiry emerged that took up this critique. It spilled into the academy in the wake of the AIDS epidemic and the activism it spawned. ACT UP's defiant, in-your-face activism in the streets reeroticized sex and refused respectability and assimilation. "Queer" came to signify a counterhegemonic sensibility that repudiated shame and rejected the cultural domination enforced by narrow categories of sexual identity. Queer studies was a departure from the first wave of lesbian and gay studies in that it drew heavily upon postmodern theories that were stirring up the humanities and the social sciences, but it also benefitted from the inroads lesbians and gay men had made in the academy.

Many intellectuals and activists influenced by the gay liberation movement and by feminism yet critical of the identity politics that overtook them argued that explanations of human being must take into account economies of desire and identification in such a way as to speak to the differences suppressed by their heteronormative organization. Those who embraced the sign "queer" recast its value, transforming shame into a standpoint for critique. Queer theory emerged as the critical effort to denaturalize how we thought about sexuality, posing it as an unstable cultural construct. It offered a critique of the straight mind—that is, of heterosexuality as a normative regime and of the arbitrary and neat distinctions it enforced.[41] It also opened the monolithic identities "lesbian" and "gay" to investigation of the ways they too were inflected by heterosexual norms that were, in turn, conditioned by race and ethnic difference.

From its earliest formulations, queer theory had a significant impact on culture study, enabling new ways of reading gender and sexual identity as performative.[42] In keeping with the long-standing tradition of immanent critique, the operations of queering disparaged analysis that began with theoretical propositions in favor of analytics that zeroed in on taken-for-granted, fixed categories in order to disclose their instability. In revealing the fluid and intersecting play of differences that undermine the presumed natural solidity of identities and norms, queer theorists deployed many of the critical strategies of deconstruction. They also drew heavily upon Michel Foucault's argument that sexuality is a historical discourse that circulates through a diffuse field of power relations, not necessarily determined by capital.

Queer theory generated new lines of inquiry and brought fresh questions to the study of literature, history, anthropology, sociology, and political science. Its attention to the cultural construction of knowledge and identity made visible heterosexuality as an institution and troubled the commonsense distinctions between hetero- and homosexual and between masculine and feminine that organized its logic, including those that feminist and lesbian and gay studies had presumed. Queer theory was also, however, a creature of the cultural sea change that accompanied neoliberalism. By the 1990s neoliberal policies were transforming the social landscape and reshaping the cultural common sense in cosmopolitan centers across the globe. An emergent neoliberal culture promoted values associated with the professional middle-class sector, among them a driving consumerism and a privatized affective life of domesticity and respectable citizenship. As these values were redefining the cultural mainstream, the once-fixed boundaries regulating normative sexuality according to a heterosexual/homosexual distinction were undergoing a parallel alteration, and gay respectability was being slowly absorbed into cosmopolitan culture. The result was not, however, a less rigid, amplified set of possibilities for human identifications and affective relations. The niche for queerness that neoliberalism opened was one that could be congruent with market rationalities, with the free subject of capital, and with multicultural diversity. Too often, academic queer theorists failed to address the relation of their knowledge work to these developments. As I discuss in chapter 6, in the context of blue jeans marketer Levi Strauss & Co., as the neoliberal normative imaginary came to include respectable queer subjects and gay families corporate America cashed in on the value bonanza gay people offered both as a labor force and as a consumer market.[43] The relationship between these two prongs of incorporation—the recruitment of queers into the labor force and into the culture—remained fraught, however, as values regulated by sexual abjection continued to supplement capital accumulation, and affect-culture was being marshaled for both.

The class politics of queer visibility under neoliberal capitalism is a component of this story, and it calls for a more rigorous materialist analysis. Some steps toward such an analysis are being taken by scholars who are "rethinking queer critique in relation to a number of historical emergencies."[44] The editors of the 2005 special issue of *Social Text,* "What's Queer about Queer Studies Now?," which marks the fifteenth anniversary of queer theory, call for a renewed queer critique that addresses pressing social issues.[45] Among those they name are the recoding of freedom as domesticity and marriage; the militarization of state violence and the escalation of U.S. empire; the clash of religious fundamentalisms; the erosion of civil rights; and the pathologizing of immigrant communities. All are important topics. Here again, though, how we see these issues affects how we organize to address them, and all too little research sees affect-culture as a feature of the political economy in which these activities take place.

Although queer theory is fascinated by the epistemology of secrets that shapes the history of sexuality, it also harbors secrets of its own. Class is one, a social relation that organizes global flows of capital, as well as everyday lives, yet is often overlooked in queer analyses. Under pressure from several converging forces—among them the violent state-sponsored sabotage of radical social movements, the systemic suppression of organized labor, and the ideological absorption of socialist thought, especially in the United States—class is seen not as a capital relation but as a cultural marker of status or lifestyle. Most people see class in abstract terms, as distinctions among sectors like the poor, lower, middle, and professional middle class, for example, or as status categories defined in terms of education, employment, or the goods people purchase. We experience this sense of class because these differences are visible and seem obvious, but this knowledge accords with the logic of the market, a logic based on what you can buy. It is a commonsense way of seeing class that keeps us from recognizing what working people know from their good sense: class is a social relation between those who own and control the resources and technology and those who own mainly or only their power to labor.

As the twenty-first century unfolds, it is more apparent than ever that the unmet needs of the 99 percent have reached a crisis point. Sexuality and sexual identity are not irrelevant to this crisis, but do we have a robust critical vocabulary that can speak to it? A new generation of scholars is reclaiming and renovating historical materialism's strong critique of capitalism and articulating it along with the insights of queer theorists into a materialist analysis that can be more fully accountable to the challenges of the present. The most notable examples affirm their debt to Marxism, feminism, the gay liberation movement, and anticolonial struggles. They insist no politics will get us very far without a critical purchase on the ways gender and sexual formations feature in the value systems of capitalism. Some examples of this work include research on queer migration and diaspora by Chandan Reddy, Martin Manalansan, Eithne Luibhéid, Cindy Patton and Benigno Sánchez-Eppler, and the late Lionel Cantú. Kevin

Floyd's return to the concept of reification is an incisive example of materialist analysis that probes the roots of queer politics in the emergence of twentieth-century consumer culture and masculine identities. Other notable examples include Jon Binnie's assessment of gay organizing in postsocialist Poland, Lisa Duggan's arguments on the neoliberal assimilation of gay culture in the United States, Lisa Rofel's dissection of the emotions unleashed by neoliberalism in Chinese sex–gender culture, and Kate Bedford's investigation of gender and sexuality in the reformed World Bank. Important work on state violence and the regulation of queer bodies elaborates ties between sexuality and the U.S.-led global war on terror.[46] Some scholars are also undertaking valuable research on the mapping of bodies and practices by indigenous cultures, colonial heritages, and the legacy of slavery and diaspora, disclosing in these sectors of capitalism's history sexual identities that belie queer Western assumptions and gender schemes.[47] The work of Cathy Cohen, Roderick Ferguson, Michael Hames-García, and others advances understanding of the sexual politics of U.S. racial formations as they have been articulated through varied forms of state and institutional violence. Scholarship on state and family formations within and across the global north and south has also extended queer analysis of changing private and public spaces. Latin American researchers have made major contributions to this developing materialist queer critique. Notable among them are Nelly Richard, Marta Lamas, the late Carlos Monsiváis, and Héctor Domínguez-Ruvalcaba. Much of this research detaches the study of sexuality from psychoanalysis in order to break out of the Western body and the model of sexual difference it presumes and into a fuller understanding of the embodied subject living at the crossroads of cultural and economic value. It is in alliance with these efforts that I offer this argument on the value of a second skin.

I think Tony Kushner has it right when he suggests that socialism and homosexual liberation converge in an "irritation of the skin." Irritation is embodied and affective. It is the sense you carry in your flesh that things are painfully out of joint, unjust, wrong. A socialism of the skin makes visible the historical reasons for this irritation, and it puts forward an alternative social ontology.[48] Ontology in the philosophical sense involves the study of the nature of existence.

Social ontology underscores that human existence and well-being are made possible through interactions with the natural world and other humans, relations whose affective components span economic, political, and cultural forms. These relations are there all the time. That we often do not see them speaks to the ways in which our activities are made meaningful through what Iván calls "narrow ways of knowing." When they are naturalized or abstracted, second skins can be powerful irritants that provoke competition among sectors of the working class, but they can also be the irritation that provokes fuller understanding of cultural domination's complicity with exploitation. A queer social ontology is a sensible understanding of sexuality and class because it takes into account the human capacity for sensation and affect that is invested in identities as second skins that add to the exchange value of labor power. In this ontology identities matter not because their recognition is embraced as a political goal but because capital harvests their cultural value and the sensibilities that comprise their affective registers. To reclaim sensibility from capital, to hope for a world that enhances the joy of living through the equitable meeting of needs, does not mean harboring nostalgia for a time before civilization but promoting socialism and its communist supplement. It is from this standpoint that the sensibility of one's affective-cultural second skin is the filter for good sense.

Capital pursues workers whose labor power is cheap. Helping to sustain that supply of cheap labor are the norms that devalue some human beings as worth less, as feminized. Whether signified as "queer," "maricón," "marimacha," or "woman," feminized second skins are sewn into the commodities workers produce and into their service labor as retail clerks, janitors, wives, mothers, and stay-at-home dads. If not all queer workers wear the same second skins, this may tell us much about the relationship of culture to class or, as Iván would have it, about the points at which cheese becomes milk. Together, cultural and economic values sustain human being and mark the crux of the most far-reaching and incisive liberatory politics. They beg for further critical work—across universities, community centers, workshops, and encuentros and within and across national borders. And that work has only just begun.

« 6 »

Feeling Bodies, Jeans, Justice

Though "neoliberalism" may not be the name that springs to mind when most people characterize the social changes of the past four decades, those who have lived its losses know all too well what it means. This chapter considers neoliberalism's impact on the regulation of life, including affects as biocultural mediators of sexual identity's second skins. The manufacturing and marketing of blue jeans as a garment that became quite literally the second skin of the working class is a part of this history. After discussing neoliberal biopolitics and sexualities, I turn to the story of the multinational blue jeans manufacturer and marketer Levi Strauss & Co.[1] Levi's move offshore to a maquiladora assembly workforce and their simultaneous adoption of gay marketing strategies crystalize the impact of neoliberal deregulation on bodies north and south and its entanglement in the changing contradictory affective value attached to homosexuality and perceptions of what's real.

Bioderegulation

The reorganization of capitalism that began soon after World War II ushered in changes that altered the shape and quality of everyday life for people around the globe. Management of the crisis of over-accumulation after the war led to a new direction for political economy that extended U.S. foreign capital investment and ultimately moved manufacturing jobs in the global north offshore, gutting the economic base of cities and towns and leaving many people unemployed or slowly moving into information technology and service jobs. Increasingly, land and natural resources, mainly from Latin America, Russia, Eastern Europe, China, Southeast Asia, and Iraq, were being absorbed by multinational capital into an unbridled global marketplace. Relaxed state regulation of capital drove public policy to support an array of free-market strategies. Over the course of the next half century, this deregulation of capital translated into privatized social services, increased labor flexibility, weakened or abolished legal structures protecting workers, and increased tax breaks to the wealthy. As the state's power to meet broad-based social needs was rolled back, the political agenda driving change substituted corporate control over government for democratic accountability, muzzled citizen dissent, and undermined efforts to think and act collectively. By the end of the first decade of the new millennium, the consequences of these structural adjustments registered in intensified immiserization of the poor, increasingly precarious lives for the social majority, and a historic gap between the richest few and the laboring majority.[2]

In *Globalization and Its Terrors,* Teresa Brennan argues that neoliberalism has made the cost of life prohibitive by intensifying a long-standing strategy of speeding up social reproduction in the effort to maximize profit. Human and natural reproduction take time, which is to say that they cost. Capitalists deal with this drag on profits in two ways: by minimizing the linear time it takes to reproduce natural resources, daily labor power, and the next generation and by traveling across space to find another supply after it uses them up. The consequence of shortening the needed time for natural and human reproduction is that life is damaged. As the pace of capital expansion outstrips the time required for regeneration, life is increasingly deregulated. Eventually, this deregulation impinges on the very conditions of survival.

In order to survive individually and as a species, humans must reproduce the means to meet the conditions of life, a process that depends on interactions with one another and with the natural world. Basic bodily and social needs include the affectively infused relations of well-being, what Brennan calls "the opportunity to enjoy life."[3] Poverty, she reminds us, detracts from the enjoyment of life; so does ill health. Without the ability to exercise the opportunity to enjoy life, the human organism becomes depressed; depression lowers immune function and thus diminishes the chances for physical survival (17). Similarly, the natural environment on which human life relies needs time to replenish when its resources are harvested or its cycles are disrupted by agriculture, industry, or commerce. Deregulation aims, however, to enhance capital accumulation by removing the constraints that time imposes on human and natural reproduction.

Deregulation is most familiar as the set of policies that have rolled back the state's check on capital accumulation by privatizing social services formerly regulated by the state, like education, transportation, utilities, and aspects of health care. Deregulation can also be understood as the broad-ranging squeeze on the regular cycles of rest and regeneration. In this respect it is a technology of biopower deeply entangled with affect-culture. Child care, health care, and elder care give people the security and time to grow up, be well, and grow old with relative stability. These caring activities have in a sense also been deregulated. They are time consuming and costly, and as such, they are a drag on capital accumulation. Their deregulation aims to lower their costs to capital by removing the constraints that time imposes on these areas of social reproduction.

Brennan calls this deregulation of the survival conditions of natural and human life "bioderegulation" (20, 32). It sets the constraints that impact the affective components of survival: interaction and personal contact are restricted when people are made to labor longer and harder, and migration becomes a matter of course, either by commuting longer distances to work or by relocating from homelands in order to survive. Bioderegulation registers in an alienated life rhythm of rushing and insecurity, where a permanent job is no longer guaranteed and where multiple jobs, overtime, job instability, and unemployment break down affective relations within families and communities (25).[4] Anxiety over survival disturbs the harmonious interplay of the body's cycles, and the disruption registers in growing personal isolation and stress. The deregulated body is one that goes without enough sleep, rest, or proper food—taking prescribed drugs to silence chronic illnesses and escalating allergies or taking illegal drugs to numb pain (24). Bioderegulation's effects cross the degrees of separation between exploitation and hyperexploitation, and for this reason it is a useful concept for enabling people in seemingly disparate situations to identify common forces in the social relations they occupy.[5] Many in the one-third world who have ostensibly benefited from global capitalism suffer its negative impact on their bodily and affective well-being, as do those who labor to survive in the two-thirds world.

At the intersection of capital's spatial expansion and its abandonment of the generational and daily reproduction time needed for survival stand those whose personhood is devalued by way of patriarchal gender cultures. The feminization of social subjects is built into the technologies of bioderegulation. As I explain in chapter 5, the feminization of certain subjects has served historically to justify a cheap, flexible, and disposable source of labor power, the most valuable commodity for capital accumulation. The squeeze exerted on the feminized worker's time, life rhythms, dignity, and well-being makes her hyperexploited. If exploitation is never itself value free, because it is structured by the second skin of cultural value embodied in labor power, then surplus value is also accumulated through the cost-saving, bioderegulating practices in the workplace that deplete the worker's flesh, life span, and sense of integrity.

As a discourse intimately involved in the regulation of bodies, sexuality has been deployed as a feature of the feminizing of subjects and a component of the cultural technologies of bioderegulation. What is the use of thinking sexuality this way? I answer that question by considering the deployment of sexuality across far-flung localities and by tracking its relation to the affect-culture accompanying the loosening of patriarchal gender norms, the feminization of cheap labor, and neoliberal investments in both assimilation and social stigma. Finally, thinking sexuality as a feature of neoliberal bioderegulation also has a political usefulness, as it can raise awareness of its mediating role both in these historical developments and in collective efforts to reclaim common resources and civic personhood.

"La Realidad Vivida en Carne Propia"

As she summed up the corrosive impact of free trade on her life, Teresa Chávez leaned across the kitchen table, punctuating her story with an occasional thump of her fist on the flowered tablecloth. After years on the line in automotive assembly plants in Reynosa, she was no longer able to find work, because carpal tunnel syndrome in her wrists, the consequence of thousands of repetitive motions, had disabled her body. Now, she cared for the children of her sons and daughters, who lived with her, including the surviving child of Teresa's daughter Alma, who also worked in the automotive assembly plants and died several years ago from cancer. This is "la realidad vivida en carne propia" (the reality lived in my own flesh), she said.[6] Teresa's searing phrase conveys the life costs of bioderegulation for workers on global assembly lines, which stretch from north to south.[7]

In an interview Martha Ojeda, a former worker at the Sony electronics plant in Nuevo Laredo, described daily life working in the maquilas. In her words we can hear how feminized bodies were precariously poised between the company's deregulation of the times and rhythms of human being and the natural world:

> Working in the factory, you don't know what hurts more, your body or having consciousness. When the bell rings, you start, and from that moment your body begins hurting. Your back, your hands. It hurts so much you don't have any emotions. You just watch the clock. And when the bell rings again, with your whole body you say, "Oh, thank God!"
>
> The days when it rained, they would turn away the ones who arrived muddy and wet, and they would lose a day of work. Of course they were muddy. They had to travel on their own across two colonias. There was no public bus or transportation from the company, but the company could not have muddy or wet people in the factory. It had to be clean for the disks.

We hear in Martha's words the process by which quick-turnover workers waste away—their bioderegulation—as it takes place in her labor on the line: the pain in her back and hands, the pain of consciousness in which even emotion is numbed. The bodies of the men and women who arrive late to the Sony plant on rainy days are subject to a different wasting, however, as they temporarily slip outside the value calculus of the marketplace, their muddy flesh and clothes devolving them into bare life. The mud-encrusted bodies of these workers also situate them as colonia residents—that is, as people who live in the liminal spaces of civil society. Indeed, colonias are literally on the margins because as unincorporated lands outside the city proper, a rainfall can turn their roadways into lakes and make mud the gluey medium of all outdoor activity. Traces of this uncivil land on their feet and flesh cancel the potential value of their disposable labor power.[8] Seemingly of less concern to Sony than this muddy second skin and largely invisible are the toxins in the effluent chemical waste that daily stream from the factories into the air and the Río Bravo, the principal water source for the colonias where the majority of maquiladora workers live.

Bioderegulation takes place in maquiladora communities as capital harvests water, land, and human energy, flaying river, earth, muscle, bone, and mind for value. The erosion of workers' health and safety in the working day can mean lasting disabilities, stillbirths, and birth defects from chemicals and other contaminants. Rape is an apt metaphor for these violations, but it can also be the literal currency for a job. As Martha elaborated:

> I remember one day when I was the union delegate for the company and one of my tasks was to go to the plaza where workers were being hired and bring some of them to the factory. When I went, there were many women lined up waiting to be hired. On the side of the plaza was the office of the secretary-general of the CTM union. This day, he was there about to meet with some reporters. Meantime, the guy who was doing the hiring was reviewing the women. He said to me, "Here, take these, but these others leave with me. They are *carne fresca* [fresh meat]."[9] If these women wanted a job, they had to go have sex with him, and then he would bring them to the factory. I remember the look on their faces—they were so young and so afraid. And so I confronted him in front of the secretary-general and the media. I said, "They are all going with me, and you will never do this again. From now on, workers will come directly to the factory to be hired." And I denounced the secretary-general for protecting this pig.

If one's identity as a feminized worker adheres to and is enacted upon the body, then sexuality is a deeply affective technology for nailing it into place. Sexuality is a pliable instrument of bioderegulation that leverages *carne propia* (one's own flesh) into *carne fresca* (fresh meat) to be stamped as worth less and less as it is worn away and used up in bioderegulation's value-making machinery. As Martha's narrative demonstrates, however, it does not have to come to this. The body's physical and affective capacities, the meaning and the value attached to them, and the degree to which they are out of our hands and subject to the regime of waste in the making comprise a scene of struggle—which is to say, a site for constituting justice.

What's Real: Take Two

Bioderegulation relies upon ways of understanding what's real that limit what can be known. Neoliberal reality is governed by market rationalities or ways of knowing that promote the values of the unleashed free-market economy. They include the discourses of individual responsibility and competition, of volunteerism, and of cultural diversity. To these discourses the U.S. war on terror adds an arsenal of affectively loaded ideological weapons, including invocations of nationalism and freedom laced with fear and denial. Underlying this neoliberal cultural matrix is the logic of randomness. It plays out in provocations to edgy anxiety and resigned disconnection, in invitations to believe that you can never know friend from foe, that you have to be always on alert, attuned to possibility—to whatever. One effect of neoliberal bioderegulation is the articulation of this random logic into how human reproduction is understood. To think about the meeting of human survival needs as random is to see the process as unpredictable and uncontrollable and human subjects as governed by the logic of "whatever." Indeed, "whatever" has become the catchword of the new millennium, a word that speaks to an increasingly normative acceptance of social instability. Its effect is to dispel causality, to implicitly insist that social relations are at best contingent and explanation is impossible or irrelevant.

Sexuality and sexual identity are key discourses here because they are ways of naming and knowing human affective capacities that are weighted with cultural value. As neoliberalism's random cultural logic has gradually seeped into the mainstream over the past thirty years, the norms and values shaping sexuality and sexual identity have also undergone a parallel sea change, redrawing the margins of tolerance and acceptability. Lisa Duggan argues, I think rightly, that neoliberal cultural politics in the United States has actually gone through several phases, and each has revolved around different myths of sexual belonging. The rhetoric of official neoliberal politics shifted during the 1990s from the sex panics of the culture wars to a superficial multiculturalism compatible with the global aspirations of U.S. business interests. As new versions of liberal inclusion were formulated, the once-fixed boundaries regulating normative sexuality according to a heterosexual/homosexual distinction also changed. Queer, transgender, and postgay identities began to be incorporated into the cultural real. However, the result has not been a less rigid, amplified set of possibilities for human affective relations. Rather, the new gay mainstream has promoted a narrow form of equality forged by a rhetoric of homonormativity and anchored in the privatized affective life of domesticity and consumption.[10]

By the new millennium assimilation seemed to be removing from U.S. mainstream culture the stigma attached to being gay. *Time* magazine's October 2005 cover story, "The Battle over Gay Teens," affirmed the trend. In it reporter John Cloud argued that although gay teens were coming out at a younger age, both those on the Christian Right and those on the progressive Left seemed to be moving toward a depoliticized, postgay identity. In the words of Rich Savin-Williams, who is quoted in the article and the author of *The Gay Teenager*, "Just because they're gay they don't have to march in a parade."[11]

The "whatever" rhetoric of postgay assimilation masks a contradictory reality. Lee Badgett's *Money, Myths, and Change: The Economic Lives of Lesbians and Gay Men* discloses that in the United States, when it comes to the exchange value of lesbian and gay labor in the workplace, lesbians are still women and gay men are, well, not quite men, considering that "lesbian/bisexual women earn about the same as heterosexual women. And gay/bisexual men earn 17 percent less than heterosexual men with the same education, race, location, and occupation."[12] The homonormalizing discourse of gay assimilation, however, overlooks these discrepancies and the ways homosexual abjection continues to supplement capital accumulation as it gets sewn into the terms of the exchange of labor power. Legitimizing gay marriage does little or nothing to undercut these economic facts. As

Duggan suggests, it might actually reinforce a depoliticized, normal-ized gay culture by severing identities from wage work and the care work that takes place in the family.[13] In this respect the terms of the gay marriage debate have limited available political choices by keep-ing invisible the gendered class politics of insecurity under neoliberal capitalism.[14]

Marriage does offer gay couples certain rights, many of them property rights that mostly benefit the middle class. The majority of lesbian, gay, and transgendered subjects are, however, deprived of property in any case. In response to the question, Shouldn't one par-ticipate in the struggle over gay rights precisely for the sake of redress-ing the terms of gay abjection that capital takes advantage of? we have to ask whose material security that normalizing would most benefit.

On this question the conservative backlash against gay marriage deserves consideration for the ways it has actually addressed, albeit ideologically, the material conditions and insecurities of home. In an article in the *Nation,* Duggan and Richard Kim refer to the mar-riage debate in the 2004 U.S. election as the "other security issue." They argue that the Bush administration actually created the back-lash against gay marriage as a deeply emotional "homeland security" program that provided a powerful supplement to the ideological ar-senal of the war on terror. Marriage offers an imaginary promise of a secure home, but a fundamental contradiction exists between the symbolic appeal of marriage as a guarantor of security (both con-serving it for male–female couples and democratizing it for gays and lesbians) and the reality most people live. The defense of the domestic home front in this sense shores up the hopes of many who live the hopelessness of an unraveling social compact and rely on family supports to compensate—supports that are no longer able to provide all that is required of them. The affect-culture surrounding marriage and weddings is potent. It promises a sense of belonging and in fleeting doses delivers it, but a gay rights position that focuses solely on access to marriage obscures the more lasting reality of home insecurity and the toll that neoliberal economic policies have taken on all kinds of families. They are evident in the freewheeling cor-porate practices that led to thousands of home foreclosures and to the relegation of care for children, the elderly, and the sick to private households. The point here is that the deregulation of capital and the privatization of social security are making individual families and property-based kinship networks the primary resources for survival, as opposed to more ample democratic and collective endeavors. The defense of heterosexual marriage and the call for gay access to marriage are rallying points for unmet needs, both physical and affective, but these needs remain obscured so long as they are framed only in terms of marriage rights.

The discourses of both postgay assimilation and gay rights in the United States are parts of a neoliberal logic that has helped advance narrow understandings of what's real. They are narrow because they promote a model of well-being and civic life that valorizes the family as a private institution. This cultural logic is materially linked to the feminization of a cheap workforce both within and outside the overdeveloped sectors, and I here turn to a particular chapter of that story.

Urban Modernists, Jeans, and Justice

Levi Strauss & Co., headquartered in San Francisco, offers an instructive example of the disparate and overlapping ways sexuality as a strong attractor of affect-culture features in bioderegulation. The company began as a maker of work clothes and prides itself on being the inventor of jeans, pants that are now so popular and so much a part of people's identities that consumers and the company itself refer to them as "second skins."[15] These second skins now have a symbolic value that includes a deeply affective and sexualized relationship to the body, but this is only one part of the story. With registered trademarks in 110 countries, contractual agreements with approximately 600 external suppliers, and joint ventures and product license agreements at approximately 350 additional facilities, Levi's has a global reach to its trademark and a reputation as a company that responds to workers in proactive ways. Pursuing how that reputation lines up against how Levi's products are made and marketed takes us to a series of events in which the incorporation of postgay identities meets up with more brutal forms of bioderegulation that rely on homosexual stigma.[16]

Levi's investment in a values discourse dates back to its founder Levi Strauss's canny combination of work clothes' manufacture and philanthropy. When Strauss brought his family's dry goods business to California during the gold rush years of the 1850s, he quickly realized that the canvas he sold to meet one set of needs—making tents and tops for covered wagons—was much better put to use meeting a more pressing demand: durable pants for miners. He secured the first patent with Jacob Davis, a Nevada tailor who had the idea of reinforcing the pants with steel rivets. By the time he died in 1902, Strauss had established himself as a community leader in San Francisco, supporting charitable work, orphanages, and the synagogue. The company is still owned primarily by indirect descendants of Levi Strauss, and its U.S. factories have never been unionized. From its earliest years, Levi's values discourse was integral to its reputation. By the end of the twentieth century, these values were being shaped by two sequential and converging global crises: the AIDS epidemic and structural adjustments to U.S. manufacturing in the face of competition to maintain wide profit margins. The former would lead the company to a major corporate commitment to HIV education, support for its San Francisco workforce, and AIDS-related philanthropy; the latter would lead them into a decades-long process of moving production offshore. That Levi's adopted a marketing strategy explicitly targeting young gay and transgendered subjects in the mid-to-late 1990s was conditioned by both crises.

In 1982, in response to rank-and-file pressure, Levi's developed what became a model program that would establish it as an international corporate leader in AIDS advocacy. The pressure began when a group of workers at the San Francisco headquarters who were grieving the loss of friends and lovers proposed that an AIDS booth be placed in the lobby. Then–chairman and CEO Robert D. Haas supported the project and subsequently endorsed a series of initiatives that grew into a multifaceted campaign that included AIDS education, health care, and community outreach.

This program made Levi's a major philanthropic resource for the entire San Francisco population. Since then, nonprofit agencies, medical clinics, chambers of commerce, and community action groups have all turned to the Levi Strauss Foundation for direction on AIDS education and training.[17] By 1992 the Levi Strauss Foundation was giving over $3 million a year in grants, many of them devoted to AIDS-related work. The foundation has also funded many LGBT projects and cultural events, including Frameline (the San Francisco international LGBT film festival) and the Hetrick-Martin Institute. They were also one of the foundations that discontinued funding the Boy Scouts of America because of that organization's antigay discrimination.

In 1991, almost a decade after Levi Strauss & Co. had taken the lead in progressive gay advocacy, it became the first multinational company to establish a comprehensive ethical code of conduct for its manufacturing and finishing contractors. The code document has been modified over the years to include Levi's "Terms of Engagement" for its product suppliers and its "Country Assessment Guidelines." Both are included in their *Social and Environmental Sustainability Guidebook.* Levi's "Terms of Engagement" addresses such items as child and prison labor, working hours and wages, freedom of association, health, safety, and environmental protections. It rates these practices according to the action the company will take regarding violations, from zero tolerance through efforts toward continuous improvement. The principal motivation for what amounts to Levi's code of conduct was blowback in the form of workers' protests and a fair amount of media attention to the relocation of Levi's production offshore, where minimum wages were lower, collective bargaining was lax or nonexistent, and workers had minimal to no safety protections. Working conditions in its U.S. factories were, however, far from exemplary, as well. The women workers at their San Antonio plant described the pressure exerted on them to produce quotas and to work fast. They said they were not allowed to go to the bathroom or get water, and they suffered multiple injuries, including carpal tunnel syndrome and herniated disks.[18]

Between 1981 and 1990, the company shifted about half of its production out of the United States and Canada.[19] By the 1990s it had subsidiaries and contractors in developing countries around the world.[20] At this point Levi's had also begun to compensate for the impact of automating production at some of its U.S. plants by laying off workers at several of its older operations in Tennessee, Arkansas, and Texas.[21] The closures had a severe impact, since these areas of the U.S. south already suffered from high unemployment rates and depressed wages, and Levi's offered paltry severance packages. The move offshore proved very lucrative. Through the early 1990s, Levi's profits swelled, and by 1993, with sales of $4.9 billion, the company had become the world's largest brand-name apparel manufacturer.

By the end of the decade, Levi's was also aggressively moving into a transgendered and gay marketing niche. In 1998 the company created its first gay-specific advertising campaign, an effort to target young, hip buyers for their Dockers brand. The ad ran as an insert in *OUT* magazine and featured profiles of ten openly gay heroes, including people like James Dale, whose case against the New Jersey Boy Scouts went to the U.S. Supreme Court.[22] Mark Malinowski, senior marketing analyst for Levi's, said of the project, "We're trying to reach 25 to 34 year olds who we call urban modernists. When we looked at who made up that group, gay men and lesbians are a large part of it."[23] Those involved in the campaign said it became more meaningful after the 1998 beating death of Matthew Shepherd, the openly gay University of Wyoming student.[24]

That same year, Levi's also launched its What's Real ad campaign, a series of interviews with "real" people. The campaign inaugurated what would become one of Levi's signature advertising strategies— featuring ordinary-seeming young people in everyday life and an offhand, oblique message. In one of the first ads, an awkward teen named Dustin recounts a conversation with his dad:

> We were talking about my neighbors, because my neighbors hated
> me and stuff. They didn't like the music I listened to, because I used
> to listen to my music really loud and dance around in my room.
> We were talking about how they hated me and stuff. He was like,
> "That's just the type of people they are" (they're like him) "they
> don't like homosexuals, they think you're a drug user." I said, "Dad,
> they don't know that I'm gay." He said, "What did you say?!" And I
> said, "'I mean, they don't know that I do drugs!" And then I'm like,
> "I mean . . . !"[25]

The mix of assimilationist and gay-vague rhetoric evident here nor- malizes Dustin as literally the boy next door, a "whatever," postgay kid. During the same year that consumers watched him and other Levi's characters represent What's Real, the economic restructuring that NAFTA's passage exacerbated kicked in for Levi's. In 1998 they closed their plants in McAllen, Harlingen, El Paso, and Wichita Falls, Texas; Mountain City and Johnson City, Tennessee; Valdosta, Georgia; Morrilton, Arkansas; Warsaw, Virginia; Murphy, North Carolina; and Cornwall, Ontario. In 2002 they closed six more U.S. plants, and by September 2003 another 5,900 Levi's workers had lost their jobs. In January 2004 the two remaining U.S. plants, located in San Antonio, closed their doors, and their production moved to Costa Rica. Two sewing facilities in Edmonton and Stoney Creek, Ontario, as well as a finishing center in Brantford, Ontario, closed in March 2004, completing Levi's move out of North America.[26]

If it is accurate to say Levi's attention to the AIDS epidemic conditioned its gay marketing strategies of the mid-1990s, then is it also fair to say its transfer of production offshore was materially related to its marketing of gay assimilation? Levi's What's Real campaign incorporated gay youth into the cultural mainstream as subjects whose gay identities were normal, even cool. What relation did this normalizing of a postgay subject have to the deregulation of the bodies of workers assembling Levi's jeans? Is bioderegulation a concept capacious enough to contain the spectacular deployment of homonormative bodies in transnational commercial sectors and the wasting of bodies elsewhere? If so, how do the borders defining sexual identity feature across that transit? Is it a mistake to presume that gay and postgay consumers and offshore factory workers are worlds apart? What are the implications of such a possibly false presumption?

In 2005 workers at one of Levi's suppliers in Gómez Palacio, Durango, confronted the company when their efforts to organize an independent union were aggressively thwarted. Their struggle confirms the interface of sexual identity and the value of feminized labor power under neoliberalism. To understand how their story complicates what's real in the spectacle of Levi's urban modernists, we cannot pit sexuality against labor or segregate gay consumers and citizens in the north from workers in the south. Moreover, unraveling that complexity confronts us with the challenges that sexuality poses to the politics of transnational organizing.

By the late twentieth century, the La Laguna region, located on the border of the states of Coahuila and Durango in the north-central region of Mexico, had become the blue jeans capital of the world.[27] It is still the country's largest center for garment manufacturing and export, outstripping Puebla and Tehuacán in the south. Historically an agricultural district, especially for cotton, La Laguna did not have any large foreign investment in the garment industry until the mid-1990s.[28] The reform of Article 27 of the Mexican Constitution in 1992 hastened the privatization of the *ejidos* (common lands) across Mexico. Along with the devaluation of the peso in 1994, it ushered in a new phase of development. In order for the neoliberal model, which supported private property and foreign investment, to be established in the region, the *ejido* dwellers had to be removed, and they became a displaced population. Many moved closer to the area's three urban centers, Torreón, Gómez Palacio, and Lerdo, where garment assembly for export was becoming the major industry, with blue jeans as the leading item. It was during this time that the Lajat Manufacturing Company was founded.

Formally known as Maquiladoras y Manufacturas Lajat, the Lajat Manufacturing Company is a model of neoliberal business practice. A subcontractor of at least one and perhaps several other subcontractors for major multinational garment marketers, including Levi's, Mudd Jeans, and Aeropostale, Lajat is owned by the five Bello brothers, who have strong political ties in the states of Durango and Coahuila. By 2006 they employed approximately twelve thousand workers in several plants in the region.

A decade earlier, NAFTA had ramped up foreign investment in the region's blue jeans assembly, reorienting it to the U.S. market, but the signing of the Dominican Republic–Central America–United States Free Trade Agreement (CAFTA-DR) in 2005 and the end of the Multi-fiber Agreement on January 1 of that year threatened the region's garment industry. The new trade agreement and the removal of protective tariffs brought Central America and Asia into the global garment market. La Laguna continued to maintain a strategic advantage, however, because of its position in the lowest of Mexico's three minimum-salary regions, allowing it to compete with the low-wage areas in the country's south and still provide companies with distribution access to the big consumer market in the United States. Nonetheless, an atmosphere of job insecurity prevailed across the region.

In January 2005, the same month that the Multi-fiber Agreement ended, Lajat announced that production was moving from their Gómez plant to the city of Torreón and that if workers wanted to keep their jobs, they would have to work there. The Torreón plant was about ten kilometers outside Gómez. The company said it would transport workers, but it would do so in the backs of open eighteen-wheeler trucks, not in buses, and the workers would have to find their own way home after work each night. The majority of the workers were young women and single mothers, and for them this was an insurmountable obstacle. The announced move to Torreón was also the last straw for the workers, who were enduring horrific conditions in the Gómez plant: They were forced to work up to twelve hours without being paid overtime. There was no potable drinking water. Management would not give workers permission to go to the restroom or would chase out those who dared to go. The toilets were often out of order, and two of the three restrooms had no running water. Production quotas were excessive, and workers could not leave the factory until they met the quotas. Finally, workers used many chemicals to stonewash jeans by hand, but they weren't given any protective equipment.[29]

In the face of these conditions, that spring workers began the process of forming an independent union, and they approached the international Coalition for Justice in the Maquiladoras (CJM) to ask for support. Because Levi Strauss and Co.'s code of conduct honored workers' right to freedom of association, CJM exerted pressure on Levi's to abide by their code. Meantime, the workers' efforts to organize their independent union were blocked at every step by the Mexican labor authorities and the CTM. As the workers pushed for an election to ratify their independent union, the labor board and governor increasingly came down on the side of the company. Then in September 2005, with an election victory for the workers almost assured, Lajat announced it was closing the Gómez plant because of a lack of production. Since Lajat could not legally lay off the workers, they cut their pay from 850 to 350 pesos per week (US$85 to

US$35) and stopped paying into their legally mandated health care and housing funds.[30] Workers who were organizing the union were fired and blacklisted.

That fall, as a result of international pressure, Levi's acknowledged its responsibility to enforce its code of conduct, but in doing so, it employed a double discourse. On the one hand, the Levi Strauss & Co. code did not allow a supplier to close a factory and transfer its production to another in order to thwart workers' organizing efforts. On the other hand, despite workers' evidence to the contrary, throughout negotiations Levi's claimed they had no official production in Gómez when the workers began their organizing campaign.

Usually when the Mexican Labor Board delays the process in workers' struggles for freedom of association, the workers give up because they cannot endure the long-term oppression that invariably accompanies an organizing campaign. As the negotiations dragged on, however, the Lajat workers grew stronger, and in the end they set important precedents in the region. They formed the first legally recognized workers' coalition in a maquiladora. Although Lajat never formally acknowledged the independent union, it did so de facto by negotiating a collective labor agreement with the Lajat workers' bargaining committee, bypassing the monopoly of the CTM. The negotiations forced Lajat to pay the workers from the Gómez plant 100 percent of what Mexican federal labor law required as severance pay, as well as 100 percent of the overtime owed them, even though companies often got away with paying only a portion of what was legally required. The Lajat workers had exposed the unethical actions of a huge multinational corporation in international public forums, and they built a strong social movement in the region. Most important, they won the official registration of the Lajat Workers' Union—the first union whose leadership positions were all filled by women.

These victories were the result of the workers' determination and courage, the support of consumer actions in the United States and Canada, and effective cross-border organizing. Coordinated efforts brought several of Levi's top executives to La Laguna to open the final session of negotiations between Lajat management and the Lajat Workers' Union. Their participation was in itself precedent setting. Throughout the negotiations, though, Levi's maintained the position that it had taken during the months of talks between the company and the workers' representatives—that they had no official production in Gómez when the workers began their campaign. Legally, Lajat was obligated to pay severance or keep the workers, but their condition was that the workers had to resign from the independent union. Levi's said they would not force Lajat to negotiate differently. They would not also insist Lajat return production to the Gómez plant, because, they said, "we can't tell our suppliers how to run their business."[31] Of course, if this was so, then what was the point of having a corporate code of conduct?

Corporate codes of conduct were developed during the NAFTA decade of the 1990s as a strategy for redressing the global exploitation of workers. In the case of the Lajat workers' struggle for an independent union, these codes proved useless. Though designed to guarantee the protection of workers' rights, they can function actually as a cover for sabotaging those rights while preserving brand reputation. In the case of Mexico, during the years of the Lajat workers' struggle maquiladora workers did not need codes of conduct because they already had a progressive labor law. What they needed was to be able to practice their legal right to free association, a right that gave them the collective agency to decide what they needed. The Lajat workers' case demonstrates that codes of conduct drafted by a corporation rather than workers themselves—let alone any democratic or national body—can actually short-circuit workers' most powerful leverage, the right to collective organizing. Critics of codes of conduct have made this point forcefully. When companies or consumers write the codes and decide whether and how to enforce them, unsurprisingly the codes do not function in the workers' favor.[32]

The story of the Lajat workers' struggle is a tale of workers' refusal to accept their bioderegulation and feminization through repressive practices. Eduardo González, a Lajat worker, explained the kinds of treatment they endured:

> When I entered this plant, I met a powerful, reckless, and envious chief. He did not recognize the effort we put into our work. . . .
> Sometimes the engineer, Tomás Bello, showed up to demonstrate

that his word was law, swearing and firing workers everywhere and insulting us by saying "m—r f—ers."

I remember that every December the rumors started that they were going to close the plant because there was no work, and I felt this uncertainty and instability in my job, and that affects my family, not to mention causing personal problems.[33]

Among Eduardo's unmentionable personal problems was a daughter, Normita, born with a heart defect. She needed daily medication and several surgeries and oxygen for the lung problems that her condition involved. When Eduardo's health benefits were taken away during the workers' struggle and he was unable to pay for the oxygen, Normita died.

The company intensified its biopolitics against the workers once they started organizing. The police were called into the plant the workers occupied, and they teargassed a group of women huddled in the cafeteria. One of the women, who was pregnant, lost her baby. Late at night, management visited workers' homes, threatened their family members, and finally, cut their salaries and benefits— all of which increased the company's squeeze on the workers and their families. Sexuality was also a ready instrument of domination. Women workers reported being sexually harassed by supervisors and managers, and sexuality also featured in more subtle and unspeakable ways.

When the workers began organizing, one of their leaders and the person they initially chose to be secretary-general of their union was a man I will call José. In an informal conversation, José acknowledged he was gay, but this fact was never mentioned in the official discourse of the workers' struggle. He had a wife he cared for, and at the time she was not well. He also had a son. He was proud of being gay and indicated it was not a secret. He said that working in the maquila was one of the few options he had as an openly homosexual (that is, feminized) man. Though José's homosexual identity was not mentioned in official reports from the workers' struggle, it did feature in the harassment and intimidation against him that became relentless as the workers' campaign heated up in the summer of 2005.

Anonymous phone calls and late-night stalkers knocking at his door and yelling threats at him in the streets were punctuated with derogatory references to his being gay. Managers from the plant came to his house and threatened him, using gay-bashing, abusive language. When he caved, quit the union organizing committee, and took his severance payment rather than endure more of this abuse, he was told by the company that he would not be placed on a blacklist. That was a lie. Much to his regret and remorse, he said he felt he betrayed his fellow workers.

I do not know how much weight the company's use of his gay identity as a lever in their retaliation should have in any calculation of José's accountability. From what I understand, collectively the workers were not able or willing to address the targeting of José's homosexuality, either as a divisive strategy on the part of the company or as a feature of the devaluation of their labor. José's homosexuality was also absent from the Jeans with Justice campaign that CJM launched in support of the Lajat workers. If a sexual politics of abjection underlies but does not excuse José's betrayal of his coworkers, then it also conditions the disappearance of the homosexual body from the NGO's strategy sessions and from the public record of the workers' organizing effort. Unfortunately, the Lajat/Levi's workers' struggle is only one of many instances in which sexuality and sexual identity have been embedded in the emotional habitus of organizing and in which lesbian- or gay-identified leaders have been harassed and intimidated, yet sexuality and sexual identity are almost never addressed in the transnational strategizing of social justice organizations. In other words, a one-time union leader who lost his commitment is not the only casualty in this story. So are all the Lajat workers' allies, the international NGO, and even Levi's workers in San Francisco, who never learned about José.

Taken together, these tales of one company's history confirm that neoliberal capitalism both directly and indirectly feeds off the reality lived in one's own flesh, in uneven and varied ways across national boundaries. The fact that at the turn of the twenty-first century corporate advertising and marketing campaigns like those of Levi Strauss & Co. began to assimilate transgendered and gay subjects is well documented. Its coincidence with and material dependence on the intensified feminization of labor elsewhere is less understood. The Levi's story suggests that these events are not simply two faces of the same coin—that is, capitalism's continual progressive and exploitative movement—for the operations of bioderegulation defy this simple binary.

The appearance of the postgay subject as a familiar and accepted member of the flexible, neoliberal workforce and as a member of an acceptable new family does little to modify the effects of bioderegulation on most working people north and south. Moreover, postgay workers labor overtime, on part-time contracts for minimum wages, and manage multitasking, flexible hours. Before, sometimes during, and after their workdays, they provide elder and child care. They too take up the slack of deregulated capital that enriches an elite minority. Their appearance as cool "whatever" subjects in Levi's ads does not change these material realities. In fact, it might even be said to have helped sanction them.

Levi's story attests to one of capital's underlying contradictions: it continually relies upon feminizing devaluation and its affective accompaniment as an accumulation strategy even as it is indifferent to who in particular bears a feminized second skin. At the same time that capital accumulation is indifferent to the persons that constitute its feminized labor force, it is deeply interested in cultural differences as it pursues new markets and consumer subjects. When political theorists engage in heated debates that pit a politics of recognition against a politics of redistribution, they are, in essence, missing the point. As a social totality, capitalism is simultaneously engaged in expanding recognition through assimilation and maintaining the unequal distribution of wealth. The particulars of each strategy change and can even be liberating for some groups, but the structure of the relations that make capital a profit-driven mode of production grounded in property ownership and labor remains.

The evolving particulars are evident in Levi's recent manufacturing and marketing decisions. While the company continues to use subcontractors in Mexico, it has also expanded its assembly into Asia's cheaper labor markets. Because of China's pervasive violation of human rights,[34] Levi's withdrew its manufacturing from there in 1993, but by 1998 it returned, putting aside human rights concerns in favor of China's compelling cheap labor and exploding consumer markets.[35] In August 2010 Levi's launched its new global brand in Shanghai, calling it dENiZEN (which combines part of the word "denim" and "Zen"). By 2010 along Shanghai's main shopping street, one could find multiple Levi's shops and banners and see Levi's ads on televisions, in taxis, and plastered on the sides of city buses. Meanwhile, in the United States, by 2009 Levi's storefronts were discreetly displaying white knots that expressed solidarity with the gay marriage movement.[36]

In July 2010 the Levi's brand inaugurated a new version of their What's Real ad campaign, which they called Ready to Work. Its message connected Levi's jeans to their original work clothes purpose but also reached out to a new version of the neoliberal subject. In keeping with advertising's ever-inventive ability to capture the affective edges of people's unmet needs, this campaign focused on the widespread preoccupation with lost work in the United States due to the economic recession. With the tag line "Real People + Real Work = Real Change," the ads echoed the 1990s' What's Real campaign. The ads also extended Levi's 2009 Go Forth campaign, which appealed to the "pioneering spirit" of a new generation of American workers by inviting them to "roll up their sleeves to make real change happen."[37] The Ready to Work campaign reached across the Americas, from Canada through the United States and Mexico and into South America, but its U.S. campaign spotlighted a story of the eviscerated town of Braddock, Pennsylvania, and Levi's investment in its economic recovery.

Located in the eastern suburbs of Pittsburgh, just upstream from the Monongahela River, Braddock was once a thriving steel manufacturing town, home to one of Andrew Carnegie's first mills and his first public library. Now, having lost 90 percent of its population to deindustrialization, Braddock is one of the many ghost towns across the Rust Belt whose remaining residents are challenged to put in place some economic alternatives. A scant forty years after Levi Strauss & Co. moved its blue jeans production offshore to escape a workforce that had become too costly, in the process undermining local economies and leaving people in towns across North America without jobs, it positioned its brand not as the emblem of the urban modernist but as the champion of the American worker. Levi's told the Braddock story in a series of slick videos and photos. "A long time ago things got broken here. People got sad and left," a young girl's muted voice-over says, as if sharing an intimate, shameful story, while images of the town's disintegration roll across the screen. In combining its philanthropic and marketing investments, Levi's deployed a timeworn strategy similar to Andrew Carnegie's. The Levi's brand was helping to refurbish a community center and supporting an urban farming project in Braddock. It enacted commitment to "the new American worker" by attaching craft-making "workshops" to its retail outlets in other cities. Significantly, it did not open garment factories in any of these towns, and Levi's profits remained high as a result of its global expansion into low-wage markets elsewhere. Certainly, this contradiction belies the populist message in Levi's Ready to Work ads that "everybody's work is equally important."

Significantly, the Ready to Work campaign pitched its spectacular message to men, specifically to anxieties triggered by the disproportionate number of men on the unemployment rolls and the crisis of masculinity it had provoked. The ad's tag line addressed the new American worker with a cliché that shored up manhood and home security by recoding the metrosexual as an updated wielder of patriarchal authority, a new man implicitly defined against an invisible and subordinate feminized subject. In the words of the ad, he is "one that embraces strength and sensitivity and ultimately encourages men to once again *'Wear the Pants.'* "[38]

It is more than a historic coincidence that workers assembling jeans for the very same company that pioneered a hip, postgay image in garment advertising would be deprived of their legal right to organize while their bodies were being poisoned by lint and bleach, the rivers and streams of their communities made to run blue. The fact that a decade later the same company that closed its North American factories would embrace U.S. communities devastated by deindustrialization and celebrate their workers may seem shocking. But it shouldn't. These events merely illustrate a contradiction that Marx long ago recognized: capital's bioderegulation is entangled in its modernizing, emancipating movement. That Levi Strauss & Co. epitomizes both is noteworthy precisely because of its progressive reputation for democratic workplace policies and philanthropy for causes on the edge of the mainstream. Like other businesses, Levi's is ultimately ruled by the bottom line. Company spokesperson Linda Butler said it well in 2003 when she addressed Levi's decision to move its production completely offshore: "A business needs to be profitable. The question is how does one implement tough business decisions with compassion, while avoiding decisions that have a negative impact on stakeholders?"[39] The answer is that tough (read, "profitable") business decisions will always have a negative impact on someone. Compassion is its fetish.

Corporations deploy bioderegulation in their labor practices and respond to the unmet needs it provokes by devising strategies that at least partially speak to those needs, the more affectively and compassionately, the better. It is well known that even companies like Levi's, who have won awards for their responsible practices, simultaneously deploy exploitative labor practices while mollifying the crises of unmet need they provoke through philanthropy and by crafting consumers' compensatory desires through appeals to new subjects that in turn provide the company fresh marketing niches. Neoliberal logic accepts this contradiction as one more "whatever" irony. Less acknowledged is the affective charge accompanying sexuality and sexual identity that features across these relations of labor and desire, but the last word on this reality need not be left to the cynics.

Constituting Justice: Arming Oneself as "Un Ser Integro"

In October 2006 representatives from the Lajat Workers' Union attended a four-day legal labor defenders workshop organized by CJM in Monterrey, Mexico. The workshop was a part of a program in the CJM Worker Empowerment Project, a train-the-trainers educational initiative that teaches organizers Mexican labor law. Maquiladora workers who have participated in the program acknowledge that the law in Mexico, as in other democratic states, functions most often to legitimize and advance corporate interests, but they also know that it can be used as a lever for justice. Making use of the law as a short-term strategy means learning how to wield this weapon to advise and represent fellow workers in the labor courts. Most workers are unaware of their legal rights, a fact that makes them especially vulnerable. In 2006 the Mexican federal government was pushing to reform the labor law, and companies were already practicing the de facto rollback of rights with the complicity of the official unions and labor boards. At the same time workers were receiving training in the law, and many were pursuing longer-term goals by developing projects that support regeneration of the life rhythms of their communities.

The Monterrey workshop brought together thirteen workers, ten women and three men, who came from across Mexico. Two of them were former Lajat workers. The workshop was led by a lawyer and a social scientist, who devised a methodology that combined conceptual and pragmatic knowledge. By integrating lessons in the specifics of the law with body–self awareness exercises, the workshop aimed to develop the participants' capacity to advocate for someone. The lawyer, Estela Ríos, was a deliberate, expert teacher, well versed in legal concepts and adept at devising exercises that required participants to show what they understood and to sort out collectively what they did not, to problem solve as teams and to draw upon each other's know-how. As a cultural anthropologist, Adriana Monroy offered lessons in self-confidence, body awareness, and reflection on the holistic human process that legal advocacy entailed. "Attitude, aptitude, and awareness: these are the keys to being an effective *abogada* [legal advocate]," Estela announced. All three remained central to the workshop, as her lessons in the law were punctuated by Adriana's exercises on the affective and corporeal components of speaking truth to power, of using one's body strategically, and of arming oneself as "un ser integro con todo que soy yo" (a complete being including all that I am).

The workshop was not revolutionary, but it did offer participants an important step toward helping each other combat the corporate investment in feminized subjects. Their work did not tackle bioderegulation explicitly, nor did they broach the topic of sexuality, but by situating legal advocacy within a broader frame of biopolitics, the workshop offered an indirect opening toward both. One of the core lessons was that as an organizer and a legal advocate, one needed to "constitute justice" and that doing so involved one's whole being: knowledge (aptitude), self-confidence (attitude), and consciousness (awareness). By extending the task of constituting justice from knowledge of the law to the bodies and affects of those who practice it, the workshop interrupted market rationalities (of fear, of accepting "whatever," of going quiet) and posed alternatives. Its methodology might readily extend to the explicit consideration of sexuality as an instrument of bioderegulation in the workplace and in organizing.

The story of Levi's/Lajat marks out several axes in the deployment of sexuality as a technology of bioderegulation: its relation to the feminized disposable laboring subject; to the "whatever," post-gay, gender-flexible consuming subject; and to the heteronormative presumptions of cross-border organizing. Against them, the example of embodied empowerment in a popular education workshop on the law is a frail, though I think noteworthy, counterinstance where combating bioderegulation is made an explicit feature of the process of political education. Attention to the affective interface of body and mind in mustering a confident attitude and critical consciousness is a pedagogic practice that can be amplified. In itself it is an exercise in gathering the collective power of bodies, affects, and minds to creatively intervene in corporate and legal formulations of what's real while making the road to what can be.

« 7 »

The North–South *Encuentros*

Changing the Way to Change

In *grupos de base* (small grassroots communities) across Mexico's north and south, women are taking leadership positions, and both men and women are recasting the culture of daily life.[1] Out of struggles that vary in their short-term goals but share a long-term vision of alternative possibilities, new political subjects are emerging.[2] Woven into these efforts to build sustainable alternatives for supporting life are adjustments to gender norms. They are a measure of the accomplishments of autonomous community organizing and a component of the cross-regional network building that is reimagining the fundamental basis of the modern nation. In this chapter I use the phrase "subversive gender adjustment" to refer to this erosion of patriarchal gender norms. Gender norms are learned and ideologically organized, and they channel affect-culture into ways of being-in-relation that are felt and transmitted in daily activities of labor and pleasure. Adjustments to these norms are transgressive but not necessarily transformative. The measures of equality they enact are not being won through state or World Bank–sponsored campaigns focused on the gender perspective or women's rights. Rather, they are being accomplished as members of autonomous grassroots communities modify the gendered dimensions of their cooperation with one another and strive for lives with dignity. Mobilizing to end the violence enabled by the patriarchal organization of gender—for example, in campaigns for women's reproductive health or against rape and domestic abuse—is, of course, valuable and necessary given the widespread violations of women's well-being, and inroads into these and other issues by Mexican feminists have had important impacts on many lives.[3] The less visible spaces where the patriarchal organization of gender is interrupted when women step up to be active community leaders or men do the work of care are also significant arenas shaping social change, and feminism's future lives here, too.

With a governing political party that is center-right and a political economy that has been increasingly militarized and driven by foreign investments and the drug business, Mexico seems remote from socialist hopes, even though it has been an international reference point for progressive social movement ever since the Zapatistas' uprising in 1994. During the last decades of the twentieth century, widespread debate about the meaning of democracy, women's organizing around rights, coalition building among women's organizations, and the spread of women's NGOs in Mexico were parts of the political conjuncture that framed the irruption of the Zapatistas into the national and international spotlight. Since then and against the rising tide of neoliberal structural reform and the cartels' reign of terror, grassroots urban and rural communities across the country have confronted the state's neglect and impunity, among them the Popular Assembly of the People of Oaxaca (APPO) and the mobilizing around women murdered in Juárez. In many of these confrontations, women have been key leaders.

A less examined example of Mexican grassroots organizing efforts is a series of meetings between maquiladora workers and the Zapatistas. Carved out of a fight for basic survival needs and political education that builds on the lived awareness of the violence of capitalism, the meetings eventually developed into a sequence of formalized exchanges that English speakers referred to bilingually as the North–South *Encuentros*. These encuentros began with a historic meeting on the occasion of the Zapatistas' March for Dignity to the Mexican capital in 2001, at which maquiladora workers from the northern border first met with representatives from the EZLN's autonomous communities in Mexico City. The following year, CJM invited Zapatista representatives to visit maquiladora workers' organizations in several towns on the northern border. Out of these initial meetings, slowly over time, a series of encounters between maquiladora workers and indigenous communities began building a political network that would link Mexico's "most forgotten ones" in the north and the south.⁴ In the process they painstakingly and persistently fostered critical knowledge and developed communal practices for sustaining life. Though they would not call themselves either socialist or feminist, the women and men in these small Mexican communities have become a creative political force, challenging the neoliberal model, enacting new forms of leadership and gender identification, and forging democratic processes that both preserve and reinvent traditional values within and across regions.

The meetings with the Zapatistas had a profound impact on the emotional habitus of the maquila workers' organizing efforts as they spilled into the colonias. This impact was especially evident in the colonia Blanca Navidad outside Nuevo Laredo, which eventually developed strong ties to the Zapatistas. The encuentros catalyzed a new phase of hope and action for the colonia residents, whose efforts to get the city government to provide basic resources like land rights, water, electricity, and roads had settled into frustrated despair. The encuentros inspired them to take autonomous action to provide these and other resources themselves. Two somewhat elusive aspects of this impact were the affective aura that surrounded their engagement with the Zapatistas and its relation to the subversive gender adjustments the meetings foregrounded and fortified.

Before detailing these features of the encuentros and their bearing on organizing in the north, I want to sketch the broader historical and political significance of these meetings. Throughout Mexico's history the north and the south of the country have been seen as provincial areas, far from the center of power in Mexico City in both a geographic and a political sense. Though the peoples of Tamaulipas and Chiapas are diverse and culturally distinct, each state has been stereotyped in mainstream Mexican culture as marginal, backward, and unsophisticated. This profile for Chiapas has been underscored by its sizable indigenous population. The Zapatista uprising in 1994 made visible the unspoken racism and colonial history in Mexico's myth of national belonging, a myth in which the indigenous population was simultaneously excluded from the nation and romanticized as its origin.⁵ It drew the attention of all Mexicans to *las indigenas* and inserted a new version of indigenous people's lives and voices into the Mexican national imaginary. It also provoked widespread debate on political representation and democratic governance.[6] In the ensuing years, the indigenous struggle in Chiapas had widespread popular support among workers and the poor in northern border states, even if the realities of life in the Lacandona jungle were remote from their daily concerns. Across the ideological and geographic distance separating north and south, the encuentros developed ties of support that brought together two axes of grassroots social movement: a model of autonomy enacted in the Zapatistas' pursuit of sustainable economic projects and self-governance and labor organizing in the north.

The exchanges took place in both northern and southern locations. The participants shared knowledge of neoliberal capitalism as it was lived in the flesh and amplified one another's critical perspectives. Through the encuentros, the Zapatista communities came to know the realities of factory work and the conditions of life on the northern border. This history was especially valuable because increasing numbers of people were migrating to northern border cities due to the restructuring of the agricultural economy in the south.[7] Many migrants looked for jobs in the maquiladoras, but few had experience with factory work. During the encuentros workers in the north spoke with the indigenous community members about their history of labor organizing and the strategies they had developed for making use of the law and for capacity building among workers. The legacy of women's strong leadership in the factories was a particular point of interest for groups in the south. The Zapatista communities brought to workers in the north a decades-long history of community building and autonomous participatory governance. They offered knowledge about how to implement shared decision making and how to make use of local conditions and resources to develop sustainable economic, health, and education projects. They brought, as well, a spark of inspiration.

In sum, the North–South *Encuentros* were part of a process of "changing the way to change," not through political parties, vanguard leaders, or state-sponsored programs but from below and for below.[8] Working across regional and ethnic divisions and emerging from the grassroots, the encounters developed local and autonomous footholds on capitalism's outside. As men and women from these forgotten urban and rural spaces listened to and learned from each other, they marshaled biopower from within bare life, and in that process they gradually subverted patriarchal traditions.

Some History of Standing on Two Feet

The shared history of maquiladora workers in Tamaulipas and indigenous peoples in Chiapas hinged on events in 1994, when the passage of NAFTA on January 1 coincided with the Zapatista uprising. NAFTA had a horrific impact on the majority of Mexicans, throwing more people into a growing disposable workforce, either as peasants no longer able to live off the land or as factory workers in unsafe, precarious jobs. It also gave birth, however, to intensified organized resistance. In April 1994, only a few months after NAFTA was initiated and the Zapatistas rose up, two thousand Sony workers in Nuevo Laredo, the majority of them women, staged their wildcat strike over the right to an independent union.[9] Many of the strikes that followed were also in Tamaulipas, and in each instance women were in the lead. By the late 1990s the struggle to survive was making economic alternatives a pressing concern for many maquiladora workers. In addition, organizing campaigns that focused solely on the workplace were proving to address only a portion of workers' needs. As a result, some of the workers who had been fired and blacklisted for organizing in the maquilas began developing organizing strategies that extended beyond the factories. Faced by the need to provide for their families and inspired to continue organizing and educating, small groups of former workers in several communities developed fledgling cooperatives. They were challenged, however, by the novel collective process and were often thwarted in their efforts to sustain it.

Between 2001 and 2007, eight encuentros between maquiladora workers and the Zapatistas sparked new developments in community organizing. The first occurred in March 2001, when leaders of the insurgent people of Chiapas led the March of Indigenous Dignity from the community of La Realidad in Chiapas through twelve states to Mexico City to meet with the Mexican Congress. The event was the last in a series of negotiations between the Zapatistas and the federal government. Under President Carlos Zadillo the Mexican government had already reneged on the San Andrés Accords on Indigenous Rights and Culture, which was negotiated with the Zapatistas and signed by both parties on February 16, 1996.[10] During and after the negotiations, the Zadillo government continued conducting a multilevel counterinsurgency war against the Zapatistas. In 2001 the new president, Vicente Fox, entering office on the triumphal wave of the demise of the PRI's seventy-year-long reign, proposed resubmitting the accords to the Chamber of Deputies. Fox's offer was hardly in good faith. After his election he continued low-intensity warfare against the Zapatistas, as he was eager to clear the way in Chiapas for his Plan Puebla Panama, which would expand the region into a major trade corridor open to foreign investment in bioresources and a new network of maquiladoras. Despite the Zapatistas' appeals in the Mexico City meeting, the federal government continued to refuse to honor the accords, so the EZLN representatives returned to Chiapas to pursue their goals on their own. During their visit to the Zócalo, however, they met with representatives from social sectors across the country, including a delegation of maquiladora workers from the north.

The historic significance of this north–south encounter was not lost on either side. In that same spot in 1915, Emiliano Zapata, leader of the peasant uprising in the south, finally met Pancho Villa, the Centaur of the North. Addressing the maquila workers that day, Subcomandante Marcos said, "We are paying attention to everything you are doing, including when you are silent. You and us, we know very well how to handle silences. When the powerful think that they have already won or that the rebellion has passed, that is when it rises up stronger." The message about strategically handling silence resounded on both sides. The Zapatistas returned to their communities, where they embraced a purposeful public silence while pursuing a major internal reorientation from leadership based in the Army of National Liberation to new structures for self-government aimed at sustaining the autonomy of their communities. The workers who returned to their factory towns in the north also began to realize the limits of their demands upon the state, especially the right to free association as an avenue to democratic decision making. They shifted their focus onto sustaining the community-based organizing efforts in Nuevo Laredo, Río Bravo, Reynosa, Valle Hermoso, and Gómez-Palacio, which had begun developing projects like schools, soup kitchens, sewing cooperatives, and workers' centers that aimed to meet the needs of sustaining life in the colonias.

Without question, the affective charge surrounding Subcomandante Marcos was an intense attractor for the workers in the north. Marcos's public persona as warrior, poet, storyteller, and spokesperson for the indigenous, along with his mestizo background, handsome masked face, humor, and light touch, made him as charismatic as a rock star. By most accounts he used this persona strategically to keep the public spotlight on the substance of the indigenous struggle. To the degree that it worked, it did so precisely because he managed to direct his charisma at advancing a political education that hooked national and international audiences. Certainly, his appearance with the Zapatistas was romanticized by workers hungry for heroes and hope, and the image of Marcos, rivaling that of Che Guevara in popularity, encapsulated that desire. A powerful something, however, exceeded this reification of Marcos. He was and remains a mediating figure, a manifestation of a shared hidden transcript that few others have had the courage to declare in the teeth of power.[11] This transcript was the substance of the alliance that the encounters eventually formed. Becoming allies took time and effort, though, and through this effort, a process of gender adjustment displaced this image of Marcos—a process in which both the Zapatistas and the northern colonia residents engaged.

In the Zapatistas' historic appearance before the Mexican Congress, it was not Marcos but Comandanta Esther who rose to speak. She began by pointing to a widely shared but mistaken expectation:

> Some might have thought that this platform would be occupied
> by Sup-Marcos and that it would be he who would be giving this
> main message of the Zapatistas. Now they see that it is not so. Sub-
> comandante Insurgente Marcos is that, a Sub-comandante. We are
> the Comandantes, those who lead jointly, the ones who govern our
> people by obeying. We gave the Sup and those who share hopes and
> dreams with him the mission of bringing us to this Congress. They,
> our *guerreros* and *guerreras,* accomplished that mission, thanks

to the support of the popular mobilization in Mexico and in the
world. Now is our hour.[12]

Esther's use of the past conditional tense ("some might have thought")
reaches into the public's romance with Marcos and wrenches it into
a different frame of reference, a different present ("now is our hour")
where the body and voice of an indigenous woman bears the Zapatistas' central message. She prefaces her speech with a subversive adjustment to the gender and racial imaginary that Marcos straddled.
Indeed, Marcos was not even in the room. When Comandanta Esther
superimposes the indigenous woman's body and words over the public's romance with Marcos, she inserts into the national record the
women of the EZLN who led the armed occupation of San Cristóbal,
Ocosingo, and Las Margaritas, and who continue to sustain community life. Despite her speech, however, the erotic aura that maintained
the mystique of Marcos and threatened to overshadow the collective indigenous subject to whom he was subordinate remained. This
aura was in evidence when Marcos in 2005 traveled with a caravan of
comandantes and supporters across the country.

Marcos's appearance brought crowds and the press, as well as a
spark of confidence and hope, to urban outposts in the north, and
the maquiladora communities' new direction in organizing, which
had developed over the previous four years, had prepared the way. In
2004, out of the recognition that in order to survive, grassroots organizations needed to maintain the "two feet" of political education
and sustainable resources, CJM developed the program Standing on
Two Feet. The program's name alludes to testimony given by one of
the Zapatistas, the president of the autonomous municipality of San
Andrés Sak'emchén, who called himself Don Emiliano. During an
interview in 2003, he declared:

> The government wants to send quantities of money so that we do
> not keep on struggling, but thank God here we are still standing
> [*estamos de pie*]. We are working and organizing, and my people are
> making a lot of sacrifices. Even if the government wants to destroy
> us, they cannot. Even if they want to buy us, they cannot.

Don Emiliano refers to the low-intensity warfare the government waged and the federal programs that divided indigenous communities by enticing farmers to buy imported low-cost, genetically modified seeds that undermined generations of indigenous farming practices and destroyed future crop yields. The Spanish phrase *estamos de pie* that he uses echoes the words of Emiliano Zapata, who famously said, "Prefiero morir de pie que vivir de rodillas" (I prefer to die standing up than to live on my knees). Like Zapata, Don Emiliano asserts a stance of resistance and, more properly, a platform for going forward with a social alternative. At the same time, this stance can be adopted anywhere. To affirm that we are still standing is to recognize that human life depends on nourishing the entire *ser* (being), the well-being and dignity of a collective, and the natural world that grounds us.

The aim of Standing on Two Feet was to advance these affirmations by enabling maquiladora workers in the north and indigenous community members in the south to learn from each other's experiences and develop strategies that responded to the onslaught of the multinationals and the government's neglect of their needs by taking matters into their own hands. The program also focused on supporting women's leadership because the women of both regions were profoundly, though somewhat differently, affected. The short-term goal of the encounters was to strengthen the two feet of each participating group by helping to consolidate capacity building and by developing sustainable economic projects or enhancing those that already were under way. Out of each encounter, diagnoses were developed as the basis for further organizing and strategizing across regions. As a first step, in November 2004 representatives from the Red de Defensores Comunitarios, Las Abejas, Pueblo Creyente de Comitán, Red de Defensores Humanos, and Centro de Investigaciones Económicas y Políticas de Acción Comunitaria, all from Chiapas, met with maquila workers from the north and visited several cities along the border. Many were shocked to witness the toxic impact of free trade and to learn about the increased emigration, the intensified militarization, and the labor and human rights violations.[13] The following year, a delegation of five women workers from northern maquiladora towns traveled to several Zapatista communities in Chiapas. They shared the experiences of women workers in the factories and learned about the strong political education being fostered at the grassroots level and about the political, economic, and social alternatives being developed in Chiapas.

The fourth encuentro took place on November 21, 2005, when Marcos visited Blanca Navidad. During the first half of that year, as Mexico's presidential election approached, a Zapatista caravan journeyed across the length of the country in what they called the Other Campaign. The direction of the Other Campaign had been determined by a series of meetings in August and September 2005 in the villages in the canyons leading to the Lacandona jungle. Here, the Zapatista high command and the EZLN's diverse constituencies discussed their needs and the possibility of devising alternatives during this time of political openings.

In an effort to consolidate a nonelectoral, anticapitalist Left, the Other Campaign called for the enactment of a new national constitution that would bar privatization of public resources and end other neoliberal violations. The campaign was backed by the EZLN's new statement of objectives, the Sixth Declaration of the Selva Lacandona. The declaration announced the Zapatistas' intention to build another way of doing politics by forming alliances beyond Chiapas in order to cultivate a popular consensus calling for the transformation of capitalist property relations and a new constitution.[14] It was, as one commentator put it, "designed to be a first step toward the self-determination of the people *in spite of* the state's continual (and continually troubled) biopolitical administration of its juridical and economic powers, privilege, and abundance."[15] This proposal for a new constitution was itself an appeal for a democratic political practice that did not yet exist, or had not been recognized, but that perhaps could be made outside, autonomous from, the existing state.

Subcomandante Marcos (whose alias for the event was Delegado Zero) was sent out as a scout on a six-month caravan to create connections with other organizing efforts and resistance groups. He was accompanied in each city by EZLN supporters, and one of their stops was the colonia Blanca Navidad on the outskirts of Nuevo Laredo. In the exchanges that took place, representatives from north and south acknowledged that they were fighting the same forces. They committed to support each other, and they called their agreement Los Jodidos Apoyando los Jodidos (The Ones Who Are Screwed Supporting Each Other). In December, in fulfillment of their promise, the Zapatistas sent 1,000 boxes of coffee, corn, and beans to Blanca Navidad. The trailer truck arrived just in time for Christmas.

Three other encuentros followed this one. In May 2007, as part of the Other Campaign's effort to maintain strategic links to key communities in the north, the EZLN sent three comandantes— Myriam, Eucaria, and Zabadeo, two women and a man—to Blanca Navidad for a longer stay. For almost two weeks, through rainstorms and mud, they met with scores of people under a tent in the colonia. Maquiladora workers from the region gave testimony on the conditions and organizing efforts in their workplaces. Colonia residents told of their struggle to keep their land and to acquire water. Men and women from the area came forward to tell of health problems provoked by unsafe work conditions and the contaminated environment: cancer of the nose, skin, and lungs; lead poisoning; and babies born with spina bifada. They spoke of NAFTA's erosion of their communities, of government impunity and inaction, and of fear and determination.

One by one, the comandantes Zabedeo, Eucaria, and Myriam spoke. Zabadeo talked about what it meant for the Zapatistas to organize themselves over ten and twenty years and the committees for health and education they formed. People listened attentively, but when Comandanta Myriam took the microphone, the audience was riveted. She told of the changes that had taken place in women's lives, and she acknowledged that women's situation remained an arena of conflict and struggle. She said that women in the Zapatista communities needed to meet separately as women but that they were also learning "to join hands with men" and participate in the Boards of Good Government that were set up as part of the reorientation after 2001. She spoke about the challenges of gender discrimination and labor exploitation that women faced and about the cooperative projects women were running. She also shared a song about women's oppression and strength, and this song struck a chord for women in the audience. Several who took the microphone afterward commented on the song and said that they shared these experiences and wanted to learn more about what the indigenous women were doing to address them. "We have two struggles," Zabadeo said, "to conquer the hearts of men and to fight for justice. We recognize that women have more work and suffer more. That is how we have grown. But it is difficult to work with men and convince them that in the home you must share the work."

After the initial days of formal presentations and testimonies, something in the group dynamic shifted. It happened one morning when Comandanta Myriam opened the meeting under the tent by asking the gathered community members to begin the discussion. But no one spoke. As the seconds passed, the silence became more and more awkward. Then, Myriam began to sing, and as she sang she started to dance. Eucario and Zabadeo joined in and gestured for the others to join the dance. Soon, everyone was dancing, dancing and singing. Awkwardness evaporated. Something had shifted. Something akin to joy had taken hold of this dancing group—the affect Spinoza formulates as the body assuming its potential, a posture that intensifies the powers of existence. Collective leadership and action followed as the group decided to acquire the water the residents needed by tapping into the line that the city had installed at the technological college bordering the colonia, even though it was farther outside the city. Over the next few days, the visitors helped to lay pipes and install faucets on several streets. The Zapatistas' visit also inspired residents to build a small clinic, launch a collective process for dealing with their land disputes, and develop proposals for economic initiatives, including a tortilla-making facility. In the exchanges that generated these actions, women's energy and labor propelled much of the planning and discussion.

Over the course of a week or so, the colonia's sense of itself had changed. An initial awkward reception of three visitors who arrived surrounded by the aura of the Zapatistas had evolved into an action plan that gave the residents much more than water. The community's emotional habitus had shifted from frustration to an energized sense of possibility, and both northern and southern participants in the encounter came away with a tighter alliance. On their website, Enlace Zapatista, the Zapatistas published the story of the visit to Blanca

Navidad, and the following summer, twelve people representing Blanca Navidad traveled to the autonomous communities in Chiapas.

In July 2008 the highland communities of Oventic, Torbellino de Nuestras Palabras, and Roberto Barrios received representatives from the colonia. The visitors learned about the Juntas de Buen Gobierno (Boards of Good Government) and how the communities preserved their traditions; ran their own cooperatives, clinics, and schools; and conducted community education. The trip was a huge step in the evolving alliance. Blanca Navidad residents were struck by women's leadership on the Board of Good Government in Torbellino de Nuestras Palabras, Morelia, and by women's work as health promoters. The experience bolstered their confidence and spurred their determination to develop sustainable projects back home. Upon their return to Blanca Navidad, they gave talks on what they had learned to the residents, and these events offered women the opportunity to demonstrate their leadership. The women shared the recipes they had gathered for curing ailments and for making shampoo and soap. Men and women began community gardens of fruit trees, vegetables, and medicinal herbs that could thrive in the arid soil of the north. Don Marcelino and his wife started a community chicken farm and began building ecological stoves. Kata built a wind generator.

In January 2009 a small delegation of Blanca Navidad residents, both men and women, journeyed by bus to Mexico City and San Cristóbal, Chiapas, to participate in the First World Festival of Dignified Rage, where they presented the colonia's history to an international gathering organized by the Zapatistas. They met other organizations from the autonomous communities in Chiapas and also from Juárez, Atenco, Oaxaca, and Chile, as well as some of the Mothers of the Plaza de Mayo from Argentina. When they returned to the colonia, they articulated their social location in expanded terms. The festival's panels had been organized around four different axes of oppression—those being exploited, evicted, repressed, or scorned—and Blanca explained in her speech and in her report to her neighbors that colonia residents were in "all four of these axes."

The north–south alliance formed through an incremental process of making the road while walking.[16] It would not have been possible without the EZLN's armed uprising and the Sony workers' strike, which prepared the path to the encuentros of the new millennium. The aura of the Zapatistas was an animating spark for workers in the north, who were translating their workplace organizing efforts into sustainable urban economic projects, but the alliance grew out of the shared information and trust developed over years. A key element in the glue that sealed the relationship was the realization by colonia residents that the Zapatista women in some communities were among the strongest voices in the rotating leadership. Likewise, the Zapatistas saw women among the organizers in the north as a force of possibility and change.

Blanca Navidad

Like the Zapatistas' autonomous communities, the colonia Blanca Navidad does not exist on the state's official map, even though it is located at the crossroads of international trade. This stretch of unincorporated land lies just outside the city limits of Nuevo Laredo, on the road that passes under the International Free Trade Bridge, where the narcos have made their shrines to Saint Death. Some residents work in the assembly plants, or they used to; most survive through the informal economy. Many residents suffer health problems from poor working conditions or chronic diseases provoked by poverty and the toxins dumped in the colonia. Until 2007, the area had no water, and it still has no electricity, sewage system, or paved roads. Since invading the land in 2004, residents have petitioned the municipal government to provide these utilities, a reasonable request from people who work in the city and pay city taxes. Only after enduring several years of government violence and neglect and being encouraged by their encounters with the Zapatistas did they decide to channel their energies into sustaining themselves.

The initial residents of Blanca Navidad were among the many migrants dislocated from farming towns to the south, drawn to Nuevo Laredo by the prospect of work in the factories. Like other migrants who flocked to the assembly plants, many quickly realized that their low wages were not enough to pay for food and rent and other basics. Blanca Enríquez was one of them. One of the founders of the colonia, she came to Nuevo Laredo from Veracruz to look for a job in the factories. She found work in the Sony plant but soon discovered her salary was not enough to make ends meet. As Blanca recounted the story, in late December 2003 a group of about fifty families came together because they were unable to pay rent from their meager factory wages, so they decided to invade this land that had once been part of Mexico's *ejido* system. They cut the trees and *nopales* (prickly pears) and built small lean-tos of cloth and wood for shelter. Their first night there, a small miracle occurred—it snowed—an extraordinary event on the border. It had not snowed in Nuevo Laredo for a hundred years. Embracing this sign of the heavens' approval, they called the new settlement Blanca Navidad.

Soon after the first group arrived, a woman named Hermes appeared, claiming that the land was hers, and she managed to procure payments from each of the families. When the settlement came to the attention of Pepe Suárez, the mayor of Nuevo Laredo at the time, he negotiated with Hermes for a parcel of the land, but the deal went sour. The mayor had her arrested and evicted the settlers. Undaunted and lacking sufficient resources to support themselves, the families soon returned. This time, they carved out lots and roads, established a land register, and built stronger houses. In February 2005, a year after the founding group and their families reinvaded the land, the new PRI mayor, Daniel Peña, sent in bulldozers and torched the houses. Community resistance was immediate, and women were in the lead.

According to Blanca, the morning of the eviction the city sent in water delivery trucks as a pretext for checking if the women were alone. As she reported:

> About three hours later, the eviction began. But they didn't take into account how strong we were. We women began to climb on the machines and remove the keys. We grabbed rocks and sticks. When they saw that we weren't driven away, they returned at night when everything was dark, and they burned the houses that were still standing. We used the little water we had left from what they had delivered that morning to pour on our burning houses. Another morning, they came again. This time, we were stronger. We made fences and ditches, and we blocked the streets with the

wood they had knocked out of our houses, so that the machines
couldn't pass. Women guarded the entrance so that the men could
check the streets.

Javier Méndez, Blanca's husband, another founding member of
the colonia, agreed that "the women made us strong. They gave us
the courage to keep fighting." José (Poncho) Herrera concurred. "The
women helped more than we men did," he said, but it was through
everyone's persistence "together all as partners, that we won enough
of a victory to be able to stay." Now, over eight hundred families
live there.

The land that comprises Blanca Navidad is part of a large tract,
the *ejido* Pancho Villa, whose custodian, Don Margarito, fought
in the Mexican Revolution and then used this land to raise corn.
The ejidos were established in Article 27 of Mexico's revolutionary
constitution, the legacy of Emiliano Zapata's struggle to maintain
peasants' access to land. Article 27 stipulated that ultimate title for
farmlands remained with the state, with officially recognized peasant
beneficiaries receiving hereditable rights of individual or collective
use.[17] In other words, ejido lands could be passed on but not sold
or rented. The *ejiditarios* lived on the land and farmed it but did not
own it. In 1992, as a condition for signing NAFTA, President Carlos
Salinas de Gortari led the revision of Article 27 to allow the privatization of the ejidos. This change meant that in order to legitimize
ownership of land, families who were custodians of ejidos, like Don
Margarito's, had to apply to the secretary of agriculture for a title
that would certify ownership. In the late 1990s, as a part of the terms
imposed on Mexico by NAFTA and the World Bank, federal subsi-
dies to Mexican farmers through the National Company of Popular
Subsistence were eliminated. Not only did farmers suffer from the
lost support, but many ejiditarios who had outstanding loans were
required to repay them as a condition for receiving land ownership.
Consequently, after the reform of Article 27, some farmers never
sought land title, for fear of being pursued for outstanding seed or
equipment loans. Part of the legalizing ownership process also entailed transfer of the lands from the National Agrarian Land Registry to the Public Registry of Properties in order for a property title

to be granted. Don Margarito did not apply for land title from the secretary of agriculture, however, and this technicality provided the opening for the settlers' invasion. Various other claims to ownership surfaced after Don Margarito died, and they remain unresolved. According to civil law, though, if the squatters occupy the land in a peaceful and public way for ten years, it can become theirs. In the meantime, out of its outlaw existence, the colonia Blanca Navidad is still standing and articulating a northern border community's version of political autonomy.

Autonomy as a Political Stance

After their representatives visited Chiapas in 2008, Blanca Navidad residents decided to become an autonomous community. They had already pursued several frustrated appeals to their local government. Residents were not only twice evicted by two different mayors but also courted by several rounds of municipal political candidates who visited the colonia in election season bearing gifts and empty promises of government support (for electricity, waterlines, roads, health care, a school) in exchange for votes. The colonia's decision to renounce this bad government was also shaped by an evolving sense of its own social and political location in relation to national and international forces and to the possibilities its representatives were learning about in other regions of Mexico. On their way to visiting Chiapas, a group of Blanca Navidad residents met with residents of communities in Oaxaca, where land and water were being harnessed by foreign investors for the energy needs of U.S. consumers while indigenous people, like the residents of Blanca Navidad, were living without electricity. Reflecting on what he saw, Don Marcelino, one of the older Blanca Navidad residents who was in that delegation, said, "Here, we are without electricity, lighting ourselves with a candle. That's not fair. Why? Because four or five are millionaires and here we are screwed and with nothing. We have to open our eyes and learn what others have learned. And that's what we are doing right here in Nuevo Laredo."

The self-determination that the colonia embraced in large measure was the result of their eye-opening encounter with the Zapatistas'

practice of autonomous government and with a long history of indigenous efforts to survive the government's failure to provide services
like clinics and schools.[18] In contemporary political discourse, no
consensus exists on the concept and practice of autonomy by either
indigenous people or the rest of Mexican society.[19] Its circulation
as a political goal and practice echoes the popular social movement
mobilized in the aftermath of the 1985 earthquake in Mexico City,
which reoriented social change away from political parties or a revolutionary vanguard and toward what was characterized then and in
the years following as civil society. As Gustavo Esteva and Carlos
Pérez point out, even as Mexican popular movements and organizations embraced autonomy as a political stance, there were and still
are competing concepts and practices in circulation and under debate.[20] One version, the European autonomous tradition adopted by
Nicaragua, situates autonomous communities within the existing
nation-state, conceiving autonomy as a part of a process of political decentralization. On the heels of the Zapatista uprising, in 1998
the indigenous people of the state of Oaxaca, which is adjacent to
Chiapas, succeeded in amending the state constitution to recognize
indigenous peoples' right to self-determination within the terms of
the Constitution of the Republic. This version of autonomy as decentralization within the nation-state was rejected by the Zapatistas
in the San Andrés Accords. The accords do not call for the state to
manage indigenous communities. Rather, they ask for recognition of
what the indigenous communities already laid claim to: territory and
their own *usos y costumbres* (uses and customs) with which to govern
themselves. As part 2 of the accords states, "Autonomy is the concrete
expression of the exercise of the right to self-determination, within
the framework of the National state."[21] This version of autonomy is
meant to be the starting point for recasting the very structure of the
nation and the state's relation to capital and property. By insisting on
the capacity of indigenous and other peoples to determine their way
of life, it is calling for new forms of democracy.[22]

   After the Mexican Congress refused to endorse the San Andrés
Accords, it drafted weaker legislation on indigenous culture and
rights that became law in August 2001. Consequently, the Zapatistas'
thirty-eight autonomous municipalities declared themselves commu-

nities in resistance and concentrated on putting in place self-sufficient economic projects and good government. Good government is guided by the mandate to *mandar obediciendo* (lead while obeying) through community decision making and collective participation based on regular rotation of officeholders and equal treatment of political allies and opponents.[23] The Zapatistas' autonomous governance operates through five centers, which they call *caracoles*. The Spanish word *caracol* carries multiple meanings. It means "snail" as well as "conch shell," the trumpet that has been used for generations in Mayan villages to call the people together. The autonomous communities speak about their movement as analogous to the snail that lives close to the earth, moves slowly and deliberately, and inhabits a home whose structure radiates outward. Like the snail, the autonomous communities are rooted in traditions that honor the earth. They are making change slowly and locally while, like the conch shell, also broadcasting to others.

Although they publicize news and issue periodic declarations, the Zapatistas refuse to advance their practice of autonomous governance as appropriate for everyone, because they do not see their version as the only or the best way. Nonetheless, their mandate to lead while obeying has been a model for democratic governance elsewhere. During the comandantes' 2007 visit to Blanca Navidad, the colonia adopted the figure of the caracol. Calling themselves the Caracol of the North, residents painted the snail into the murals on their community buildings, depicting women workers and indigenous women together.

From the beginning, the Zapatistas' new form of relating included women's concerns as fundamental to revolutionary change. The Women's Revolutionary Law, ten demands annexed to the First Declaration of War of the Zapatista National Liberation Army in 1994, calls for women's rights to health care, education, choice, and leadership and to freedom from beatings, mistreatment, and rape.[24] Women also called for a most extraordinary set of rights: to rest, to think, and to be.[25] These demands appear in an abbreviated form in a section of the San Andrés Accords that calls for child care, job training, and other support programs that might enable women's right to well-being.[26] Unlike the accords, the Women's Revolutionary Law targets issues internal to

the indigenous communities, and as such it has an uneasy relation to
the formulation of demands from the state and to how the Zapatistas
enacted the accords in the next decade. Certainly, the Zapatistas are
exceptional for their rhetorical promotion of women's value and rights
and for their situation of women as soldiers in the front lines and, later,
as key spokespersons. Their new governing process also aims at recruiting more women participants, but because cultural change occurs
slowly, gender norms that devalue and oppress women persist in their
communities.[27]

Gender surfaces in arguments by opponents of indigenous autonomy who call upon the state to protect indigenous women from
traditional customs that oppress them.[28] For Zapatista women the
concept of autonomy has also been contested terrain, but they refer
the struggle over traditional customs back to the democratic principles of community governance, not to the nation-state. During
the preparation of the accords and in the National Indigenous Con-
gresses held in Mexico City in 1996 and 1997, indigenous women
broadened the Zapatista notion of autonomy.[29] They held out an integrated vision of human being and called for women's full participation at home, in the community, and in the nation. They demanded
the equal division of domestic labor, land rights, and respect for their
bodies and persons. In these ways, women eventually modified the
indigenous traditional customs so integral to the formulation of
autonomy by incorporating the proviso that these customs should
not be oppressive to women.[30] Various comandantas have forcefully
advocated for reorienting traditional ways that deprive women of
their dignity, yet within the Zapatistas' new system of governance,
women's full participation remains uneven and contested. Here, too,
have been subversive adjustments, not transformations. Some visitors to the communities who have witnessed the way of life they are
building report remarkable changes in gender relations: more men
participate in child care and cooking, and more women participate
in public arenas.[31] Women are still seriously underrepresented in the
governing councils, however, and the communities are not always
supportive of women's activities that defy expected roles.[32] Some research on the internal dynamics of the communities suggests that
the Women's Revolutionary Law has not changed long-standing cus-

toms.[33] In this context encounters with colonia residents from the north have been occasions to provoke further discussion of adjustments to patriarchal gender culture.

Gender Adjustments and the Biopower of Standing on Two Feet

The autonomy and subversive adjustments to traditional gender norms practiced in these grassroots communities exercises a form of biopower that reorients the concept. The North–South *Encuentros* enable us to understand biopower as a positive force, a notion that is quite distinct from the understanding of biopolitics that is widely adopted in political theory, most notably in the work of the Italian philosopher Giorgio Agamben. Agamben elaborates Michel Foucault's analysis of biopolitics as the form that power takes in modern societies when the king's sovereignty is replaced by a more diffuse circulation of power. Like Foucault, Agamben formulates biopolitics as the increasing tendency for power to take control of life itself. Through an array of technologies and institutions, biopolitics penetrates populations, bodies, and life forms. Agamben is interested in the invisible exclusions biopolitics enacts in this regulation of life through its juridical and normative technologies. His name for this often concealed nucleus of biopolitics is "bare life." Bare life is that which is included in modern democratic politics as an exception—that is, an area of life that the law has abandoned but that is also the counterpart to its sovereign violence. He traces the genealogy of bare life across Western history and claims that a major change occurred in modernity as sovereign power mutated into biopolitics. The result was that an exceptional zone of bare life came to be integrated into modern democracies as their hidden inner ground, an exclusion embedded in the very structure of citizenship itself.[34]

Although Agamben's analysis offers a fresh perspective on the operation of power in modern states, it misses several crucial points. First, he does not address the ways in which bare life is materially bound to the outlawed needs upon which capitalist accumulation depends and which the nation-state's regime of law protects. Second, in formulating bare life as a zone where political distinctions no longer matter, he ignores the fact that biopolitics relies upon the power

relations encoded in cultural distinctions—gender, race, and ethnicity, for example—to legitimate and configure forgotten zones.[35]
Finally, he fails to see these zones as sites of struggle and resistance.[36]
The North–South *Encuentros* offer an instructive counterexample.
They demonstrate that forgotten people are confronting the violent
biopolitics of neoliberal capitalism in places where life has been deregulated and citizens abandoned. These forgotten spaces may be the
necessary exclusions of modernity's biopolitics, but in them people
are mustering biopower as a part of their invention of alternative social relations. And gender adjustments are an affectively loaded feature of this material, ontological, and epistemological struggle.

The inhabitants of neoliberal capitalism's forgotten places are hy-
perderegulated, which is to say they are socially abandoned to a degree that others are not. The difference in degree is what constitutes
capital's ideal labor force: one that is just shy of slavery. This labor
force is available to be tapped and discarded, and for them life is defined by an extreme degree of outlawed need. The forgotten ones are
the surplus population whose social location marks them as valuable
precisely because they are disposable and inconsequential. Bare life
accumulates as multiple life forms are used up and capital investment
moves elsewhere. Of course, commodity production also relies on
consumption, and herein lies one contradiction that has to be continually managed: too much bare life deprives capital of its markets.

Slavery, the economic relation in which human lives are purchased outright, requires subjects who are economically valuable but
politically dead—nonpersons in the eyes of the law whose existence
is excluded by the sovereign state but necessary within the social relations of capitalism's early development. Hyperexploited workers are
in a similar situation, but their exclusion is modified by their non-
slave status, which affords them liminal incorporation into the social
body of the democratic state.[37] Their recognition as subjects of the
modern state is continually negated by legal controls that guarantee
continued minimal terms for their material existence. Cultural difference is the ideological pretext that facilitates the perpetuation of
this zone of abandonment and the repression or public forgetting of
these losses.

As I discuss in chapter 5, feminization is one tag for the negative personhood built into the exclusions of liberal citizenship and the symbolic scaffolding of modernity. Historically, it has served to thrust workers and indigenous peoples into bare life. Free-market exchange capitalizes on the political and cultural dispossession of feminized subjects, a dispossession that is a pretext for extracting natural resources and labor. It is an ideological code for devaluation, abandonment, and in the extreme, social death.

In the colonias of the north and the highlands of Chiapas, where bare life is regulated by both the legal political economy and its shadow narco economy, death oozes into life. In the north, neoliberal policies have taken a deadly toll as the invasion of foreign investment has intensified the exploitation of human labor, contaminated and crippled bodies, poisoned the environment, and snatched up common farmlands. As a northern border state and one of the prime sites for multinational investment, Tamaulipas has paid dearly in human and environmental costs. Blanca Navidad is only one of many similar colonias in this and other northern states where workers live on the fringes of industrial parks that spill chemical effluent directly into water sources, the land, and the air. In Blanca Navidad this bioderegulation is palpable every day, but the colonia's location in the cross hairs of the narco economy and the criminal state is no more evident than when it rains. After a rainfall water accumulates in deep holes, and on hot days children once swam in them, but they no longer do, since too many dead bodies have been dumped into them by the narcos.

Neoliberal political economy has taken a lethal toll in Chiapas, too. As the state that has the highest level of poverty in the country, it also generates almost 50 percent of the nation's electricity. Yet, one-third of the households do not have running water, and over 40 percent have no sewage system. Transport is scarce, and medical assistance can be many miles away. Capital's legal and extralegal sovereignties also control daily life here as official and paramilitary troops continue low-intensity war against the autonomous communities and as the drug cartels control the shadow economy and migration routes north. During the past fifteen years, the region's natural resources have been stripped by agribusiness and biopiracy. Life expectancy for women in Chiapas is two years less than that for men, and the state has the highest maternal death rate in Mexico.[38] Since the uprising, women are targets of military and paramilitary intimidation and sexual violence. The stress caused by the militarization manifests itself in women's bodies as they lose their milk and cannot breast-feed their babies, fail to menstruate, and suffer other maladies.[39] Many women and children die from the lack of medical attention.

During their visit to Blanca Navidad, Myriam and Eucaria spoke of women's efforts to combat this violence and the subversion of patriarchal culture they were provoking. Some adjustments were evident in the very syntax of their descriptions when they referred to women with the word *nosotras,* transgressing the standard masculine first-person plural, *nosotros,* by feminizing it. It was a small modification to be sure, but one many of the colonia women remarked upon when they asked about the ways the Zapatista women had been organizing to confront their oppression. For their part the women of Blanca Navidad have been recasting traditional gender schemes that value men over women. Although many of these adjustments are situational, they range over everyday activities that impact the sexual division of labor and the processes of decision making and governance. In addition to being the principal voices of the colonia, women are full participants in the economic projects and are integrated into the vigilance committee, whose members guard the entrance gate and keep a registry of visitors. Some of the men are actively involved in the labor of child rearing. Doña Bety, one of the colonia's many single mothers, proudly boasted that she built her house herself. The community has also accepted and welcomed as "just one more" two gay couples who were being harassed in their former residences.

Gender adjustments like these have been conditioned by the fact that many of the women in Blanca Navidad have been or still are wage earners in the maquilas. Earning wages outside the home puts women in a situation that to some degree alters their economic dependence on husbands and fathers. The eviction thrust women into being the community's strength, and as they were also providing household incomes or heading families as single mothers, a collective pride in women's leadership began to congeal. Though the women and men of Blanca Navidad have not radically transformed traditional gender values, modifications to them have accompanied the consolidation of the community's collective interests.

The women from the north assert that they have become leaders because, as Blanca said, they "are more tenacious [than the men]." She continued, "When confronted with a lot to accomplish, we keep going." Many reiterated that their determination is inspired by the Zapatistas' accomplishments, saying, "If they can do it, we can, too." This doing is the forming of new political subjects who are creating their own laws and devising alternative measures to meet common needs. As Blanca explained:

> Now that we have met with the Zapatistas, we know that to meet together and decide among all of us is an improvement for the colonia. Two people from every block know the needs. These people come and talk, and it is like it is in the Zapatista communities, where people from different communities take to their communities what was decided in the *caracol*.

This fortified collective standpoint does not target patriarchal gender culture as a root cause of injustice or see gender reform as its sole remedy, but it does include attention to oppressive gender hierarchies as a crucial step in the process of standing on two feet.

In Blanca Navidad, as in the Zapatista communities, affect is embedded in the rearticulation of bare life into the pursuit of life with dignity. It hovers in the demands of the Zapatistas' Revolutionary Women's Law. Each of its points recasts the feminine subject as healthy and educated, potentially a leader, someone whose desires and relations are respected. Affect-culture is also integral to the ontology and epistemology of the elsewhere here imagined as the result of women's organizing, both before and after the uprising, and of their investigation into the other world the Zapatistas' declaration of autonomy proposes.

The political stance that has emerged from the North–South *Encuentros* echoes what some call *feminismo comunitario* (community-based feminism).[40] Born in Bolivia in the 1990s, feminismo comunitario is autonomous, outside the bureaucracy of state institutions. It denounces the discourse of gender equality as reiterating neoliberal *machista* and individualism, and it disparages Western feminism's focus on rights. Instead, feminismo comunitario claims an epistemic birthplace in indigenous women's history and memory. The community is like a body, says the Bolivian organizer Julieta Paredes, formed by men and women side by side, with the intersexed in between.[41] The North–South *Encuentros* have enacted a similar understanding of the gendered social body and nurtured its integrity through adjustments to the traditional *cargos* of men and women.

In describing Blanca Navidad's current situation, Poncho Herrera said he often remembered the words Comandante Zebedeo spoke during his visit, and he added:

> We are continuing to form alliances not only in our own country but also around the world, looking for another way of life so that future generations may have the chance to choose what works for them. We have a lot to learn as we know practically nothing. But we are still standing [*estamos de pie*].

In the phrase *estamos de pie* can be heard echoes of Zapata, the CJM program Standing on Two Feet, and the concept of autonomy that the Zapatistas have developed in their decades-long struggle. The phrase conjures, as well, the community's exercise of biopower through its gender-adjusted autonomous governance and its efforts to build sustainable life against the violent neoliberal deployments of biopolitics. When Poncho asserts, "We are still standing," the we he refers to is a collective rooted in a particular place, but one whose existence is shaped by affiliations formed with others elsewhere. To be still standing affirms a position as capable social and political subjects who are, in fact, not standing still. It carries the sense of refusing to give up or give in, of being unvanquished and in a position to act. To be still standing in the sense Poncho gives it is to do more than survive. It is to have arrived through knowledge and determination at the crossroads between necessity and freedom, where far-flung alliances in resistance inspire and educate. Here, a feminism without the name plots the future.

III

The Utopian Question

<< 8 >>

Love in the Common

The utopian question is a simple one: what possibilities today
lie beyond reality?

Carlos Monsiváis, "Millenarianisms in Mexico"

What does love have to do with labor and community organizing in
Mexico or elsewhere? The question seems preposterous, even untimely, yet we know that affective capacities are a part of the dynamic
process by which political identities are formed and that they bind
people to one another and, sometimes, to a common cause. Like
sexuality—and often entangled with it—love is a historical discourse that is suffused with affect. It names an emotion freighted
with norms that shape desire and direct attachments to objects, relations, and pleasures. As such, it can enhance or undermine individual or collective well-being. If we are cynical, we may disparage love
as a useless term for politics or dismiss it as a mystification, even a
distraction. Yet many of us who recognize all of the above may also
harbor a loyalty to love, a sense that the positive social bonds that
love conjures may be necessary to survival, tied to a fundamental
condition of dependency on relations of care that sustain life and
to the passions that motivate action on behalf of others and for a
better world.

In this closing chapter, I propose that we think about labor and
community organizing as acts of love.[1] When people mobilize themselves into a campaign for better working conditions or community
resources, they aim to redress, in some fashion, their unmet needs.
Those unmet needs are a surplus that is fundamental both to capitalism and to its potential undoing, the source of profit and the ground
for critical resistance. Organizing is an effort to activate and reorient

that surplus from the standpoint of living labor. The term "living labor" connotes the common human capacity for action in collaboration, a capability through which survival needs are met. It is enacted in the marketplace and in the home; it draws upon knowledge from the past and can realize imagined possibilities. Living labor is a necessary component of the social relation that constitutes capital. It is the form-giving fire harvested as surplus labor, but because that harvest is never entire, the remainder continually threatens capital's undoing. Antonio Negri and Michael Hardt suggest that "love" might serve as a name for the affective material that facilitates the reclamation of this common resource. In what follows, I elaborate on their proposal as part of a recent shift in the political imaginary of the Left that has opened a space for entertaining the intelligibility of love as a political concept. I turn to Hardt and Negri's *Commonwealth* (2009) because it renarrates love as a political value and a material force fundamental to the constitution of the common. In critical conversation with their work and that of others on the common, I entertain the potential of "love" as a name for the affect-culture of collaboration and passionate reason that accompanies the conversion of living labor into organized resistance. I place alongside these arguments some love stories from struggles to reclaim the common that were led by women workers in grassroots communities in northern Mexico. Though their context has its own particularity, the issues these stories raise highlight the ways the twin surpluses of unmet need and surplus common feature in collective action and the belief in possibility it requires. For this reason, these stories may resonate in organizing efforts elsewhere. They are, in any case, testimonies to the continuing pertinence of utopian hope. Any organizing effort carries with it a promise that change for the better is possible, and it is this future prospect that makes hope one of the positive affects that organizing solicits. This chapter on love therefore begins and ends with a consideration of hope, a feature of affect-culture that arises not from an ideal abstraction but from the exercise in the historical here and now of capacities that enable our attachments to one another and to the imagination of a better future.

The Future Is Not What It Used to Be

Recently, culture theorists on the Left in the overdeveloped sectors have begun to question the efficacy of negativity as the driving discourse of social change and to reassert a politics of affirmation.[2] As many of their arguments make clear, a politics of affirmation is not a rejection of critique—the practice of unsettling official and common knowledge and revealing its history and ties to power. What affirmative politics turns away from is the cynical refusal of a possible outside or alternative to capitalism, a refusal that defines much of late twentieth-century postmodern culture theory. Now, under pressure from the ground swell of organized resistance across the globe against the gaping disparity between the wealthy few and the social majority, intellectuals are rereading Marx, the Frankfurt School, Ernst Bloch, Herbert Marcuse, and the revolutionary Left in Latin America for the utopian possibility they voice. The turn to imagining alternatives is surfacing in work on ecology and sustainability, affect, queer subjectivities, and counter- and alter-modern histories, and it joins the demands of *plantóns* and social movements that are rejecting negativity and the "whatever" postmodern pose. In short, the future is not what it used to be.

As I mention in chapter 2, some of this work is embracing Spinoza's materialist formulation of affect as one reference point for an affirmative critical reorientation, and it is this formula and its utopian implications that I want to briefly reconsider. "Joy" and "sorrow" are Spinoza's names for the two primary affects. "Joy" is his term for the positive affective register that entails a change to the better in a state of the body. It enables the capacity to act, and it is best achieved with others. Sadness is the opposite. I am interested in joy because this formulation of the enabling affective register speaks to one of the great unsolved riddles of human history: what motivates individuals to act to improve their lives and to do so in concert? Spinoza's insight that embodied affective intensities accompany change for the better and that this improvement in well-being is best achieved in collaboration suggests that the decision to join a labor or community organizing effort may be tied up with this primary affect in that it projects an improvement in one's life, an improvement tied to the lives of others.

One of my presuppositions throughout *Fires on the Border* is that labor and community organizing are by definition efforts to redress the systemic erosion of well-being that capitalism's deregulation entails and, thereby, to improve the quality of life. This drive toward a common enhancement of well-being is also the basis for the utopian aspiration of organizing. In his discussion of utopian desire, Fredric Jameson considers the legitimate though unanswerable question of the utopian premise, or what can be affirmed as the goal of an emancipated society. He turns for an answer to Theodor Adorno, who reframes the question of utopia, restoring its material basis. Adorno's answer is as follows:

> He who asks what the goal of an emancipated society is is given answers such as the fulfillment of human possibilities or the richness of life. Just as the inevitable question is illegitimate, so the repellent assurance of the answer is inevitable. . . . There is tenderness only in the coarsest demand: that no-one shall go hungry any more. Every other seeks to apply to a condition that ought to be determined by human needs, a mode of human conduct adapted to production as an end in itself.[3]

Rejecting as illegitimate a question that begins with the fetishized image of an emancipated society, Adorno comes down to earth and lands upon a feeling: tenderness. Yes, tenderness. With this surprising affect-laden word, he recasts the problematic in which the question is couched to begin not with an abstract image of freedom but with a demand: "that no-one shall go hungry any more." Elegant in its simplicity, Adorno's formula underscores that care in the fullest sense, as empathy, even love, inheres in organized resistance that begins with unmet needs and demands freedom from want.[4]

In organizing to confront and redress their exploitation and the imposition of bare life in their communities, maquiladora workers enact the tenderness of the "coursest demand" that fundamental needs be met, and in so doing they highlight injustices that are widely shared by others. In this respect their campaigns join far-flung grassroots efforts to reclaim the common. They also keep company with intellectuals who have put forward proposals for marshaling the capacity-building affects of hope and love. Among them are Silvia Federici, David Harvey, Myles Horton, Naomi Klein, Walter Mignolo, and James Petras. They draw upon a long line of utopian thinking in Western Marxism and in indigenous thought.[5] The Zapatistas are not the sole example of hope put into practice in Mexico. Other grassroots movements, like the struggles over land and other natural resources in Atenco and for education and democratic governance in Oaxaca and the Yo Soy 132 movement against electoral corruption in spring 2012, are sparks of determined resistance. In the past fifty years, communities around the globe have been spreading seeds of hope as they develop short- and long-term initiatives to combat capitalist bioderegulation.[6] We can find examples in AIDS activism and grassroots feminism where the tenderness of demands for dignity have been pursued through shared labor, care, and leadership. Like the struggles of maquiladora workers, whose factory-based organizing has spilled into their neighborhoods, these pockets of hope are capitalism's underside, and as such they are a history to hold on to and learn from in political education for the future. As Jameson affirms against those who dismiss utopian aspirations as impractical, a utopian horizon will not necessarily at once make visible the outlines of practical politics for the era of globalization, but we will never come to one without it.[7]

The utopian aspiration is intrinsically infused with affect-culture because it aims to make impossible the belief that there is no alternative, but this does not mean that it promotes a feel-good politics. The critical pedagogy that accompanies utopian aspirations can also provoke the tenderness of exposed hurts. *Fires on the Border* offers many instances in which this critical undertaking was articulated in feelings that were disturbing and discomforting, if also at times inspiring. The feminist theorist Sarah Ahmed stresses that such a complex affective culture is invariably attached to troublemaking. Revolutionary consciousness is accompanied, she reminds us, by feeling at odds with the world or feeling that the world as it is given is odd. Indeed, "the revolutionary is an affect alien."[8] To be willing to let the present get under your skin is to confront that alienation and convert it into a collective aspiration, the belief that an alternative existence is achievable and an unfinished history can be pursued. Letting the present get under your skin can feel like a painful flaying as you open yourself to a perspective that refuses to go along and listens for alternative possibilities. As Ahmed reminds us, although refusing to be well adjusted may feel bad, joy can be found in it and in laboring with others to open alternatives for living.

Ernst Bloch's three-volume magnum opus, *The Principle of Hope*, explores the epistemological and ontological dimensions of future-oriented thinking and makes a strong case for the fundamental value of hope's critical readjustments and joyful affirmations.[9] For Bloch, hope takes utopian forms that are both affective and cognitive. In its utopian function, hope entails a dual affective temporality. It is directed, on the one hand, at critical assessment of the past and present and, on the other, at aspiration toward a better future. This affective temporality is fundamental to Bloch's concept of utopia and his renarration of realism. Contrary to the charge of liberals who dismiss utopian hope as unrealistic, Bloch maintains that it is actually a brand of radical realism. He stresses that utopian hope is not about escaping reality for some ideal other world. Rather, it is a way of knowing that attends to dimensions of reality that encompass not only what has come to be but also its potential to become something else. Here, Bloch's concept of the "Not-Yet-Conscious" that inhabits the present is pertinent.[10] This knowledge is anticipatory and looks "towards the side of something new that is dawning up, that has never been conscious before, not, for example, something forgotten" (11). The Not-Yet-Conscious lies at the edges of what is knowable, at the threshold of unrealized possibilities that inhabit the past and the present and, with some effort, can be attended to. Bloch claims this more ample knowledge has an objectivity that suggests an altered conception of realism, one that entails an affective relationship to time in that it includes anticipatory elements that regard individual and collective relationships to the past as alterable and looks to rescue from the past a more viable present (197). This is "a different concept of reality than the narrow and ossified one of the second half of the nineteenth century" (197). For Bloch these anticipating elements that are a component of reality operate in the field of hope. This hope is not to be taken *"only as emotion,* as the opposite of fear . . . but *more essentially as a directing act of a cognitive kind"* (12).

The chief affective obstacle to utopian hope's affective investment in the future is fear (193–95). Kathi Weeks reminds us of Thomas Hobbes's analysis of the political effectiveness of fear: "It enables subjects to give up their power and submit to the will of the sovereign" (198). For Hobbes, fear is a politically disabling affect because the fearful subject contracts around the will to self-preservation. In contrast, the hopeful subject embraces an expansive affective orientation, pursuing a range of connections and openings. She is the agent of the future who points toward the possibility of a break with the present, however partial (220). This combination of critical attention and hopeful aspiration holds fear at bay. It is the driving force that infuses the actions of those organizers who bravely speak back to intimidation on the border and elsewhere.

In all of these respects, utopian hope shares an epistemological and political affiliation with the practice of bearing witness that I detail in chapter 3. Bearing witness is a vigilantly cognitive and hopefully affective act. Its vigilance provokes estrangement from past and present common sense and awakens openings that envision and move toward an alternative future. The hopeful witness brings forward unrealized possibilities that hover in the activities and texts of everyday culture. She clings to daydreams as a surplus that Bloch calls a "substratum of the claimable cultural inheritance" (156). This surplus culture is produced as the "effect of the utopian function," or the dream of a better life (156). This dream taps what Bloch calls "the Real" in history—"namely the events produced by working people together with the abundant interweaving process-connections between past, present, and future" (198). Here, Bloch hints that surplus culture, the dreams of possible alternatives, are bound to a common resource: the collective activity of working people. Knowledge of this kind mobilizes subjects (198), and as I address in more detail, it awakens a common wealth that we might daringly call "love."

Like utopia and hope, love is weighted with past and present cultural investments, its material history often obscured, frozen in the sentimentalized, commodified, and abstracted forms love takes. Any renarration of love must acknowledge that it has been the vessel for many of Western culture's most violent delusions and the cultural instrument of much suffering. What would an alternative, materialist version of love look like? Might such a version of love help us recognize the integral importance of affective capacities to cultivating a forward-looking, hopeful, passionate reason? Antonio Negri and Michael Hardt offer one answer with which to begin.

Common Wealth

Commonwealth is the third book in Hardt and Negri's series that includes *Empire* (2001) and *Multitude* (2005). In this volume they elaborate their argument that new levels of biopolitics are escalating the erosion of the natural world and the deregulation of bodies, consciousness, affects, and other features of human life necessary for social interaction. They are not alone in discerning that capitalist biopolitics is creating openings for alternative social and economic relations, and they concede that the concept of biopower resonates with feminist attention to bodies and affects as features of social and political life. Their argument does not tell us much, however, about women's involvement in anticapitalist struggles, nor do they draw very extensively upon the work of materialist feminists or substantially attend to gender or sexuality as they feature in the deployment of biopower. Nonetheless, their book shares an affinity with feminist goals, and given the prominence they assign to affect and to love, it is relevant to the question of love for organizing toward alternatives to capitalism.

Despite the shortcomings with Hardt and Negri's formulation of biopolitics that I detail in chapter 2, their concept "common wealth" includes a dimension of social life that is undertheorized—namely, the affective components of cooperation. The common (sometimes figured in the plural as "the commons") comprises the substantive goods that enable the regeneration of nature and human life. In the long history of its uses, the concept of the common has generally referred to the resources of the material world—the air, water, and fruits of the soil.[11] The common also includes social resources made available through human labor not only in the production of goods and services in the marketplace but also in the labor that takes place outside the market—for example, caring for children, the sick, and the elderly; dealing with waste; and acquiring food or water. More recently, attention has been given to the intellectual and cultural common organized around shared conceptual, creative, and artistic resources, to which I would add the good sense of critical knowledge produced in many social sites. Finally, some analysts have extended the concept to include the species' common—for instance, resources like body parts and genes.[12] Some of the most significant feminist theoretical work on the common has attended to the history of women's labor and bodies as a part of the appropriation of common resources. As capital accumulation historically proceeded through the dispossession of commonly held lands, women themselves became a communal good, and their work, defined as a natural resource, replaced these lost common assets in the long centuries of primitive accumulation.[13]

Hardt and Negri are especially interested in capital accumulation that advances through the appropriation of cooperation that entails common forms of knowledge, social relationship, and affect.[14] The name they give to this common of cooperation is "love." They recognize that one difficulty in identifying love with this common resource is that love is "deeply ambivalent and subject to corruption," and they concede that love alone is too weak to overthrow the current ruling powers.[15] Their proposal therefore rests on the argument that love in the sense of common cooperation must be animated by an intellectual force, "the revolutionary passion of reason" that emerges from the margins of history.[16] Unfortunately, this intriguing conception of love also rests upon their troubling theory of social relations as fundamentally biopolitical.

In chapter 2, I discuss in more detail the ways this problematic concept of biopolitics, so fundamental to their understanding of social life, eclipses the intimate material relations that involve embodied affective capacities in the accumulation of surplus labor and in organized efforts to redress capitalism's unmet needs. When Hardt and Negri locate biopolitics in "the power of life to resist," they foreclose our ability to understand the unmet needs that capitalism produces as the basis for resistance. Their concept of biopolitics also obscures the material interfaces among bodies, the labor through which needs are met, and culture. In other words, in mistaking the matter of bodies for their materiality, Hardt and Negri, like Brian Massumi, substitute biomatter for the dialectical relation between nature and history, bodies and culture, unmet need and social struggle. An accompanying casualty is affect. The human capacity for affective attachment is nonetheless an important common resource and a component of the surplus potential they call "love," from which resistance to capitalism's violent deregulation springs.[17]

I explain in chapter 2 that a historical and materialist approach to affect does not understand it as ontological matter but rather as one name for culturally mediated sensations and capacities for attachment that are made meaningful through historically variable languages and practices, many of which adhere to the embodied labor to meet human needs. As such, affects are part of the physical/ psychic/emotional material of living labor, whose appropriation accumulates surplus value. Affects saturate the unmet needs that capitalist relations of production produce. They leaven the cooperation that is required in the labor of the formal marketplace and in the labor of social reproduction outside it. Though affective capacities are appropriated as part of the human personality that is commodified and sold as surplus labor, the potential to form affective attachments (of cooperation, accommodation, anger, frustration, and so forth) is never completely consumed by the social relation that constitutes capital. It is a surplus that is both immanent and external to it.

Let me say more about this surplus. Capitalism produces unmet needs, but unmet needs also pose a constant threat to capitalist interests. They are in this sense a surplus, capitalism's continual outside. They are also the basis for social unrest, and so for this reason they must be reckoned with continually. Hardt and Negri refer to unmet needs as the deprivation that leads to antagonism. As they point out, this antagonism is transformed into revolt only when it is reinforced by another surplus that cannot be expropriated by capital. This surplus is crucial to the generation of revolutionary change. It consists of the common wealth, which for them is a surplus of intelligence, experience, knowledge, and desire.

In his responses to the work of Hardt and Negri, Cesare Casarino asks from where the transfiguring power of this surplus arises if it is the generator of revolutionary becoming. His answer is that the power of this surplus lies in the fact that it escapes capital's reach and that it does so because it is an absolute and not a relative potential. The potential wealth of intelligence, experience, knowledge, and desire is wealth only if the term "wealth" is disengaged completely from its capitalist determination. It is not measurable or even comprehensible in terms of value. Rather, it is absolute wealth, or in the terms Marx uses in reference to labor power, it is "the general possibility of wealth."[18] This surplus wealth is the human potential that capital tries to subsume into surplus value, but it can do so only relatively because if it did so absolutely, it would foreclose the very human potential that it requires. It is this potential that persists as surplus common, an externality that will always to some degree exceed capital's reach. It is the "living" feature of living labor. Living labor is, David Harvey reminds us, a concept that not only emphasizes the fundamental qualities of dynamism and creativity but also indicates where the life-force and the subversive power for change reside.[19]

As living labor, surplus common is an unexploitable potentiality that is incorporated in our bodies and expressed in social relationships.[20] It includes a mind–body circuit that connects "sensation-emotion-perception-feeling-thought," to use Antonio Damasio's terms, a circuit that draws upon both affective capacities and passionate reason.[21] As Casarino recognizes, this surplus potential is a feature of "solidarity, care for others, creating of community, and cooperating in common projects" that "is an essential survival mechanism."[22] If unmet need is the surplus seedbed of organized struggle against exploitation and oppression, then surplus common is its glue. Enmeshed in capital's labor relations as the monstrous possibility that haunts it, surplus common includes the affective attachments that cling to the cooperation and care of living labor and to the motivation to act on behalf of collective interests. If we choose "love" as the name for the activation of this potential, then we must grapple with both its ideological appropriation and its utopian aspiration.

In organizing campaigns, the radical potential of surplus common gets narrowed when commonsense formulations of property or attachments undermine the critical force of passionate reason, but it can also nurture the critical standpoints from which alternative ways of knowing and surviving emerge. In other words, the affective attachments of surplus common are sites of struggle and possibility in social movement. As a witness on the border, I learned that the labor of organizing invariably involved the arduous navigation of both.

Love in the Labyrinth

I first went to Mexico in 1999, inspired by the accounts of women on the global assembly lines that I had been reading and teaching for over a decade. The experience transformed my life. Listening to Mexican organizers' testimonies, analyses, and informal talk, I began to discern the affective attachments that accompanied efforts to reclaim the common resources of labor power, clean air and water, land, dignity, and collective action. They punctuated these struggles in many forms and often disrupted gender and sexual norms. From my witnessing vantage point, it was clear that the fundamental premise of the commitments I joined was a crazy kind of love.

One of the challenges in an organizing campaign is to maintain that love. J. K. Gibson-Graham refers to this process as "cultivating subjects."[23] Cultivating subjects is an implicit part of the process that the Mexican organizers signify in the verb *organizarse*. *Organizarse* literally means "organize themselves," and as no word in English can, it captures the reflexive dynamic that organizing entails as workers organize themselves to see their place in history from a new perspective. *Organizarse* translates the cultivation of subjects into a collective undertaking that requires the effort, time, and care of all involved. The transposition of the kinds of cooperation that occur in a factory during the workday into the collective cooperation that takes place in a labor organizing campaign is not automatic or easily done. The political education it involves is cognitive and affective, and in both respects it draws upon and reorients individuals' capacities for cooperation and care. Participants fall in love with the possibilities held out by a collective movement. They fall in love with their leaders and with each other. These loves are levers that activate good sense and courage. They generate attachments and identifications, some of which adhere to the strong pull of familiar norms. The challenge is to simultaneously maintain and transform these loves as the organic fertilizer of the common.

Certainly, as I discuss in chapter 4, the affect-culture circulating in an organizing campaign can also be toxic, as it can corrode a group's fragile hold on each other and their collective goals. The joy-full potential of the surplus common is, though, what I want to dwell on here. As many of the labor campaigns on the border illustrate, the activation of this surplus common and the claims made in the name of capital's outside may not be lasting, but the very fact of their existence against tremendous odds is a foothold on possibility, a glimpse of a better world unveiled in the here and now. As workers organize themselves, leaders emerge, outsiders get involved, and new relationships become a component of the collective surplus. Sometimes, the outsiders are allies who contribute their labor, resources, and ideas. They may facilitate workshops, circulate information, contribute expertise, and recruit allies. Those who become effective agents in the cultivating of subjects must be insiders enough to be trusted, especially by those who are on the front lines of a campaign. These trusted outsiders walk a tightrope of attachments and projections on which they are hurled and turn it into a launching pad for critical vigilance, for often collective consciousness is first cultivated through the affective disorientation inspired by one of these trusted outsiders.

One of the Duro workers, a woman I will call Claudia, told me about her initial meeting with such a trusted outsider and the feelings it provoked:

> She is real special. You don't know if she is good or bad. When I first saw her, I didn't speak to her. I only wrote down what I was feeling in that moment after I arrived home. I wrote her a letter. But it took me three days to deliver it to her. I said to myself, "Will I send it? I don't know. How would that seem? What is she going to think? Maybe she won't care." I didn't know what to do. I only remember that I wrote her that when I first saw her, when I heard her and listened to her talk, I felt that she was a really special person. A strong person, that is what I saw, but at the same time a person with a heart that breaks for the needs of everyone else. Later, she

told me that she really liked what I had written. She said that little
message was a good luck charm for her and now she always carried
it with her on the road. "For me it is a talisman," she said, "something really beautiful, really profound, that I identify with." Except
for my husband, she was the first person to whom I ever wrote
something so deep. I think that he fell in love with me because I
wrote him such things. But I never wrote such things to a person
I didn't know. So from then on, I began to feel surer of myself. For
me it was something fundamental—that a person would tell me
such beautiful things.

Claudia's story confirms what we know but do not often admit—
that critical consciousness is leavened by attachments that open the
possibility of affective mapping and alternative ways to be. For her
this organizer-teacher is disconcerting—"you don't know if she is
good or bad." She is a gender transgressor, a woman who lives on the
road and breaks the rules, but she is not simply a rebel. That her heart
"breaks for the needs of everyone else" hints that for Claudia this
outsider represents a third way beyond good or bad—a way of knowing and acting we might call the "tenderness of the surplus common" that gestures toward utopian possibility. This outsider opens
for Claudia an affirmation and a path toward becoming "we." Both
will lead her to feel surer of herself and eventually put her life at risk
by speaking on behalf of others during the Duro workers' strike.

In her story Claudia acknowledges that her feelings for this
organizer-teacher nudge right up against the familiar discourse of
romantic love, and much of her eloquence lies in so gracefully distinguishing the two. Attachments almost invariably get entangled
in the norms regulating gender and desire. Claudia's tale recognizes
that they feature in this outsider's affirmation. Feeling sure of herself
is the product of an exchange of gifts whose value cannot be divorced
from the gender transgressions that script this unnamable love. She
takes the risk of delivering her message, and her gift is returned. The
teacher has made Claudia's letter into a good-luck charm. The charm
is proof that she is not alone on the road and, perhaps, also proof that
she too is vulnerable. That a person would tell her "such beautiful
things" may be as important to this woman as it is to Claudia—even,

as Claudia recognizes, fundamental. It eases the brave and risky process of prying oneself loose from a familiar way of knowing and living in order to embrace the perilous and potentially deadly standpoint of advocating justice. The affective attachments formalized in affirmations like these motivate action. They are good-luck charms that arm one against fear and despair.

Claudia's story tells us a lot about the role of psychic processes in cultivating subjects who desire to channel their capacity for joy toward collective action. In his discussion of charisma and the arts of resistance, James Scott gives us a way to think about this relationship as more than simply a crush or hero worship. He draws our attention not to the individual enthralled by another's person or personality but to the medium of charisma itself and to the affective intensity it elicits. "Charisma," he proposes, "is not a quality—like, say, brown eyes—that someone possesses in any simple way." It is, he writes, "a relationship in which engaged observers recognize (and may in fact help inspire) a quality they admire. . . . Understanding that charismatic act, and many others like it . . . depends upon appreciating how [a] gesture represented a shared hidden transcript that no one had yet the courage to declare in the teeth of power."[24] The hidden transcript encoded in Claudia's encounter with this woman whose gesture so inspired her is part projection and part identification. It lies in a series of actions and exchanges that draw out the latent possibility of surplus love. It is, more specifically, the tenderness of this affirmation that enables a change for the better in a state of the body, a better capacity to act.[25]

As you may have discerned, Claudia's story is enfolded in another, the story of what made possible her telling it to me. If there was a certain level of trust that allowed Claudia to share this story with me, the description of transference I offer in chapter 3 captures some of the conditions that made that sharing possible. Lines of triangulation, loss, and desire crisscrossed the breach over which this *profesora de los Estados Unidos* and this Mexican maquiladora worker gave ourselves to the other, each of us humbled, shy, and self-consciously groping toward common ground. The transference that took place— if "transference" is the right word—felt to me like an electrifying safety net for the fatal leap we each had taken in the shadow of that other woman—the one who was neither good nor bad—for she had powerfully touched my life, as well.

Claudia's story and mine are snapshots from a process of giving oneself into the hands of the other that an organizing campaign provokes, even requires. They offer only glimpses of the attachments that propel individuals here and there into a chain of witnessing. They do not disclose much of the material history in which these attachments are entwined, though we can surmise what such an account might address: that some of these actors come to a common struggle from different locations in capitalism's uneven development; that the attachments formed by those on the front lines are leavened by wage and subsistence labor that does not even minimally meet their needs, whereas the lives of others who lend support are tempered by labor that more amply provides; that the attachments of women in organizing efforts are frayed by the pull of their greater share in the labor at home; that in becoming organizers women weigh these attachments against the expectations of their mothers and grandmothers, their fathers, husbands, and children; that the actors in these scenarios live the contradictory emotional landscapes of late-capitalist gender formations quite differently from one another, hedging their duties and desires against available options with differing calculations and costs; and that the strong attractors of race, ethnicity, and nation shape these attachments and are transmitted in the discourses of an eros that circles around and beyond the normative disciplining of desire.

The Common as Plantón

An organizing campaign is metaphorically and at times literally a *plantón*. A plantón is a public demonstration that reclaims the common, a demonstration that does not go away. It is a spectacle of civil resistance that inserts the hidden transcript of utopian demands into public discourse and spaces. It requires collective participation and months, sometimes years, of labor and time. *Plantón* in Spanish means both "seedling" and "long wait." It sprouts from the grassroots as evidence of surplus common and class consciousness. Maintaining a plantón requires critical thinking and hope, determination and a lot of work. It also requires sustaining the cultivation of new subjects and attachments. In Mexican workers' campaigns, this cultivation takes place in workshops on topics that arise out of the workers' needs. They might focus on the concept of the wage, the gender perspective, women's leadership, or how to deal with the limits of the law. The plantón draws upon this conceptual and strategic education and continues it through discussions on the spot that help connect critical knowledge and experience. This labor of *organisandose* draws upon the time of the seedling and the long wait, but in waiting, it is not passive. Its waiting is an activity that pushes the irritation of unmet needs toward the deliberate irruption of crisis.

I saw a plantón in action when the Duro workers went on strike in 2001 after their demands for better working conditions and for recognition of their newly formed union were ignored. On June 20 the judicial police entered the campground that the workers had set up for their protest outside the factory. They tore down their strike banners and began arresting and beating the striking workers. In the ensuing months, the workers moved their plantón to the plaza in front of the city hall. During that time they faced repression and intimidation. While some workers stayed in the plaza day and night, others pursued a frustrating, circuitous path through legal channels in order to be able to hold an election for the union that would officially represent them.

Claudia told me that her experience in the plantón gave her a new bond to others that was neither that of coworker nor that of friend. As she described it, this relationship took place through daily decisions that were both spontaneous and guided by values emerging from the process of political education that enabled her and others to develop a new way of being with each other. Its impact on her life was immense and fragile. "What I can now do, express, feel, or transmit I learned in this struggle," she said.

> I began to let out my feelings, to let out what I had really guarded inside myself. I began to talk with the others, sometimes about really deep things. It could be about marriage, sickness, or worries about one of their children. All that I learned, I learned with them. All of them, even if they don't know it, taught me to rebel and to say, "No, we don't like this," or, "This should not be this way," or to

go and say, "I am coming on behalf of someone." All of that they taught me from their participation, from listening to them, from knowing them.

Over the course of the sixteen-month strike, women formed ties with one other and forged a dramatically new way of knowing and acting, epitomized in Claudia's formulation "I am coming on behalf of someone." The testimonies of many of the worker-organizers involved in this plantón conveyed that they were driven to do what they did out of a determination for justice that intensified as the repression against them increased. A new economy of care took over during the days and weeks of the plantón. Women like Ana, Carmen Julia, Kuiquis, Silbia, Luisa, and Margarita went to the plantón in the morning. Some left at midday to get children or younger sisters from school, returned with them, and stayed until six or seven at night, when they would go from house to house giving out flyers. Those in the plaza began to take care of one another in new ways. Even after the workers lost the union election due to fraud and intimidation, many of the women who spoke with me asserted that they did not really lose, and in that assertion one could hear the sense of dignity that the plantón achieved. As Ana said:

> They didn't give us our jobs back, but that doesn't mean that we lost. We won because we won an experience that was very beautiful. We had many experiences, and all of us were united. They say, "Ah, they lost," but we feel we won because we took the struggle to the end. But we took it. We didn't leave in the middle of the road. We didn't lose. We won our dignity.

The sense of dignity that those who stayed with the strike took from it was a crucial component of the surplus common they claimed. When it is earned as a result of painful decisions that break away from traditional expectations and reframe the very scaffolding of one's life, dignity can be a powerful reward. As Herbert Reid and Betsy Taylor have written in discussing the common, dignity is the hinge between the individual and the collective, between independence of thought and the common as a civic body. Dignity is both highly charged affectively and the incarnation of political principles that are no longer abstract but embodied in the fabric of one's being in the world, in social interaction and speech.[26]

When a struggle occupies a public space day and night, it rends the veil of denial that maintains normalcy. It puts unmet need on display and moves the demand for its redress into a different temporality, the time of the seedling and the long wait. In this sense the plantón also disrupts the time of capital, of bioderegulation, of the stressful working day, of rushing. In the enactment of the space of surplus love, dignity is mobilized as the catalyst of collaboration, and a new political imaginary is born out of the losses capitalism incurs. In this sense, the plantón materializes the temporality of utopia, the space-time of elsewhere. This "elsewhere" signifies the daring risk of imagining an alternative to the exploitative labor relations so fundamental to capitalism, an alternative that for too long has been erased in the Left's discourse and culture theory. It is an outside grounded not in the transcendence of historical time but in the excavation of the potential encrypted in the past and simmering in the present. This elsewhere draws the surplus of unmet needs and the surplus of collaborative potential into the seedling of transformative change.

"Demiurgic Strength . . . Modestly Concentrated"

In the epigraph to this chapter, Carlos Monsiváis reminds us that the utopian question is an outrageous and simple one: "what possibilities today lie beyond reality?" His essay "Millenarianisms in Mexico," in which this quote appears, was originally published in 1994 on the heels of the Zapatista uprising. It chronicles millenarian movements in Mexico stretching from the uprising against church and state in nineteenth-century Sonora to the postrevolutionary Christeros, who fervently rebelled against the revolutionary government's separation of church and state, to the student movement for an end to authoritarianism sparked by the Massacre of Tlateloco in 1968. His reflections are a reminder that there have been utopias of the Right as well as of the Left. Against the anti-utopian profile of neoliberal culture that squelches the imagination of alternatives and delegitimizes the very word "utopia," Monsiváis underscores the daring intervention into mainstream politics that the mere claim to hope announces and the preposterous entitlement to imagine it enacts.

> In politics one of the main guarantees of the credibility of a project lies in making sure that it has no utopian content. Pragmatism is foregrounded, as is a vigilant eye for the concrete, not to mention a healthy distance from the excesses of the past . . . to safeguard the idea of legitimate causes that entail, in whatever order of things, the transformation of the world. This is the deep rationale of today's utopian language whose demiurgic strength is modestly concentrated in the mere possibility of its existence.[27]

The world-transforming force of utopian language is contained in a seedling: the mere fact of its articulation. An assertion like, "Another world is possible!" is a powerful intervention into the public imaginary precisely because of the wish it pronounces. The other world it lays claim to exceeds the confines of "what's real." It is a hidden transcript that irrupts into the present and connects surplus need to surplus common. In other words, a utopian political imaginary begins from a standpoint that takes as fundamental living labor. This is the living labor that capital harvests when it leaves unmet the basic needs of so many, but it is also the surplus wealth that capital cannot appropriate, the capacity for cooperation and creativity that drives organizing efforts. Affective attachments mediate this capacity and its enactment. A utopian political stance affirms the joyful and critical potential of this surplus wealth and perhaps even calls the passionate reason that articulates it "love." It is indeed untimely and out of step with the fashions of our time, even as it speaks to the most pressing issue of today: how to realize the possibility of reclaiming and nourishing the common ground on which we live.

Until recently, the major challenge for social movement in the United States has been the failure of hope. The labor and civil rights organizer Myles Horton once said that it made no sense to work with people who had given up hope. "Only people with hope will struggle," he said.

> If people are in trouble, if people are suffering and exploited and
> want to get out from under the heel of oppression, if they have
> hope that it can be done, if they can see a path that leads to a
> solution, a path that makes sense to them and is consistent with
> their beliefs and their experiences, then they'll move. But it must
> be a path that they've started clearing. . . . If they don't have hope,
> they don't even look for a path. They look for somebody else to do
> it for them.[28]

Horton's words remind us that hope is the affective leavening of
social movement that makes growth possible and the long wait bearable, yet hope cannot do its work unless people embrace it themselves. Horton reminds us that "a revolution is just the last step of
a social movement after it has taken a prerevolutionary form. Then
it changes again—qualitatively—into something else."[29] Perhaps, it
is too daring to say that we are in a prerevolutionary phase in the
United States, but signs of hope sprouted in plantóns across the country in 2011. Like the organizers on the other side of the southernmost
U.S. border, these occupiers were cultivating new strategies for addressing the outlawing of dissent.

When I first began writing this book ten years ago, an organized
labor movement against neoliberalism was simmering in northern
Mexico, articulating itself as part of a broader transcontinental coalition of organizations calling for an end to free-market capitalism's brutality. Over the past decade, many of these alliances have
thinned or been redirected in the wake of 9/11 and a series of U.S.
economic recessions. More recently, the reign of the narco-despotism
that muzzles almost all dissent in Mexico has been a major obstacle to organizing in maquila-based communities. Sustaining labor
and community organizing in Mexican border communities has
become more challenging than ever as unemployment rises, job options inside and outside the maquilas diminish, and cartel violence
intensifies the struggle to simply survive. In this context, to speak of
love and hope may seem naïve, even arrogant, but in communities
that might seem hopeless and forgotten, a scattered few continue to

pursue openings in an impossible, deadly present. To say, as these workers and colonia residents courageously do, "La lucha sigue!" (The struggle continues!), is to maintain against all common sense an illuminating horizon of hope for another, more just world kindled from the passionate politics and living fires of cooperation and care.

Acknowledgments

This book was a long time in the making and would not have been possible without the generous support of many people and organizations. Principally, I thank the workers and organizers from grass-roots groups along the northern Mexican border and in central and southern Mexico who welcomed me into their lives and shared their struggles. In addition to the individuals who appear in the book and those who gave their testimony anonymously, I thank members of the following groups for their conversations, insights, and support: residents of the colonia Blanca Navidad, Nuevo Laredo; Centro de Trabajadores (CETRAC), Nuevo Laredo; Custom-Trim/Auto-Trim Workers, Valle Hermoso; the Duro Workers' Collective (DUROO), Río Bravo; Derechos Obreros y Democracia Sindical (DODS), Reynosa; Key Safety System Workers, Valle Hermoso; the Lajat Workers' Coalition, Gómez Palacio; Las Abejas, Chiapas; LG Workers, Reynosa; the Zapatista autonomous communities of Oventic and Morelia, Chiapas; the newspaper *El Mañana,* Nuevo Laredo; Pastoral Juvenil Obrero (PJO), Matamoros and Juárez; Servicio, Desarrollo, y Paz (SEDEPAC), Monclova and Frontera; Factor X, Tijuana; and Youth with Justice, Río Bravo. I am deeply indebted to the staff of the Coalition for Justice in the Maquiladoras (CJM), who introduced me to these organizations and who were an enormous asset to my research, giving me countless hours of their expertise. Cynthia Uribe was especially helpful with the transcription of interviews.

Funding from various sources enabled my research, and I thank the following for their support: the National Endowment for the Humanities' summer institute at Texas State University–San Marcos on Traversing Borders: History and Cultures of the Southwest (2000); the Rockefeller Humanities Residency Fellowship Program at the University of Arizona–Tucson (2001–2); the University at Albany–SUNY for a travel grant (2002), a College of Arts and Sciences Research Development Grant (2003–4), and a Faculty Research Award (2003–4); and a United University Professions Individual Development Award (2003). Sabbatical leaves from the University at Albany–SUNY in fall 2001 and fall 2005 and from Rice University in 2011–12 gave me time to research and write at crucial stages of the project.

I am grateful to colleagues at Rice for giving their time and thoughtful commentary to this book's manuscript. The Feminist Research Group of the Center for the Study of Women, Gender, and Sexuality was a valuable resource, and I am indebted to those who attended the seminar on drafts of selected chapters and shared their readings and helpful suggestions: José Aranda, Sergio Chávez, Krista Comer, Julie Fette, Rebecca Hester, Betty Joseph, Susan Lurie, Courtney Morris, Martha Ojeda, Robin Paige, Nanxiu Qian, and Abigail Rosas. I owe a very special thank you to Melissa Wright, who read the book proposal and the final manuscript multiple times and led the seminar. Her generous and wise suggestions at each step of the way refined and deepened my arguments. Whatever flaws remain are mine.

I am also indebted to Miranda Joseph for believing in the potential of this project before any of it was written and for hosting me in 2001 as I began the research as a fellow in the Rockefeller Residency Program that she directed at the University of Arizona–Tucson. Over the years many other colleagues read or published or listened to parts of what became the manuscript. Their interest prompted me to clarify my arguments, and the opportunities for discussion they offered provided helpful commentary that sharpened my thinking on material for several chapters. Among them are Tina Chen and David Churchill, Susan Comfort, Davina Cooper and Didi Herman, Ann Ferguson, Frigga Haug, Stevi Jackson, Anna Jónasdóttir, Liz Kennedy, David McNally, Breny Mendoza, Paula Rabinowitz, Diane Richardson, Janice Mc Laughlin, Mark Casey, and Joan Sangster.

I am grateful for the opportunities given to me by many individuals and organizations to present portions of the book as it was taking shape. I thank Julie Rak and the Distinguished Lecture Series at the University of Alberta–Edmonton; Rahel Jaeggi and Daniel Loick of the Rethinking Marx Conference, Berlin; Christina Kaindl,

Christoph Lieber, Oliver Nachtwey, Rainer Rilling, and Tobias ten Brink of the Capitalism Reloaded Conference, Berlin; Murat Aydemir and the School for Cultural Analysis, Amsterdam; Anna Jónasdóttir and the GEXcel Center for Gender Excellence, Örebro, Sweden; Christian Klasse, Susie Jacobs, and the Feminism and Political Economy Workshop at Manchester University, United Kingdom; Gordon Brent, Bill Leap, and the Reinstating Transgression Colloquium at American University, Washington, D.C.; Breny Mendoza and the Gender and Women's Studies Department at California State University–Northridge; the organizers of the Global Queeries Conference in Western Ontario; Tracey Deutsch and the Markets in Time Collective of the Institute for Advanced Study at the University of Minnesota; Davina Cooper and the Research Centre for Law, Gender, and Sexuality at the University of Keele Law School, Stoke-on-Trent, United Kingdom; the Center for Gender and Law, Westminster University, London; the organizers of the Humanities Graduate Conference at the University of Utah; the Marxist Reading Group at the University of Florida–Gainesville; Seth Marnin and the Rainbow Center of the University of Connecticut; Joan Sangster and the Graduate Studies in Historical Materialism Conference at the University of Trent, Ontario; Jyotsna Vaid and the Women and Gender Studies Program at Texas A&M; Jennifer Wingard and the English Graduate Student Conference at the University of Houston; and Erin Schell and the organizers of the Historical Materialism Conference at New York University.

I owe a debt of gratitude to the graduate student research assistants who gathered and synthesized materials for me at Rice University— Amanda Branker-Ellis, Heather Elliott, and Marite Preti—and to Sydney Boyd, who worked on editing the bibliography. Jean Niswonger, GIS support specialist at Fondren Library, Rice University, did meticulous and patient work designing the map. I was fortunate to be introduced to the inimitable Theresa Grasso Munisteri, who worked her magic as a copyeditor on the first draft of the manuscript. For their assistance, I thank the staff in the English Department at the University at Albany–SUNY and in the Center for the Study of Women, Gender, and Sexuality and the English Department at Rice University, especially Liz Lauenstein, Brian Riedel, Angela Wren Wall,

Marcia Carter, and Linda Evans. I am grateful to my editor, Richard Morrison, for supporting the project and for welcoming the book into the University of Minnesota Press. The editorial and production team at the Press has been outstanding. Many thanks go to Erin Warholm-Wohlenhaus, Rachel Moeller, and Wendy Holdman for their editorial and design work and to Mike Hanson for his exquisite copyediting. Sallie Steele's skillful indexing was also invaluable.

I am infinitely fortunate to have family and friends whose love, intellectual curiosity, and fierce commitments have animated my work. Over the years this book was in the making, my daughters, Molly and Kate Hennessy-Fiske, joined in the chain of witnesses to the struggles of Mexican workers and migrants, and they continue to testify on their behalf in their own work as a journalist and a high school history teacher. My mother and father, Mary-Jane and John Hennessy, taught my six sisters and me to love reading for the other worlds it takes you to. Their interests in literature, art, and history shaped my life and provoked me to try my best to make this book accessible to readers like them.

Finally, from start to finish, the generous and loving guidance of the legendary worker and organizer Martha Ojeda, who introduced me to the passionate politics of organizing on Mexico's northern border and who continues to inspire and transform my life, made this book possible. It is dedicated to her.

Mil gracias a todas y todos.

Notes

Introduction

Epigraph. "La dignidad es esa patria sin nacionalidad, ese arcoíris que es también puente, ese murmullo del corazón sin importar la sangre que lo vive, esa rebelde irreverencia que burla fronteras, aduanas y guerras."

1. The common noun *frontera* means "border." The city of Frontera in the state of Coahuila, which appears in chapter 3, also bears this name, perhaps because it is relatively near the northern border.

2. The archive of recent work on affect is considerable and growing. Some notable examples in feminist studies include Ahmed, *Cultural Politics of Emotion*; Berlant, *The Female Complaint, Compassion,* and *Cruel Optimism*; Brennan, *The Transmission of Affect*; Clough, *The Affective Turn*; Cvetkovich, *An Archive of Feelings* and *Depression*; Flam and King, *Emotions and Social Movements*; Gould, *Moving Politics*; Massumi, *Parables for the Virtual*; Probyn, *Blush*; Ramos-Zayas, *Street Therapists*; Rei, *Feeling in Theory*; Stewart, *Ordinary Affects*.

3. Some of these studies offer workers' testimonies on the impact of free trade in their communities. In addition to Ojeda and Hennessy, *NAFTA from Below,* see Bacon, *Children of NAFTA*; Kopinak, *Desert Capitalism*; Lugo, *Fragmented Lives*; Peña, *Terror of the Machine*; Sklair, *Assembling for Development*.

4. Among the most notable of these are Carillo and Hernández, *Mujeres fronterizas*; Cravey, *Women and Work*; Fernández-Kelly, *For We Are Sold*; Fuentes and Ehrenreich, *Women in the Global Factory*; Prieto, *Beautiful Flowers*; Kamel, *Maquiladora Reader*; Lugo, *Fragmented Lives*; Nash and Fernández-Kelly, *Women, Men*; Pearson, "Male Bias"; Salzinger, *Genders in Production*; Tiano, *Patriarchy on the Line*; Wright, *Disposable Women*.

5. See, for example, Balderston and Guy, *Sex and Sexuality*; Cantú, Naples, and Ortiz, *Sexuality and Migration*; Chávez, Silverman, and Librata Hernández, *Reading and Writing the Ambiente*; Domínguez-Ruvalcaba, *Modernity and the Nation*; Limas and Hernández, "Tránsitos de género"; Kelly, *Lydia's Open Door*; Lumsden, *Homosexuality and the State*; Luibhéid and Cantú, eds., *Queer Migrations*; Mongrovejo, *Un amor que se atrevió*; Monsiváis, *Amor perdido*; Prieur, *Mema's House*; Quijada, *Comportamiento*.

6. See Cantú, Naples, and Ortiz, *Sexuality and Migration*; Carrier, *De los Otros*; Díaz, *El SIDA en Mexico*; Kelly, *Lydia's Open Door*; Pérez, "El infierno"; Wilson, *Hidden in the Blood*.

7. One exceptional example is the work of Efraín Rodríguez Ortiz on the organizing being done against homophobia in Ciudad Juárez.

8. The Coalition for Justice in the Maquiladoras (CJM) was founded in 1989 as a binational coalition of U.S. and Mexican labor, faith-based, and women's organizations. During the years of my research, the coalition expanded to become international and to include over 125 organizations, over a quarter of them Mexican grassroots labor organizations. From 1999 to 2006, I met and spoke with many of these groups during CJM annual and regional meetings, site visits, and phone conferences.

9. Among them are those of Ruth Behar, Joseph Carrier, Matthew Gutmann, Patty Kelly, Oscar Lewis, Alejandro Lujo, Devón Peña, Annick Prieur, Leslie Salzinger, Lynn Stephen, Eric Wolf, David Bacon, Lourdes Benería, Lionel Cantú, Laura Carlson, Héctor Domínguez-Ruvalcaba, Patricia Ravello, Alicia Gaspar de Alba, Eithne Luibhéid, Kathleen Staudt, and Melissa Wright.

10. Gramsci, *Prison Notebooks*, 171.

11. See Badiou, *The Communist Hypothesis*, and Hardt and Negri, *Commonwealth*, respectively.

12. Colonias are squatter communities that ring border cities. Many maquiladora workers live in them and have built their homes out of cast-off wooden pallets from the factories or other found materials. Because colonias are unincorporated lands, residents have no property rights and pay no taxes, and the city does not provide paved streets, sewage, electricity, or water.

13. Marx, *Grundrisse*, 361.

14 See Mignolo on the Zapatistas' discourse of dignity in *The Darker Side of Western Modernity*, 215–19.

15. I use a lowercase *m* in *marxist feminism* throughout the book in order to signify feminist critical engagement with Marxism. A key distinction between marxist feminism and socialist or materialist feminism is the priority marxist feminism gives to relations of labor necessary for survival, a process in which culture, including gender and sexuality, prominently features. Marxist feminists approach the oppression of women, sexual dissidents, and people of color as integral to capitalism and pay special attention to the ways ideologies of race, gender, and sex legitimize the devalued labor that feeds capital accumulation.

16. Hale, *Engaging*, 20–21.

17. Many of these struggles are documented by Elena Poniatowska; see, for example, *La noche del Tlateloco* on the repression of student protests in 1968 and *El amanecer en el Zócolo*, which documents the seven weeks of massive protests in Mexico City after the 2006 presidential elections.

1. Labor Organizing in Mexico's Entangled Economies

1. Van Schendel, "Spaces of Engagement," 53; Payan, *The Three,* 28.

2. Grim, *This Is Your Country.*

3. Ibid.

4. Fraser, "NAFTA and the War on Drugs."

5. Reddy, *Navigation of Feeling,* 124. Helena Flam, in *Emotions and Social Movements,* 19–20, also mentions emotions that "uphold social structures and relations of domination."

6. Peña, "Las Maquiladoras," charts the number of work stoppages in U.S. garment and electronics industries during these years.

7. Kopinak, *Desert Capitalism,* 7.

8. "One Firm Goes to Mexico to Sort Grocery Coupons," *Wall Street Journal,* May 25, 1967.

9. Peña, "Las Maquiladoras," 168.

10. Reform of the labor law has been one of the major objectives of the PAN. The contentious reform proposals were blocked successfully until 2012, when they were passed by Congress. The reform rolls back many rights and protections for workers; it allows the companies to offer workers part-time contracts and three-month probation periods; and it gives them the freedom to engage in outsourcing.

11. Kopinak, *Desert Capitalism,* 10. Some of these changes pertained to lengthening the probation period from thirty to ninety days and allowing companies more discretion in adjusting the size of the workforce and length of the working day.

12. The term "charro union" originated during a period when union bosses first gained political control. Jesus Díaz de León, the leader of the railroad workers' union who struck deals with the government to limit workers' rights, was known as El Charro because he used to come to meetings in full cowboy, or charro, regalia.

13. For history of the CTM in the early years of the maquiladoras, see Carillo and Hernández, *Mujeres fronterizas.* On the union's role in the post-NAFTA years, see Bacon, *Children of NAFTA*; Ojeda and Hennessy, *NAFTA from Below.*

14. Carillo and Hernández, *Mujeres fronterizas,* 170.

15. Ibid., 177.

16. Baird and McCaughan, "Hit and Run," 16.

17. Ibid., 10.

18. Herbert G. Lawson, "U.S. Firms Open Plants across Mexican Line to Save Labor Costs," *Wall Street Journal,* May 25, 1967.

19. Ibid.

20. "Businessmen Promote Mexico as Source of Cheap Labor," *Machinist,* February 1969; Baird and McCaughan, "Hit and Run," 18.

21. Baird and McCaughan, "Hit and Run," 18.

22. Peña, "Las Maquiladoras," 180.

23. One example of the conflicts of interest that had become business as usual was that Pedro Pérez-Ibarra was the secretary-general of the maquiladora union in Nuevo Laredo and also one of the godsons of the national secretary-general of the CTM, who awarded him prominent positions at the local and state levels. He also had close ties to the Longoria family, who controlled several industries in Mexico.

24. Peña, "Las Maquiladoras," 183.

25. Richard Kokholm-Erichsen, "ICFTU: Behind the Wire," World Economic Processing Zones Association website, November 1996, http://www.wepza.org/bh101120.htm.

26. Ibid.

27. Peña, "Las Maquiladoras," 184.

28. Ojeda, *NAFTA from Below,* 49–53.

29. Institute for Research on Women and Gender, *Global Feminisms.*

30. Peña, "Las Maquiladoras," 189.

31. For histories of the early phases of the maquiladora program, see Baird and McCaughan, "Hit and Run"; Carillo and Hernández, *Mujeres fronterizas*; Fuentes and Ehrenreich, *Women in the Global Factory*; Lawson, "U.S. Firms Open Plants"; Peña, *The Terror of the Machine*; Prieto, *Beautiful Flowers.*

32. Kopinak, *Desert Capitalism,* 12.

33. One of them was the protracted struggle of striking workers at Solidev Mexicana in Tijuana between 1979 and 1981, when workers formed an independent labor union that was violently repressed by the government and the private sector. For details, see Prieto, *Beautiful Flowers.*

34. For more information on the number and location of plants and the impact of NAFTA on Mexican workers, see Ojeda and Hennessy, *NAFTA from Below*; Bacon, *Children of NAFTA.*

35. By 1996, CJM had become a trinational coalition, which included Canada, and in 2003, with the entry of organizations from the Dominican Republic, it became international. In 2006, organizations from Argentina, Brazil, Chile, and the Netherlands joined; in 2009 an organization from Haiti did, as well.

36. In 1992 the coalition released a documentary video, *Stepan Chemical: The Poisoning of a Mexican Community,* that had a wide-ranging impact, including prodding Stepan to redesign its pollution-control practices and train employees in handling toxic wastes.

37. Some of these early supporters included the AFL-CIO, the American Friends Service Committee, the Canadian Labor Congress, the Canadian

Autoworkers, the Environmental Health Coalition, the Interfaith Center for Corporate Responsibility, the Institute for Policy Studies, the Mexico Action Network on Free Trade, and Mexico Solidarity Network.

38. For documentation on several of these cases, see Ojeda and Hennessy, *NAFTA from Below*.

39. Peña, "Las Maquiladoras," 198.

40. Ibid., 197–98, 199.

41. The phrase "soft weapons" is the title of Gillian Whitlock's book on the management and transit of Muslim life narratives during the war on terror. It signals for her the ways in which cultural forms can be co-opted as propaganda during times of crisis to manipulate emotion and opinion in the public sphere.

42. I refer to the networks of organized crime as "cartels," even though their organization is looser than this word implies. I use the word "narco" to refer to them, as it is the word most often used colloquially to signify the other economy of the cartels. Though the *narcotraficantes* deal in drugs, drugs are not the sole commodity of "the business" (as it is also referred to colloquially). The narcos also deal in guns and human trafficking and have expanded into many legitimate commercial operations, among them resorts, hotels, restaurants, and media. Moreover, it is important to remember, when referring to the "upsurge in violence" on the border, that forms of violence—exploitation and poverty, corruption, impunity, and gender oppression, to name a few—had been features of life before the narco violence irrupted and, with it, a new form of criminal state sovereignty.

43. On the difficulty of gathering accurate statistics, see Ravelo, *Violencia sexual en Ciudad Juárez*.

44. Julia Monárrez Fragoso of the Colegio de la Frontera Norte in Juárez was the first who adopted Jill Radford and Diana Russell's notion of "femicide" to describe the killings. In their 1992 essay collection *Femicide*, Radford and Russell define femicide as "the misogynous killing of women by men." Organizers in support of the victims and their families adopted this term in order to stress the inordinate number of women among the dead and disappeared and the message explicit in the sexual violation and mutilation of the bodies: they were killed because they were women. The film *Senorita extraviada* was aired on *POV* in August 2002. It won a Documentary Special Jury Prize at the Sundance Film Festival and has circulated widely on the college circuit.

45. Notable among the many studies on the murdered women of Juárez are the following: Limas and Ravelo, "Feminicidio en Ciudad Juárez"; Tabuenca Córdoba, "Ghost Dance"; Monárrez Fragoso, "The Victims of the Ciudad Juárez Feminicide"; Ravelo and Domínguez-Ruvalcaba, *Entre las duras aristas*; Domínguez-Ruvalcaba and Corona, *Gender Violence*; Wright, *Disposable Women*; Fregoso and Bejarano, *Terrorizing Women*; Gaspar de Alba, *Desert Blood*; González Rodríguez, *Huesos en el desierto*; Washington, *The Killing Fields*.

46. On discourses of sexuality in the representation of the activists as public women, see Wright, "Witnessing."

47. Human rights experts have called attention to the rising numbers of women murdered in other regions of Mexico, not surprisingly in other areas of conflict, especially on the southern border. See Olivera, "Violencia Femicida."

48. Debbie Nathan, "Missing the Story," *Texas Observer,* August 30, 2002, http://www.texasobserver.org/archives/item/13627-1011-movie-review-missing-the-story.

49. Limas and Ravelo, in "Feminicidio en Ciudad Juárez," 55, remark on the relationship between the murders in Juárez and three decades of transnational capital, neoliberal policies, and economic restructuring on the border, which widened the disparity between rich and poor in Juárez and lowered the city's human development index.

50. Ravelo, *Violencia sexual en Ciudad Juárez,* 62.

51. Schmidt Camacho, "Ciudidana X"; Balderas Domínguez quoted in Monárrez Fragoso, "Victims," 62.

52. Limas and Hernández, "Tránsitos de género."

53. Ibid., 12.

54. Several feminist critics have delineated this analysis. For example, see Monárrez Fregoso, "Victims"; Schmidt Camacho, "Ciudadana X"; and Wright, *Disposable Women.*

55. Staudt, *Violence and Activism*; and Balli, "Murdered Women."

56. Limas and Ravelo, "Feminicidio en Ciudad Juárez," 55.

57. Wright, "Necropolitics," 715.

58. González Rodríguez, *Huesos en el desierto,* 38. In September 2003 the Mexican federal attorney general issued a report on the 228 cases of murdered women in Juárez that pointed to long years of criminal activity and local authorities' tolerance for organizations like the Juárez cartel. See Amnesty International, *Ten Years of Abductions and Murders.* In August 2003 the magazine *Proceso* published an FBI file that cited the already well-known but officially unspeakable information that an official in the PAN was a protector of the Juarez cartel.

59. Segato, "Territory," 86–87.

60. For detailed analyses of the antifemicide movement in Juárez and its public discourses, see Monárrez Fragoso, "The Victims"; Rojas, "The V-Day March"; and Wright, "Justice and Geographies," "Witnessing."

61. Laura Carlsen, "The Murdered Women of Juárez," *Foreign Policy in Focus,* January 19, 2011, http://www.fpif.org/articles/the_murdered_women_of_juarez.

62. Balli, "Murdered Women"; Segato, "Territory."

63. Balli, "Murdered Women."

64. The program was initially greeted with complaints from members of the U.S. Congress that the Bush administration provided no information to congressional committee members until the deal was done.

65. Laura Carlsen, "A Primer on Plan Mexico," Americas Program website, May 5, 2008, http://www.cipamericas.org/archives/1474; see also Laura Carlsen, "Armoring NAFTA: The Battleground for Mexico's Future," NACLA website, August 27, 2008, http://NACLA.org/node/4958.

66. Carlsen, "Armoring NAFTA," 22.

67. Marc Lacey, "In Drug War, Mexico Fights the Cartels and Itself," *New York Times,* March 30, 2009.

68. Quoted in Ed Vulliamy, "Day of the Dead," *Guardian,* December 6, 2008.

69. Payen, *The Three,* 27.

70. Vulliamy, "Day of the Dead."

71. Smith, "Semiorganized Crime," 203; Carlsen, "Armoring NAFTA," 18.

72. In this sense, as Domínguez-Ruvalcaba writes in "Presentacion," 11, for the politicians the violence in Juarez gets reduced to a discourse of accusations between parties. On some of this history, see Vulliamy, "Day of the Dead"; Smith, "Semiorganized Crime."

73. Smith cites the well-documented drama involving Carlos Salinas de Gortari and his brother Raúl's involvement in the assassination of PRI leader José Francisco Ruiz Massieu, a member of one of Mexico's other elite families. Allegations flew that drug bosses ordered the murder and that their alliances went all the way to the president. Smith, "Semiorganized Crime," 203. In another notorious example, the leader of the Sinaloa cartel, Chapo Guzman, was released from prison right after Calderón took office.

74. Tamaulipas had 1,209 officially recorded murders in 2010, the third-highest rate in the country. See Dawn Paley, "Off the Map in Mexico," *Nation,* May 23, 2011, 23.

75. Jason Beaubien, "In Just One Year, a Mexican City Turns Violent," NPR website, October 16, 2010, http://www.npr.org/templates/story/story.php?storyId=130592600; see also Molly Hennessy-Fiske, "Wealthy, Business-Savvy Mexican Immigrants Transform Texas City," *Los Angeles Times,* March 24, 2013, http://articles.latimes.com/2013/mar/24/nation/la-na-sonterrey-20130324.

76. Mbembe, "Necropolitics." Melissa Wright's recent essay "Necropolitics, Narcopolitics, and Femicide" is a brilliant analysis that extends Mbembe's argument to the gendered violence in Juárez, the first to link the discourses of narco violence to the discourses around the femicides. She stresses that gender is central to necropolitics, though neglected in its analysis. It has been deployed in Juárez through patriarchal discourses that sexualize and shame public women (both the victims of violence and feminist activists). These women are represented as transgressing their assignment to domestic spaces, whereas narco violence is represented as the work of criminals that nonetheless demonstrates the masculine traits of competition, rationality, and violence enacted in disputes over business in the public sphere, which is the domain of men.

77. Paley, "Off the Map," 20.

78. On the high-school party shootout, see Ken Ellingwood, "Ciudad Juarez Police Baffled by Shooting of Teens," *Los Angeles Times,* February 1, 2010. On April 7, 2010, 134 mass graves containing at least 177 bodies were found in San Fernando; see Paley, "Off the Map."

79. Alfredo Corchado, "Mexican Criminals Expand Intimidation with Citizen Journalist Killings," *Dallas News,* September 29, 2011. See also Campbell, *Drug War Zone,* 215–26.

80. "Not Even a Grenade Can Stop the Presses in Mexico," *Dallas Morning News,* May 13, 2012.

81. Catherine E. Shoichet, "Latest Battlefield in Mexico's Drug War: Social Media," CNN.com, September 15, 2011, http://articles.cnn.com/2011-09-15/world/ mexico.violence.internet_1_twitter-users-social-media-raul-trejo-delarbre?_s= PM:WORLD.

82. CNN Wire Staff, "Mexican Editor's Death Linked to Social Media," CNN.com, September 28, 2011, http://www.cnn.com/2011/09/26/world/americas/mexico-editor-decapitated/index.html?iref=allsearch.

83. Paley, "Off the Map in Mexico," 22.

84. Gibler, "Marketing Violence," 32. See the *NACLA Report on the Americas,* May–June 2011, for several astute essays on issues ranging from women traffickers to the sexualization of the violence, media representation, and civil society responses.

85. For their code of conduct, see the Key Safety Systems website, http://www.keysafetyinc.com/pdfs/1031069.pdf.

86. Baird and McCaughan, "Hit and Run," 23.

2. *The Materiality of Affect*

1. On the affective turn, see Clough and Halley, *The Affective Turn.*

2. Hemmings, "Invoking Affect."

3. Michelle Rosaldo, "Toward an Anthropology," 143.

4. For example, see Jaggar, "Love and Knowledge"; Federici, *Caliban and the Witch*; Ann Ferguson, *Blood at the Root* and *Sexual Democracy*; Haug et al., *Female Sexualization*; Rose, *Love, Power, and Knowledge.*

5. Staiger et al. in *Political Emotions* document the work of the Public Feelings group at the University of Texas–Austin and in the Feel Tank at the University of Chicago.

6. In their introduction to *The Affect Theory Reader,* Gregg and Seigworth confirm that the concept of affect has been turned toward all manner of political/pragmatic/performative ends, and they provide a useful typology of some of them (5).

7. Damasio, *Looking for Spinoza,* 164. Following references to this work are indicated with parenthetical citations.

8. Spinoza, *Ethics,* 171.

9. Ibid., 250.

10. Massumi, *Parables*, 85. Following references to this work are indicated with parenthetical citations.

11. Gould, *Moving Politics*, 20.

12. Ibid., 27.

13. Ibid.

14. Ibid., 8.

15. Raymond Williams, *Marxism and Literature*, 134, 130.

16. Damasio, *Looking for Spinoza*, 88.

17. In her readings of popular culture, Beverly Best, "Fredric Jameson Notwithstanding," 71–73, contends that theorists like Massumi do not pay enough attention to the mediating function of the narratives in which affects circulate, many of which carry the same message. In this sense, she maintains, affects are hypernarrated, yet their ideological and discursive narrations, along with their social history, have become virtually invisible.

18. Tompkins, *Affect, Imagery, Consciousness*, 6. Following references to this work are indicated with parenthetical citations.

19. Flatley, *Affective Mapping*.

20. Ibid., 16.

21. Ibid., 18.

22. Brennan, *Transmission*, 6. Following references to this work are indicated with parenthetical citations.

23. On the stickiness of emotions, see Ahmed, *Cultural Politics of Emotion*.

24. Brennan, *Transmission*, 195n4.

25. Grossberg, *We Gotta Get Out*, 82. Following references to this work are indicated with parenthetical citations.

26. Gould, *Moving Politics*, 33.

27. Ahmed, *Cultural Politics of Emotion*, 120.

28. Ibid.

29. Ibid., 212.

30. Jaggar, "Love and Knowledge," 160.

31. Reddy, *The Navigation of Feeling*, 114.

32. Ibid., 94.

33. Ibid., 128.

34. The American Sociological Association organized its Sociology of the Emotions section in 1986. Jasper, *Art of Moral Protest*, 408n5.

35. For example, see Poletta, *Freedom Is an Endless Meeting*, chap. 6; Gould, *Moving Politics*, 28.

36. Some recent key contributions of feminist cultural theory include Ahmed, *Cultural Politics of Emotion* and *The Promise of Happiness*; Berlant, *Compassion* and *Cruel Optimism*; Cvetkovich, *An Archive of Feeling* and *Depression*; Love, *Feeling Backward*; Ngai, *Ugly Feelings*; Puar, *Terrorist Assemblages*.

37. Much of the scholarship on affect and emotion in social movement theory

acknowledges the contributions of earlier theorists of emotion, among them Émile Durkheim, Erving Goffman, Arlie Hochschild. For more recent work on affect in social movement, see Flam and King, *Emotions and Social Movements*; Flam, "Emotions' Map"; Gould, *Moving Politics*; Jasper, *Art of Moral Protest*; Klatch, "Underside of Social Movements"; Polleta, *Freedom Is an Endless Meeting*; Reed, "Emotions in Context." This research is an important resource, especially for its attention to specific social movements. Though many of these researchers concede the influence of historical materialism on their work, it is not, however, the theoretical paradigm from which they approach affect.

38. Gould, *Moving Politics*, 32.

39. Flatley, *Affective Mapping*, 23.

40. Hardt and Negri, *Commonwealth*, 31, 194, 196. It is noteworthy that their collaborative work here and in the *Empire* trilogy grows out of Negri's earlier formulations of affect and value. For example, see Negri, "Value and Affect," from 1999.

41. Ibid., 61.

42. Laclau, *On Populist Reason*, 242.

43. Ibid., 111.

44. Ibid., 115.

45. Ibid., 86.

46. Hemmings, "Invoking Affect."

47. Many feminist approaches to ontology and epistemology acknowledge emotion as a feature of both. For example, see Alcoff, *Feminist Epistemologies*; Bakker and Gil, *Power, Production*; Jaggar, "Feminist Politics and Epistemology" and "Love and Knowledge"; Rose, "Hand, Brain, Heart" and "Love, Power"; and Weeks, *Constituting Subjects*.

48. Affective attachments are not only a basic component of social cooperation but also elements in what Étienne Balibar calls the "other scene" of politics. The extremes of annihilation (of oneself or others) mark the poles of this other scene. We need a fuller accounting of the otherness of this scene and the attachments it performs precisely because they are propelled by the modulation of need by affect. Think of the act that became the spark for uprisings across the Middle East and beyond in spring 2011: Mohammed Bouazizi's self-immolation in Tunisia occurred in reaction to a slap from a female official in public, the last of a long series of daily humiliations and harassments by police as he struggled to support his family by selling fruit at his stand.

49. On the concept of unmet need, see Kelsh, "Desire and Class."

50. Weeks, *Constituting Feminist Subjects*, delineates the contributions of feminist standpoint theory to a fuller understanding of the ontology of labor and of women's laboring practices as value creating. She points to the contributions of Dorothy Smith, Hillary Rose, and Nancy Hartsock. Although Weeks stresses ontology over epistemology, she does make the critical point that much

early feminist standpoint theory emphasizes epistemology in its attention to subjectivity as a somewhat disembodied consciousness.

51. See Weeks, *The Problem with Work*, 113–74, on some of the history of this feminist argument in the context of the Wages for Housework campaigns. She also rightly points out the growing irrelevance of the distinction between productive wage work and reproductive or domestic labor in post-Fordist economies, where the reproductive labor of subject formation, education in norms, know-how, and affective relations increasingly informs labor relations in the marketplace and the reproductive labor of the household is increasingly assimilated into the wage economy.

52. Fortunati, *The Arcane of Reproduction*, 49.

53. Ibid., 95.

54. Ibid., 96.

55. Sue Ferguson, "Building on the Strengths of the Socialist Feminist Movement," *Kendine ait bir oda* (blog), August 9, 2009, http://kendineaitbiroda. wordpress.com/2009/08/09.

56. Engster, "Rethinking Care Theory," 51.

57. Ibid., 52.

58. Ibid., 55.

59. Considerable feminist research has been done on this level of caring labor—for example, Folbre and Bittman, *Family Time*; Fineman, *The Neutered Mother*; Hochschild with Ann Machung, *The Second Shift;* 1997; Okin, *Justice, Gender, and the Family*.

60. Hochschild, "Emotion Work," 563.

61. Lynch and Walsh, "Love, Care, and Solidarity."

62. Much earlier, Michelle Rosaldo had marked the difference between merely hearing a child's cry and "a hearing that is *felt*—as when one realizes that danger is involved or that the child is one's own." As Rosaldo emphasizes, this felt dimension of affect-culture, like what individuals can think and feel generally, is a product of a social formation's cultural organization. "Toward an Anthropology," 143.

63. Boris and Parrañas, *Intimate Labors*.

64. Spivak, "Scattered Speculations," 80.

65. Ibid., 79.

66. Gutiérrez-Rodríguez, *Migration, Domestic Work*, 147.

67. Berlant, "The Subject of True Feeling," 132. See also Berlant, "The Epistemology of State Emotion," as well as *Cruel Optimism*; *The Female Complaint*; *The Queen of America*; and the edited collection *Compassion*.

68. Berlant, "The Subject of True Feeling," 57–58.

69. Sedgwick, *Epistemology*, 86.

70. Gould, *Moving Politics*, 27.

71. Gutiérrez-Rodríguez, *Migration, Domestic Work, and Affect*, 147. See also

Anzaldúa, *Borderlands*; Lorde, "Uses of the Erotic"; Sandoval, *Methodology of the Oppressed.*

72. Gould, *Moving,* 28.

73. Ibid., 265.

3. Bearing Witness

1. Behar, *Vulnerable,* 174.

2. Oliver, *Witnessing.*

3. Berlant, "The Subject of True Feeling." See also her "The Epistemology of State Emotion" and fuller elaborations of this work in *Compassion* and *Cruel Optimism.*

4. There is a considerable archive of work on witnessing in Holocaust studies; notable examples include Agamben, *Remnants*; Felman and Laub, *Testimony*; and La Capra, *Writing History* and *Representing the Holocaust.*

5. Agamben, *Homo Sacer,* 185; *Remnants of Auschwitz,* 33–86.

6. Cubilé, *Women Witnessing Terror,* 2–10.

7. Ibid., 4.

8. In addition to the extensive archive of former slave narratives, see the provocative twenty-first-century representations of the lost history of the Middle Passage in Hartman, *Lose Your Mother*; Philip, *Zong!*; as well as Moten, *In the Break.* All address the affective features of this history as it registers in the sensorium of a black radical tradition.

9. On witnessing through testimony to violence orchestrated by Latin American states, see Logan, "Personal Testimony"; Strejilevich, "Testimony"; Cubilé, "Women Witnessing"; Gugelberger, *The Real Thing*; Saporta Sternbach, "Remembering the Dead"; Somer, "Not Just a Personal Story."

10. Cubilé, *Women Witnessing Terror,* 144.

11. Behar, *Vulnerable Observer,* 27. See also Beverly, *Testimonio*; Gugelberger, *The Real Thing.*

12. Somer, "Not Just a Personal Story," 118.

13. Hale, *Engaging Contradictions,* 20–21.

14. Compassion has been most recently and notoriously deployed in political discourse in the United States as the signature phrase "compassionate conservatism" during the first administration of George W. Bush. The collection of essays from the Harvard English Institute *Compassion: The Culture and Politics of an Emotion,* edited by Lauren Berlant, takes up this circulation of the discourse of compassion and offers several compelling analyses of its genealogy and significance. See especially essays by Berlant; Garber; Woodward.

15. In her analysis of the testimonies of mothers of the disappeared and murdered women of Juárez, Melissa Wright addresses the complicated emotional tenor of testimony that employs the discourse of family by referring to victims of violence as "daughters" and positioning families in the front of the organiz-

ing efforts. Her analysis demonstrates that emotional bonds can spur action but also prevent broadened support for a movement. See Wright, "Justice and the Geographies" and "Witnessing."

16. Saporta Sternbach, "Re-membering the Dead," 94–95.

17. In "Affective Economies," Sarah Ahmed argues that the bond of empathy expands the audience's own identity to include that of the testifier, such that the experience of the testifier and her quest for justice become the audience's. Geraldine Pratt, in "Circulating Sadness," also acknowledges empathy as an identification based on an emotional bond that can be a catalyst for shifting an audience from the position of spectator to witness and action. In *Affective Mapping,* Jonathan Flatley addresses empathy as it operates in the context of therapy, a space that shares certain features with witnessing in that here one can turn a melancholic relation to the past into a critical reflection upon one's subjectivity. Flatley argues that it is the emotional tie established in the space of therapy that enables one to live with the return of ghostly, melancholic memories.

18. Yúdice, "*Testimonio* and Postmodernism." For other examples of obstacles to witnessing, see Angel-Ajani, "Expert Witness"; Silvey, "Envisioning Justice."

19. Ibid., 24.

20. Clifford, *The Predicament of Culture*; Clifford and Marcus, *Writing Culture*; Hale, *Engaging Contradictions*; Scheper-Hughes, "The Primacy of the Ethical"; Speed, "Forged in Dialogue."

21. Behar, *Vulnerable Observer,* 14.

22. Hale, *Engaging Contradictions,* 20.

23. Ibid.

24. Gilmore, "Public Enemies."

25. Oliver, *Witnessing,* 7. Following references to this work are indicated with parenthetical citations.

26. Grossberg, *We Gotta Get Out,* 6.

27. Flatley, *Affective Mapping,* 7. Following references to this work are indicated with parenthetical citations.

28. Ibid., 93.

29. This phrase is taken from Robyn Wiegman, who writes in *Object Lessons* about the tutelage of the mistake that instructs her as a feminist in "how to find a way to live in critical practice without giving in to arguments that are never adequate to the world they stand for—even as I do and have and am giving in" (297). See also Halberstam, *Queer Art of Failure,* on the critical advantages of embracing mistakes and wrong turns as crucial to the democratic visions of feminist and queer resistance.

30. Gordon, *Ghostly Matters,* 43, 45. Following references to this work are indicated with parenthetical citations.

31. Gordon, 45.

32. Renato Rosaldo, *Culture and Truth,* 11–17.

33. Flatley, *Affective Mapping,* 100.
34. Gordon, *Ghostly Matters,* 46.
35. Freud, *The Standard Edition,* 14:169.
36. Ibid., 170.
37. Gordon, *Ghostly Matters,* 48.
38. Ibid., 119.

4. Open Secrets

1. The most notable examples are Foucault, *The History of Sexuality,* vol. 1, and Sedgwick, *Epistemology of the Closet.*
2. Foucault, *History of Sexuality,* 1:11.
3. Gordon, *Ghostly Matters,* 8.
4. Ibid.
5. Ibid.
6. The classic analysis of this process is D'Emilio, "Capitalism and Gay Identity." See also Floyd, *Reification of Desire.*
7. Roger Lancaster used the phrase "public secret" to refer to a "unifying thread" in the representation of homosexuality in Latin America, which is "more complex than the North American concept of 'the closet.'" Here, "one is neither completely hidden nor, short of catastrophe, completely exposed, but always, it would seem, on the cusp of the two. . . . The taboo is not against knowing or acting but against speaking." "Tolerance and Intolerance," 261. The norm he teases out involves degrees of tolerance for discourse and display in some public spaces and rigidly prescribed silence in others. His argument is aimed, in part, at claims that a recent upsurge in antigay violence is attributable to the culture of *machismo.* His point is that this backlash may be seen as an effect of the unraveling of the pact of the public secret. He does not address, however, the ways the public secret features in either the context of Mexico's northern border towns or in the practice of organizing there. Annick Prieur's research on transvestites in Mexico City echoes the point that homosexuality in Mexico is "neither socially accepted nor stigmatized . . . so long as it remains relatively invisible, so long as it is kept within a purely male context, so long as it is not talked about, so long as certain rules are respected, and so long as it is *euphemized.*" *Mema's House,* 188–89.
8. Reding, *Question and Answer Series.*
9. In his study of the cultural context of sex between men in the northern border region of Hermosillo, Sonora, Guillermo Núñez Noriega identifies the shared discourses of Christianity and medicine, in a sometimes confused amalgam, as comprising one of the principal hegemonic discourses defining the field of sexuality in the region, the other being the discourse of consumption that promotes the satisfaction of desires. He contends that the discourse of consumption has relaxed gender norms and the censorship of the body and

marginalized sexualities, but within the limits of a heteronormative paradigm. His argument could be extended to other northern border regions. See *Sexo entre varones*, 99, 105.

10. In 1999 Mexico's federal penal code was reformed to eliminate homosexual activity as an aggravating factor in corruption-of-minor cases. In 2001 Article 1 of the Mexican Constitution was amended to prohibit discrimination based on sexual orientation (*preferencias*), among other factors. In 2003 a federal law was passed that prevents and eliminates discrimination based on sexual preference, and in 2004 the Consejo Nacionale para Prevenir la Descriminación (National Anti-discrimination Council; CONAPRED) was created to implement and administer it.

11. Ley Federal del Trabajo, article 47.2, 8.

12. According to the NGO Citizens' Commission against Homophobic Hate Crimes, there were 332 homophobic killings across Mexico between 1995 and 2004. Based on 1,482 interviews with members of the general public and with 200 self-identified homosexuals, respondents indicated that discrimination against homosexuals was common in Mexican society. See Research Directorate of the Immigration and Refugee Board of Canada, *Mexico*.

13. Reding, *Question and Answer Series*. See also CONAPRED, "El combate a la homofobia: Entre avances y desafíos," CONAPRED website, 2012, http://www.conapred.org.mx/index.php?contenido=documento&id=105&id_opcion=106&op=21; and CONAPRED, "Documento informativo de homofobia," 2010, http://www.equidad.scjn.gob.mx/spip.php?page=ficha_biblioteca&id_article=1336, which indicates that 59 percent of people surveyed say being homosexual in Mexico puts you at risk.

14. Alexander Lujo considers new notions of *machismo* in factory culture. Leslie Salzinger looks at how managers' emasculation of men on the assembly lines provokes dominating behaviors. Pablo Vila reads masculinity at the border as an identifier of national difference. Kathleen Staudt investigates the backlash that has provoked increased domestic violence as a control strategy men use to direct their frustrations at the convenient target of their women partners.

15. See Cantú, *Sexuality of Migration*, esp. chap. 4.

16. Roger Lancaster makes the point that *machismo* is not simply about male dominance over women. It is as much a means of structuring power among men and securing one's association with masculine activity. "Like drinking, gambling, risk taking, asserting one's opinions, and fighting, the conquest of women is a feat performed with two audiences in mind: first, other men, to whom one must constantly prove one's masculinity and virility; and second, oneself, to whom one must also show all signs of masculinity. *Machismo,* then, is a matter of constantly asserting one's masculinity by way of practices that show the self to be 'active,' not 'passive.'" *Life Is Hard,* 236–37.

17. For example, see Parades, "The United States"; Gutmann, *Meanings of Macho.*

18. One of the classic critiques of these connotations of *machismo* is Américo Paredes's 1971 genealogy of the term, which draws out its emergence in folk and national culture after the Mexican Revolution and the cultural similarities and borrowings between North American and Mexican versions. See Parades, "The United States."

19. Cantú with Luibhéid and Stern, "Well-Founded Fear," 66–67, offers an instructive and strong critique of Andrew Reding's report for its ahistorical representation of Mexican sex–gender culture and the difficulties it poses for asylum cases, among them the equation of effeminacy with certain forms of homosexuality and the erasure of lesbians.

20. For example, see the work of Patricia Ponce or Carter Wilson on Veracruz, Lionel Cantú on tourism, Cymene Howe on gay migration from Guadalajara to San Diego, and Lynn Stephen on Oaxaca.

21. Carrier, *De los Otros*; Carillo, *Night Is Young*, 37–41; Domínguez-Ruvalcaba, *Modernity*; Kelly, *Lydia's Open Door*; Lancaster, *Life Is Hard*; Gutmann, *Meanings of Macho*. See Stephen, "Sexualities and Genders," on historical evidence of three or more genders among the Zapotec and other indigenous peoples in the Americas, as well as contemporary examples of the *biza'ah* and *muxe* of Oaxaca. On the *muxe,* see also Chiñas, "Isthmus Zapotec."

22. Cantú, *Sexuality of Migration,* 139. In her research on transvestites in Mexico City, Annick Prieur also found that the *vestidas'* (cross-dressers') gender constructions could not be understood simply in terms of masculinity and femininity.

23. Domínguez-Ruvalcaba, *Modernity,* 132. Sources for one researcher say, however, that despite this distinction, *mayates,* or men who *lo hacen para penetrarlos* (do it to penetrate), in the end *piden ser penetrados* (ask to be penetrated), testifying to the practices that undermine neat cultural distinctions. On the ways cross-border migration, class, and location are factors in the relation of sexual-object choice and the sexual role for men who have sex with men, see Cantú, *Sexuality of Migration*; Carrier, *De los Otros*; Lancaster, "On Homosexualities"; and Philen, "Geography of Sex."

24. Núñez Noriega, *Sexo entre varones,* 209–10.

25. Castillo et al., "Violence," 16–17.

26. "Los travesties suelen ser usados como dipósito de frustraciones y de males que padece la comunidad." Núñez Noriega, *Sexo entre varones,* 243.

27. See Howe, *Intimate Pedagogies,* for a discussion of the changing value attached to the derogatory term *cochona* in Nicaragua and the impact of the circulation of the new term *lesbian* (lesbian) in international human rights discourse on sexuality, sexual identity, choice, and love.

28. Ponce, "Sexualidades costeñas."

29. In his path-breaking work on sex between men in Hermosillo, Núñez Noriega addresses the limited public range of the counterdiscourse of its *ambiente* (gay community), which is mostly confined to the university, strategic

positions in the media, and a few organizations concerned with sexuality and health. *Sexo entre varones,* 116.

30. Molly Hennessy-Fiske, "On the Border," *Advocate,* June 2000, 40.

31. For several examples from the Hermosillo newspaper *Imparcial,* see Núñez Noriega, *Sexo entre varones,* 94.

32. Taussig, *Defacement,* 6.

33. Ibid.

34. EZLN, *Documentos y comunicados,* 98; see also Marcos, *Shadows of Tender Fury,* 86.

35. "Zapatistas on Gay Rights: 'Let Those Who Persecute Be Ashamed!,'" *Green Left,* July 21, 1999, http://www.greenleft.org.au/node/19235.

36. See Manolo, "Zapatistas' Theoretical Revolution," in *The Darker Side of Western Modernity,* for a fuller explanation of the process of double translation this reorientation of democracy entails and its relation to the concept of dignity as opposed to rights.

37. Taussig, *Defacement,* 238, 242.

38. Gobernación is the short name for the federal police from Mexico's National Security and Investigation Center (CISEN).

39. Interestingly, masks also feature in the history of the term *matachine,* which was adopted by Harry Hay as the name for the homophile organization he founded in 1950. *Matachines* were members of a mysterious French medieval society of unmarried figures, akin to tricksters, who wore masks and conducted rituals and sometimes public protests. See Vaid, *Virtual Equality,* 49–50.

40. McLean and Leibling, *Shadow Side,* xi.

41. Lumsden, *Homosexuality and the State,* 77.

42. Drucker, introduction to *Different Rainbows.*

43. Lumsden, *Homosexuality and the State,* 64–65; Research Directorate of the Immigration and Refugee Board of Canada, *Mexico.*

44. Taussig, *Defacement,* 62.

45. Gluckman, "Gossip and Scandal," 308.

46. In *Freedom Is an Endless Meeting,* 167, Francesca Poletta addresses friendship in social movement in the context of the 1970s' U.S. women's movement. See also Lugones and Rosezelle, "Sisterhood and Friendship."

47. Gordon, *Ghostly Matters,* 8.

5. The Value of a Second Skin

1. Prosser credits Dedier Anzieu's analysis of the "skin ego" for conceptualizing this interface between psyche and body and for highlighting the experience of the material skin as crucial in the formation of a sense of self. *Second Skins,* 65. See Anzieu, *The Skin Ego.*

2. In a reading that is critical of Prosser yet advances his general argument for the important ontological role of the body in sexed subjectivity, Sven

Brandenburg, in "The Perfection," emphasizes that psychic investment arises from perception. He contends that the notion of perception underscoring the neoconstructionist version of gender draws upon a rationalist account of perception that confuses being with appearance, idea with image. As a result, it forecloses the processes involved in the mediation of perception, the formation of the unconscious, of a gestalt, or visual field, and the role of physical difference—the bodily differences with which the subject is confronted. He contends that as one gives meaning to these differences and to one's own body both nature and culture are necessary, though neither serves as a guarantor of meaning. Brandenburg also argues that queer theory has been incapable of accounting for the irreconcilable gap between the felt gendered perception of the transsexual and the visual perception of the physical body that stands in contrast to it.

3. Haraway, "A Cyborg Manifesto," 166.

4. Harvey, "Body as Accumulation Strategy," 405.

5. For example, see the special issue of *GLQ* "Queer Studies and the Crisis of Capitalism," edited by Jordana Rosenberg and Amy Villarejo, especially the essays in that issue by Meg Wesling on queer value and by Janet Jakobsen on perverse justice and the roundtable discussion on queer studies, materialism, and crisis.

6. For a fuller development of their arguments, see Jakobsen, "Can Homosexuals End"; Joseph, *Against the Romance,* esp. chap. 2. For an analysis that carries Jakobsen's elaboration of Spivak's argument on value to the U.S. side of the U.S.–Mexico border, see Zimmerman, "Learning to Stand."

7. Spivak, "Scattered Speculations," 79.

8. Ibid.

9. Ibid., 57. Joseph makes a similar point in *Against the Romance.*

10. Jakobsen, "Can Homosexuals End," 58.

11. Butler, *Gender Trouble,* 133.

12. Flatley, *Affective Mapping,* 79.

13. Ibid., 101. The designation of confession as a "structure of feeling" is Flatley's.

14. Jakobsen, "Can Homosexuals End," 58.

15. Race also is a second skin, of course. Though in its representations skin color is often invoked, it is also overwritten by other terms of abjection, including "feminization." In Mexico racial abjection is coded "dark skinned" or "Indian." The range of signifiers it carries is evident in the description of racial discrimination offered by Alfonso Carrión, a member of the Mexican Labor Party: "Because you arrive [some place] dirty and badly dressed, or hardworking, then he or she is rendered an 'Indian.'" Saldaña-Portillo, *Revolutionary Imagination,* 228.

16. Valentine, *Imagining Transgender,* 65.

17. Grant, Motett, and Tanis, *Injustice at Every Turn.*

18. See Núñez Noriega's interviews in *Sexo entre varones*, 243–46. He also refers to similar comments on the class position of *travestis* (cross-dressers) interviewed by Annike Prieur in *Mema's House*, who suggests that the subculture of gender nonconformity is more common among the working class. For an argument that presents a more accepting perspective, see Ponce, "Sexualidades costeñas."

19. Wright, *Disposable Women*, 27–9.

20. Carmen is the name Andrés adopted. She did not discuss with me why or when she changed her name. I refer to her for the most part as Carmen, the name she used to introduce herself. The slips between Carmen and Andrés in her story mark both the gender complexity of her life and the places where feminism's attention to gender discrimination and queer attention to gender performativity meet.

21. Douglas, *Purity and Danger*, 114–28.

22. Ibid., 115.

23. Haraway, "A Cyborg Manifesto," 166.

24. Salzinger, *Genders in Production*, 36–47; Van Waas, "Multinational Strategy for Labor," 357.

25. Pearson, "Male Bias," 140.

26. Salzinger, *Genders in Production*, 43; Lugo, *Fragmented Lives*, 78.

27. Fabián, a *travesti* interviewed by Guillermo Núñez Noriega, said that he fought with many businesses that considered homosexuals denigrated persons and did not accept him and that he tried for years to get work as a janitor but was never called back. In the end he worked only where he was accepted, in the red zone. *Sexo entre varones*, 125.

28. Van Waas, quoted in Salsinger, *Genders in Production*, 37, refers to a manager during the boom years in the 1980s, when the labor supply of women was short, requesting gay men "as queer and feminine as possible," adding, "If I can't have women, I'll get as close to them as I can."

29. Nuñez Noriega, *Sexo entre varones*, 125; translation mine.

30. What he said was, "Se iba a salar porque yo era gay." *Irse a salar* is a Mexican expression meaning "to be turned to salt"—perhaps, a reference to Lot's wife. It means you have been cursed and will have to go to a *curandero* (healer) to have a *limpia* (ritual cleansing).

31. Marx, *Capital*, 1:178.

32. Ibid., 270.

33. Ibid., 271.

34. Reddy, *The Navigation of Feeling*, 104.

35. Monárrez Fragoso, "Victims of Cuidad Juárez," 62.

36. Salzinger, *Genders in Production*, 38.

37. Ibid., 39–40.

38. Ibid., 41.

39. Wright, "Dialectics of Still Life," 454.

40. For a history of some of the debates on homosexual identity, class, and socialism among radical groups from the early to the late twentieth century, see D'Emilio, *Sexual Politics* and *Making Trouble*; Hennessy, "Thinking Sex Materially"; Sears, "Queer Anti-capitalism"; Wolf, *Sexuality and Socialism.*

41. The phrase "the straight mind" is the title of Monique Wittig's now classic text. Although she does not embrace the formulation "queer," her critique of heterosexuality is an important materialist intervention. On this point, see Hennessy, "Queer Theory."

42. Butler, *Gender Trouble.*

43. Quiroga, *Tropics of Desire,* 7.

44. Eng, Halberstam, and Muñoz, "What's Queer?," 1.

45. Ibid., 2.

46. Agathangelo et al., "Intimate Investments"; Puar, *Terrorist Assemblages.*

47. Domínguez-Ruvalcaba, *Modernity and the Nation*; Geviser and Cameron, *Defiant Desire*; Green, "Desire and Militancy"; Jackson, Jieyu, and Juhyun, *East Asian Sexualities*; Johnson and Henderson, *Black Queer Studies.*

48. Bakker and Gill, *Power, Production,* 17.

6. Feeling Bodies, Jeans, Justice

1. Levi Strauss & Co., also known informally as Levi's, is the trademark name of the privately held international garment manufacturing and marketing company, makers of Levi's jeans and other brands.

2. The deregulation of life that neoliberalism has intensified is endemic to capitalism. The early writings of Marx make this point, as does much of the work of western Marxism, especially that of Walter Benjamin and Herbert Marcuse. For a more recent study that explicitly draws upon branches of this tradition regarding the impact of capitalist deregulation on affective attachments, see Flatley, *Affective Mapping.*

3. Brennan, *Globalization and Its Terrors,* 17. Following references to this work are indicated with parenthetical citations.

4. Brennan rightly points out that the most rushed of the rushed are wage-working mothers.

5. Hyperexploitation has a social geography that includes sectors of the advanced capitalist global north, though proportionately more of these conditions of life are concentrated in the global south.

6. Ojeda and Hennessy, *NAFTA from Below,* 91.

7. To give one example, in 2011 the U.S. Bureau of Labor Statistics reported a 4 percent increase in musculoskeletal disorders with days away from work. Bureau of Labor Statistics news release, BLS website, November 8, 2012, www.bls.gov/news.release/pdf/osh2.pdf. In 2002 OSHA reported that 1.8 million workers annually have injuries related to overexertion or repetitive motion, with 600,000 injured severely enough to require time off from work.

8. In many maquilas the company provides transportation, but the costs for it are deducted from the workers' wages. In one instance, the Sony workers eventually got buses only after the workers collectively organized and exercised their own resourcefulness to find three old school buses in the United States that Mexican customs finally let them bring across the bridge.

9. Literally, the phrase means "fresh meat," but *carne* also suggests "flesh" in the sexual sense.

10. Duggan, *The Twilight of Equality?*, 44–50. Lisa Duggan smartly analyses gay civil rights organizations like the Human Rights Campaign and groups them within the mainstreaming of sexual politics that she calls "Equality, Inc."

11. John Cloud, "The Battle over Gay Teens," *Time,* October 2, 2005, 51.

12. Evidence of workplace discrimination against lesbian and gay individuals has been reviewed and summarized in two reports by the Williams Institute at the UCLA School of Law: a 2009 report focused on discrimination in the public sector and a 2007 report focused on employment discrimination in the private sector. The General Social Survey (GSS), a national probability survey representative of the U.S. population, found in 2008 that of LGB respondents, 27 percent had experienced at least one form of sexual orientation–based discrimination during the five years prior to the survey. More specifically, 27 percent had experienced workplace harassment, and 7 percent had lost a job. The GSS found that among LGB people who were open about their sexual orientation in the workplace, an even larger proportion, 38 percent, experienced at least one form of discrimination during the five years prior to the survey.

13. Duggan, *Twilight of Equality?*, 44–50. See also Valverde, "A New Entity," on the emergence of the respectable same-sex couple.

14. For a much fuller argument on this point, see do Mar Castro Varela et al., *Hegemony and Heteronormativity*; Richard Kim and Lisa Duggan, "Beyond Gay Marriage," *Nation,* July 18, 2005; and Julie Torrant's insightful analysis of the new family in *The Material Family.*

15. See, for example, some of the comments of consumers interviewed in Valeria Manzano's fascinating study of the blue jean generation in Argentina. See also Levi's promotion of its dENiZEN line in Asia, launched in 2010: "Throughout your life, jeans are a constant, a second skin." See Levi's India's Facebook post from August 29, 2012, https://www.facebook.com/gauravlevis/posts/335631229863289.

16. For a detailed history of Levi Strauss & Co., see Schoenberger, *Levi's Children.*

17. For more on the Levi Strauss Foundation, see Levi Strauss Foundation home page, Levi Strauss & Co. website, http://www.levistrauss.com/about/foundations/levi-strauss-foundation.

18. Schoenberger, *Levi's Children,* 27. The piece-rate system fostered individualism and relentless competition between workers and contributed to the deterioration of social relationships among workers.

19. Miriam Ching Louie, "Life on the Line," *New Internationalist,* June 5, 1998, http://www.newint.org/issue302/sweat.html.

20. These locations include Costa Rica, Mexico, Guatemala, the Dominican Republic, Brazil, the Philippines, South Korea, China, Hong Kong, Taiwan, Macao, Thailand, Malaysia, Singapore, Bangladesh, India, Pakistan, Sri Lanka, and Indonesia. For a catalog of abuses of Levi's workers from Saipan to Mexico, see Louie, "Life on the Line."

21. Mary Owen, "Levi Strauss Workers Fight for Jobs," *Workers World,* http://www.workers.org/ww/2000/levi0316.php. Among the fired workers were the 2,000 Mexican and Mexican American women at Levi's Zarzamora plant in San Antonio, Texas. Many of these women had worked for Levi's for over fourteen years when the company moved operations to Costa Rica. They filed a lawsuit against Levi Strauss & Co. and lost, but Fuerza Unida, a group that formed in the struggle for their rights, brought Levi's sweatshop labor practices into the national spotlight by picketing and staging hunger strikes at Levi's headquarters. The organization Fuerza Unida still exists and from its San Antonio base is involved in struggles for women's and labor rights and for immigration and environmental issues. See the Fuerza Unida website, http://www.lafuerzaunida.org; see also Zugman, "Political Consciousness."

22. Stuart Elliott, "Levi Strauss Begin a Far-reaching Marketing Campaign to Reach Gay Men and Lesbians," *New York Times,* October 19, 1998.

23. Excerpts from the Commercial Closet, which monitors representations of gay subjects in advertising, including this ad, can be accessed through the Human Rights Campaign website, http://www.hrc.org.

24. Ibid.

25. "Dustin," Levi's commercial, 0:30, 1998, Ad Respect website, http://www.adrespect.org/common/adlibrary/adlibrarydetails.cfm?QID=92&ClientID=11064.

26. Shannon Jones, "Jeans Maker Levi Strauss to Cut 5,900 Jobs in the U.S. and Canada," World Socialist Web Site, February 26, 1999, http://www.wsws.org/articles/1999/feb1999/levi-f26.shtml.

27. "In 2000, firms in the Torreón area were producing an average of six million garments a week, of which 90% were exported. Jeans accounted for 75% of the exported apparel, and thus the region made over four million pairs of jeans each week. In contrast, El Paso, Texas—Torreon's predecessor as the blue jeans capital of the world and a major manufacturing center for Levi Strauss & Co. before the company closed its last factories there in 1999—produced two million pairs of jeans a week at its peak in the early 1980s." Gary Gereffi, "Export-Oriented Growth and Industrial Upgrading: Lessons from the Mexican Apparel Case," Sociology Department website, Duke University, January 31, 2005, http://www.soc.duke.edu/~ggere/web/torreon_report_worldbank.pdf.

28. For a more detailed history of the La Laguna region, see the testimony of

Julio César Ramírez and Reyes Edelmira Hernández Rodríguez in Ojeda and Hennessy, *NAFTA from Below,* 114–18.

29. The list of chemicals includes potassium, which with prolonged exposure, can cause cancer; hydrogen peroxide, which creates toxic steam; and liquid sosa caustica, which is highly toxic and corrosive in contact with the skin and when ingested or breathed causes irritation to the respiratory system and is poisonous. Sodium is used in the factory as a bleaching agent and causes serious irritation when in contact with the skin; oxalic acid, another chemical used, causes serious skin irritation and respiratory problems.

30. Companies are legally obligated to pay 25 percent of wages into a fund for workers' health benefits and housing. In time workers can participate in a housing lottery, and accumulated funds from the harvested 25 percent of wages can be used for a down payment. Only some workers are awarded housing, however, and many never see the housing to which their wages contribute.

31. Michael Kobori, vice president in charge of supply chain social and environmental sustainability at Levi Strauss & Co., in a phone conference, May 2006.

32. This point is made in a report funded by the Levi Strauss Foundation and carried out by the Universidad Autónoma Metropolitana, Mexico. See Graciela Bensusan, "Norms, Practices, and Perceptions: Labour Enforcement in Mexico's Garment Industry," Maquila Solidarity Network website, November 21, 2008, http://en.maquilasolidarity.org/node/820; Klein, *No Logo.*

33. Ojeda and Hennessy, *NAFTA from Below,* 122.

34. This decision came on the heel of debates over China's most-favored-nation trade status based on its poor human rights record, which included imprisonment of demonstrators from the 1989 Tiananmen Square event. The campaign was led in the U.S. Congress by San Francisco representative Nancy Pelosi.

35. James T. Areddy, "Levi's Faced Earlier Challenge in China," *Wall Street Journal,* January 14, 2010.

36. White Knot for Equality website, Levi's store locations, accessed May 11, 2013, http://whiteknot.org/levis.html.

37. Press release, Levi Strauss & Co. website, June 24, 2012, http://www.levistrauss.com/news/press-releases/levis-proclaims-we-are-all-workers-launch-latest-go-forth-marketing-campaign.

38. Docker's home page, Levi Strauss & Co. website, accessed May 11, 2013, http://www.levistrauss.com/brands/dockers.

39. Dara Colwell, "Levis: Made in China?," *AlterNet,* May 8, 2002, http://www.alternet.org/story/13095.

7. *The North–South* Encuentros

1. For their contributions to this account of the encuentros, I thank the residents of the colonia Blanca Navidad in Tamaulipas and the Zapatista

communities of Chiapas, who shared their history with me, as well as the staff of CJM, who organized all of these meetings. In the multiple visits I made to Blanca Navidad, colonia residents were warm and generous. They invited me to learn their stories through formal interviews and informal conversations, and they welcomed me into the audiences gathered for their public presentations. Four autonomous communities in Chiapas also graciously welcomed me in 2003 and enabled my conversations with many community members there.

2. The Spanish phrases *grupos de base* and *organizaciones de base* translate colloquially as "grassroots groups" and "grassroots organizations," respectively. They have replaced the phrase *comunidades de base* (grassroots communities), as some groups have wanted to distance themselves from the discourse of liberation theology in Latin America with which *comunidades de base* is associated. Some groups who have histories tied to Catholic-based organizing continue to use it, however, whereas others with more secular aims use these terms.

3. For an excellent overview of the accomplishments and challenges of Mexican feminism, see Lamas, *Feminismo*.

4. In her visit to the colonia Blanca Navidad on May 12, 2007, Comandanta Myriam referred to the indigenous peoples of Chiapas as the country's "most forgotten ones." For a similar concept of "forgotten places," see Ruth Gilmore, *Golden Gulag*, a work based on her powerful, engaged research on prison-based organizing in the United States.

5. Among all Latin American countries, Mexico has the largest absolute number of citizens who define themselves as indigenous—around twelve million people. States with the highest proportion of indigenous are in the south: Yucatán, Oaxaca, Quintana Roo, Chiapas, and Campeche. See Gledhill, "Introduction," 485.

6. The EZLN itself, as well as many scholars and critics, has written about the recasting of indigenous subjectivity that the uprising and the continued political presence of the Zapatistas have enacted. See Subcomandante Marcos, "Sixth Declaration of the Selva Lacandona," translated by irlandesa, *Znet*, July 2, 2005, http://www.zcommunications.org/sixth-declaration-of-the-selva-lacandona-by-subcomandante-marcos; Government of the State of Chiapas, *Los acuerdos de San Andrés*; Marcos, *Shadows of Tender Fury*; Saldaña-Portillo, *Revolutionary Imagination*; Ramírez, *20 y 10*; Womack, *Rebellion in Chiapas*.

7. Under NAFTA, all nontariff barriers to agricultural trade between the United States and Mexico were eliminated. In January 2008 NAFTA's Agricultural Provisions were completed, and they did away with tariffs on corn, dry edible beans, sugar, nonfat dry milk, and high-fructose corn syrup. The resulting impact on Mexican agriculture has been a detonator for migration from agricultural regions, including Chiapas.

8. Esteva and Pérez, "The Meaning and Scope," 14.

9. Ojeda and Hennessy, *NAFTA from Below*, 46–59.

10. Government of the State of Chiapas, *Los acuerdos de San Andrés*.

11. Scott, *Domination and the Arts,* 21.

12. Speed et al., *Dissident Women,* 16–17.

13. This visit was documented by Gustavo Castro, then director of CIEPAC, in "Las maquiladoras: Cárcel de mujeres," *Rebelión,* June 27, 2005, http://www.rebelion.org/noticia.php?id=17045.

14. Mora, "Zapatista Anti-capitalist Politics"; Gledhill, "Introduction"; Zugman, "The Other Campaign."

15. Williams, "The Mexican Exception," 147.

16. The phrase "make the road while walking" comes from the refrain of the poem "Caminante no hay camino" by Antonio Machado, which was adopted by grassroots organizers across the Americas: "Caminante no hay camino / se hace camino al andar" (Traveler there is no road / the road is made by walking). See *We Make the Road by Walking,* an exchange between Miles Horton and Paulo Friere.

17. Gledhill, "Introduction," 488.

18. Mattiace, "Mayan Utopias," 188.

19. Esteva and Pérez, "The Meaning and Scope," 253.

20. Ibid., 128–29.

21. Government of the State of Chiapas, *Los acuerdos de San Andrés,* 45–46.

22. Ibid.; Barmeyer, "Guerilla Movement"; Stephen, "Redefined Nationalism." For extended discussion of the multiple understandings of autonomy among Mexican indigenous groups, see Stephen, "Zapatista Opening" and "Redefined Nationalism."

23. Gledhill, "Introduction," 494; Ojeda and Hennessy, *NAFTA from Below.*

24. Speed et al., *Dissident Women,* 3–32; Forbis, "Autonomy and a Handful," 186. The ten points included in the Zapatistas' Revolutionary Women's Law are as follows: (1) women, regardless of their race, creed, color, or political affiliation, have the right to participate in the revolutionary struggle in a way determined by their desire and capacity; (2) women have the right to work and receive a just salary; (3) women have the right to decide the number of children they can have and care for; (4) women have the right to participate in community affairs and to hold office if they are freely and democratically elected; (5) women and their children have the right to primary consideration in their health and nourishment; (6) women have the right to education; (7) women have the right to select their partner and not be forced to marry; (8) no woman shall be beaten or physically mistreated by her family members or strangers, and the crimes of rape and attempted rape will be severely punished; (9) women can occupy leadership positions and hold military rank in the revolutionary armed forces; and (10) women will have all the rights and duties stated in the Revolutionary Laws and Regulations.

25. Belausteguigoitia, "The Right to Rest."

26. Section 3.5 of the accords—which contains the only mention of women—states the following: "Social policy must set up priority programs

for the improvement of the levels of health and nourishment of children, as well as support programs, in an egalitarian plane, for the training of women, increasing their participation in the organization and the development of the family and the community. Priority must be given to the intervention of the indigenous woman in the decisions regarding economic, political, social and cultural development projects."

27. In "Autonomy and a Handful of Herbs," Melissa Forbis observes that efforts to contain Zapatista women who got involved in health projects that broke from traditional expectations of women often took the form of rumors, gossip, and accusations of infidelity—for example, claiming that some women were going to town not to take classes but to meet lovers (196). Other conflicts involved control of resources because through the classes, women gained access to materials and skills not available to others, as health-related skills could translate into income generation. Examples of communal projects being undermined included course materials meant for the whole community that were sometimes kept by one person or communal gardens for growing medicinal herbs being invaded by marijuana growers (196–97).

28. Forbis, "Hacía la Autonomia," 236.

29. Stephen, "Gender Citizenship," 60–61.

30. Ibid., 63.

31. Nash, "Women in Between," 160; Earle and Simonelli, *Uprising of Hope,* 267.

32. Eber, "Seeking Our Own Food"; Forbis, "Hacía la Autonomía" and "Autonomy and a Handful"; Mora, "Zapatista Anti-capitalist Politics"; Stahler-Sholk, "A World"; Olivera, "Subordination and Rebellion."

33. Forbis, "Hacía la Autonomía."

34. Agamben, *Homo Sacer,* 9.

35. Ziarek, "Bare Life on Strike," 92.

36. Laclau, "Bare Life;" 14; Ziarek, "Bare Life on Strike," 92–93, 98.

37. Ziarek, "Bare Life on Strike," 96.

38. Kovic and Eber, *Women of Chiapas,* 1.

39. Speed, "Actions Speak Louder," 51.

40. In the Cumbre de los Pueblos in Mexico City in July 2012, held in preparation for the parallel meetings in Los Cabos protesting the G20 summit, a panel of Mexican women circulated as their statement this community-based, women-focused politics of *feminismo comunitario.* See Ecuador Decide website, blog post, May 14, 2012, http://ecuadordecidenotlc.blogspot.com/2012/05/f-o-r-o-el-g20-desde-una-mirada.html.

41. Ibid.

8. Love in the Common

1. The rescripting of love and the erotic have been feminist preoccupations for generations, but many of these critical undertakings do not share the argu-

ment I make. Nonetheless, the case I make here and in chapter 2 for the importance of taking into account the affect-culture of social movement is indebted to their insights. For example, see Huffer, "Eros in Biopower" and *Mad for Foucault*; Kollontai, *Selected Writings*; Lorde, "Uses of the Erotic"; Sandoval, *Methodology of the Oppressed*.

2. Among the major books published within the past decade that elaborate a politics of affirmation are Fredric Jameson's *Archaeologies of the Future*; Alain Badiou's *The Communist Hypothesis*; Slavoj Žižek's *Living in the End Times* and *The Year of Dreaming Dangerously*; Sara Ahmed's *The Promise of Happiness*; J. K. Gibson-Graham's *A Postcapitalist Politics*; José Muñoz's *Cruising Utopia*; Maria Josefina Saldaña-Portillo's *The Revolutionary Imagination in the Americas in the Age of Development*; and Kathi Weeks's *The Problem with Work*.

3. Adorno, *Minima Moralia*, 155–56.

4. Of course, not all organizing efforts are utopian in this sense. One can think of many counterexamples, and they too entail potent affect-cultures and draw ardent followers—racist or xenophobic organizations, for instance. Like other feminist standpoint theorists, I argue that we can gauge the value of the betterment an organizing effort promises by the quality and scope of the improvements in well-being it promises.

5. Weeks, *The Problem with Work*, chap. 5, offers a very useful overview of some of this theoretical work, especially in the contributions of Ernest Bloch, the autonomous Marxist tradition, and feminism to utopian demands; see also Muñoz, *Cruising Utopia*, for a queer appropriation of Bloch.

6. For example, see Reid and Taylor, *Recovering the Commons*; Gibson-Graham, *Postcapitalist Politics*. For two US-based examples, see Devón Peña's Acequia Institute in Colorado http://www.acequiainstitute.org/; and in West Virginia, the American Folklife project, "Tending the Commons" http://memory.loc.gov/ammem/collections/tending/

7. Jameson, "The Politics of Utopia."

8. Ahmed, *Cultural Politics of Emotion*, 168–69.

9. In the last chapter of her book *The Problem with Work*, U.S. feminist Kathi Weeks puts forward a reading of Bloch's argument on utopian hope that ties it to her case for the importance of utopian demands. She offers an incisive reading of the significance of Bloch's thinking in relation to affective temporality and the autonomous Marxist influence on the feminist Wages for Housework campaign. My reading of Bloch is indebted to her arguments here.

10. Bloch, *The Principle of Hope*, 114; Weeks, *The Problem with Work*, 187. Following references to Bloch, *The Principle of Hope*, are cited parenthetically.

11. George Caffentzis contends that in response to capitalism's most recent political crisis, "the commons has been used by anti-capitalists to show that collective non-capitalist forms of organizing material life are alive and struggling throughout the world in two senses: the pre-capitalist commons still exist and the subsistence of billions of people depend on them . . . and the rise of a new commons, especially in ecological-energy spaces and in computational-informational

manifolds." He argues for a sharper and more specific use of the terms, especially in light of what he calls "Neoliberalism's Plan B"—that is, the use of the commons to save neoliberalism from itself. "Future of 'The Commons,'" 24. For similar arguments, see Federici, *Caliban and the Witch*; Klein, "Reclaiming the Commons"; Žižek, "How to Begin."

12. Nonini, *The Global Idea*, 6–8.

13. Federici, *Caliban and the Witch*, 97; Shiva, *Staying Alive*.

14. Hardt and Negri, *Commonwealth*, 139.

15. Ibid., 182.

16. Ibid., xii.

17. See Berlant, "A Properly Political Concept of Love," for a provocative response to their concept of love.

18. Casarino, *In Praise of the Common*, 22.

19. Harvey, "Body as an Accumulation Strategy," 413.

20. Casarino, *In Praise of the Common*, 30.

21. Damasio, *Looking for Spinoza*, 179.

22. Casarino, *In Praise of the Common*, 180.

23. Gibson-Graham, *Postcapitalist Politics*, 128. The concept "cultivating subjects" is from Gibson-Graham, *Postcapitalist Politics*, 127–63. It is a component of the action research projects with which the authors were involved. The projects entailed sustaining positive affects through embodied, habitual, and emotional practices that mobilized individuals and groups toward new collective enterprises.

24. Scott, *Domination*, 21.

25. See Oliver, "Witnessing the Power of Love," in *Witnessing*, which draws upon the work of intellectuals on love—among them Franz Fanon, Julia Kristeva, bell hooks, and Luce Irigaray—who address love in the sense of an ethic that requires of the subject an openness to the other, vigilance, and movement beyond the desire for recognition.

26. Reid and Taylor, *Recovering the Commons*.

27. Monsiváis, *Mexican Postcards*, 139.

28. Horton, *The Long Haul*, 44.

29. Ibid.

Bibliography

Adorno, Theodor. *Minima Moralia*. London: Verso, 1974.

Agamben, Giorgio. *Homer Sacer: Sovereign Power and Bare Life*. Translated by Daniel Heller-Roazen. Stanford, Calif.: Stanford University Press, 1998.

———. *Remnants of Auschwitz: The Witness and the Archive*. Translated by Daniel Heller-Roazen. New York: Zone, 2000.

Agathangelou, Anna M., Daniel Bassichis, and Tamara Spira. "Intimate Investments: Homonormativity, Global Lockdown, and the Seductions of Empire." *Radical History Review* 100 (Winter 2008): 120–43.

Ahmed, Sara. "Affective Economies." *Social Text* 22, no. 2 (Summer 2004): 117–39.

———. *The Cultural Politics of Emotion*. New York: Routledge, 2004.

———. *The Promise of Happiness*. Durham, N.C.: Duke University Press, 2010.

Alcoff, Linda. *Feminist Epistemologies*. New York: Routledge, 1992.

Alonso, Ana María. *Thread of Blood: Colonialism, Revolution, and Gender on Mexico's Northern Frontier*. Tucson: University of Arizona Press, 1995.

Alonso, Ana María, and María Teresa Korek. "Silences: Hispanics, AIDS, and Sexual Practices." *differences* 1 (1988): 101–24.

Alvarez, Sonia E. "Advocating Feminism: The Latin American Feminist NGO 'Boom.'" *International Feminist Journal of Politics* 1, no. 2 (1999): 181–209.

Alvarez, Sonia E., Elizabeth Jay Friedman, Erika Bekman, Maylei Blackwell, Norma Chinchilla, Nathalie Lebon, Marysa Navarro, and Marcela Ríos Tobar. "Encountering Latin American and Caribbean Feminisms." *Signs* 28, no. 2 (2003): 537–39.

Amnesty International. *Ten Years of Abductions and Murders of Women in Cuidad Juárez and Chihuahua*. Amnesty International, 2003. http://www.amnesty.org/en/library/asset/AMR41/026/2003/en/a62f0982-d6c3-11dd-ab95-a13b602c0642/amr410262003en.pdf.

Angel-Ajani, Asale. "Expert Witness: Notes toward Revisiting the Politics of Listening." *Anthropology and Humanism* 29, no. 2 (2004): 133–44.

Anzaldúa, Gloria. *Borderlands/La Frontera*. 3rd ed. San Francisco: Aunt Lute Books, 2007.

Anzieu, Didier. *The Skin Ego*. New Haven, Conn.: Yale University Press, 1989.

Bacon, David. *Children of NAFTA: Labor Wars on the U.S./Mexico Border.* Berkeley: University of California Press, 2005.

Badgett, M. V. Lee. "Discrimination Based on Sexual Orientation: A Review of the Literature in Economics and Beyond." In *Sexual Orientation Discrimination: An International Perspective,* edited by M. V. Lee Badgett and Jefferson Frank, 19–43. New York: Routledge, 2007.

———. *Money, Myths, and Change: The Economic Lives of Lesbians and Gay Men.* Chicago: University of Chicago Press, 2001.

Badgett, M. V. Lee, Brad Sears, Holning Lau, and Deborah Ho. "Symposium: The Evolution of Academic Discourse on Sexual Orientation and the Law." *Chicago-Kent College Law Review* 84, no. 2 (2009): 345–79.

Badiou, Alain. *The Communist Hypothesis.* London: Verso, 2010.

Baird, Peter, and Ed McCaughan. "Hit and Run: U.S. Runaway Shops on the Mexican Border." *NACLA Report on the Americas,* 1975, 2–30.

Bakker, Isabella, and Stephen Gill, eds. *Power, Production, and Social Reproduction.* New York: Palgrave, 2003.

Balderston, Daniel. *El deseo, enorme cicatriz luminosa: Ensayos sobre homosexualidades latino americanos.* Rosario, Argentina: Beatriz Viterbo, 2004.

Balderston, Daniel, and Donna J. Guy, eds. *Sex and Sexuality in Latin America.* New York: New York University Press, 1997.

Balibar, Etienne. *Politics and the Other Scene.* London: Verso. 2002.

Balli, Cecilia. "Murdered Women on the Border: Gender, Territory, and Power in Ciudad Juárez." PhD diss., Rice University, 2009.

Bandy, Joe. "Paradoxes of Transnational Civil Society: The Coalition for Justice in the Maquiladoras and the Challenges of Coalition." *Social Problems* 51, no. 3 (2007): 410–31.

Bandy, Joe, and Jennifer Bickham Mendez. "Women Organizers Negotiating the Local and Transnational in the Maquilas of Nicaragua and Northern Mexico." *Mobilizations* 8, no. 2 (2003): 173–88.

Barmeyer, Niels. "The Guerilla Movement as a Project: An Assessment of Community Involvement in the EZLN." *Latin American Perspectives* 30, no. 1 (January 2003): 122–38.

Bedford, Kate. *Developing Partnerships: Gender, Sexuality, and the Reformed World Bank.* Minneapolis: University of Minnesota Press, 2009.

Behar, Ruth. *Translated Woman: Crossing the Border with Esperanza's Story.* Boston: Beacon Press, 1993.

———. *The Vulnerable Observer: Anthropology That Breaks Your Heart.* Boston: Beacon Press, 1996.

Belausteguigoitia, Marisa. "The Right to Rest: Women's Struggle to Be Heard in the Zapatista Movement." *Development* 43, no. 3 (2000): 81–87.

Benería, Lourdes. "Conceptualizing the Labor Force: The Underestimation of Women's Economic Affairs." *Journal of Development Studies* 17, no. 3 (April 1987): 10–28.

Berlant, Lauren, ed. *Compassion: The Culture and Politics of an Emotion.* New York: Routledge, 2004.

———. *Cruel Optimism.* Durham, N.C.: Duke University Press, 2011.

———. "The Epistemology of State Emotion." In *Dissent in Dangerous Times,* edited by Austin Sarat, 46–81. Ann Arbor: University of Michigan Press, 2005.

———. *The Female Complaint: The Unfinished Business of Sentimentality in American Culture.* Durham, N.C.: Duke University Press, 2008.

———. "A Properly Political Concept of Love: Three Approaches in Ten Pages." *Cultural Anthropology* 26, no. 4 (2011): 683–91.

———. *The Queen of America Goes to Washington City: Essays on Sex and Citizenship.* Durham, N.C.: Duke University Press, 1997.

———. "The Subject of True Feeling." In *Feminist Consequences: Theory for the New Century,* edited by Elizabeth Bronfen and Misha Kavka, 126–60. New York: Columbia University Press, 2000.

Best, Beverley. "Fredric Jameson Notwithstanding: The Dialectic of Affect." *Rethinking Marxism* 23, no. 1 (2011): 60–82.

Beverley, John. *Testimonio: On the Politics of Truth.* Minneapolis: University of Minnesota Press, 2004.

Binnie, Jon. *The Globalization of Sexuality.* London: Sage, 2004.

Boris, Eileen, and Rhacel Salazar Parreñas, eds. *Intimate Labors: Cultures, Technologies, and the Politics of Care.* Palo Alto, Calif.: Stanford University Press, 2010.

Bowden, Charles. *Murder City: Ciudad Juárez and the Global Economy's New Killing Fields.* New York: Nation Books, 2010.

Brandenburg, Sven. "The Perfection of Vision and Knowledge: The Concept of Perception and of Sexed Subjectivity in Contemporary Gender Theories and Their Political Consequences." Unpublished paper, 2004.

Brennan, Teresa. *Globalization and Its Terrors: Daily Life in the West.* New York: Routledge, 2002.

———. *The Transmission of Affect.* Ithaca, N.Y.: Cornell University Press, 2004.

Brenner, Johanna. *Women and the Politics of Class.* New York: Monthly Review, 2000.

Butler, Judith. *Gender Trouble: Feminism and the Subversion of Identity.* New York: Routledge, 1990.

Caffentzis, George. "The Future of 'the Commons': Neoliberalism's 'Plan B' or the Original Disaccumulation of Capital?" *New Formations,* no. 69 (Summer 2010): 23–41.

Campbell, Howard. *Drug War Zone: Frontline Dispatches from the Streets of El Paso and Juárez.* Austin: University of Texas Press, 2009.

———. "De Ambiente: Queer Tourism and the Shifting Boundaries of Mexican Male Sexualities," *GLQ* 8, nos. 1–2 (2002): 139–66.

Cantú, Lionel, Jr., *The Sexuality of Migration: Border Crossings and Mexican*

Immigrant Men. Edited by Nancy Naples and Sálvidor Vidal-Ortiz. New York: New York University Press, 2009.

Cantú, Lionel, Jr., with Eithne Luibhéid and Alexandra Minna Stern. "Well-Founded Fear: Political Asylum and the Boundaries of Sexual Identity in the U.S.–Mexico Borderlands." In Luibhéid and Cantú, *Queer Migrations,* 61–74.

Carillo, Héctor. *The Night Is Young: Sexuality in Mexico in the Time of AIDS.* Chicago: University of Chicago Press, 2002.

Carillo, Jorge, and Alberto Hernández. *Mujeres fronterizas en la industria maquiladora.* Mexico City: Consejo Nacional de Fomento Educativo, 1985.

Carrier, Joseph. *De los Otros: Intimacy and Homosexuality among Mexican Men.* New York: Columbia University Press, 1995.

Casarino, Cesare, and Antonio Negri. *In Praise of the Common.* Minneapolis: University of Minnesota Press. 2008.

Castañeda, Marina. *El machismo invisible regresa.* Mexico City: Taurus Pensamiento, 2007.

Castillo, Debra A., María Gudelia, Rangel Gómez, and Armando Rosas Solís. "Violence and Transvestite/Transgender Sex Workers in Tijuana." In Domínguez-Ruvalcaba and Corona, *Gender Violence at the U.S.–Mexico Border,* 15–34.

Castro, Mary Garcia. "Engendering Powers in Neoliberal Times: Reflections from the Left on Feminism and Feminisms." *Latin American Perspectives* 38, no. 6 (2001): 17–37.

Chávez-Silverman, Susana, and Librata Hernández, eds. *Reading and Writing the Ambiente: Queer Sexualities in Latino, Latin American, and Spanish Culture.* Madison: University of Wisconsin Press, 2000.

Chiñas, Beverly N. "Isthmus Zapotec Attitudes toward Sex." In *Latin American Sexualities,* edited by Stephen O. Murray, 293–302. Albuquerque: University of New Mexico Press, 1995.

Clifford, James. *The Predicament of Culture: Twentieth-Century Ethnography, Literature, and Art.* Cambridge: Harvard University Press, 1988.

Clifford, James, and George Marcus, eds. *Writing Culture: The Poetics and Politics of Ethnography.* Berkeley: University of California Press, 1985.

Clough, Patricia Ticineto, and Jean Halley, eds. *The Affective Turn: Theorizing the Social.* Durham, N.C.: Duke University Press, 2007.

Cohen, Cathy. *The Boundaries of Blackness: AIDS and the Breakdown of Black Politics.* Chicago: University of Chicago, 1999.

Collins, Patricia Hill. *Black Feminist Thought: Knowledge, Consciousness, and the Politics of Empowerment.* New York: Routledge, 1991.

Conaghan, Joanne. "Intersectionality and the Feminist Project in Law." In Grabham et al., *Intersectionality and Beyond,* 21–47.

Cravey, Altha J. *Women and Work in Mexico's Maquiladoras.* Boston: Rowman and Littlefield, 1998.

Crenshaw, Kimberlé. "Mapping the Margins: Intersectionality, Identity Politics and Violence against Women of Color." *Stanford Law Review* 43 (July 1991): 1241–65.

Cubilié, Anne. *Women Witnessing Terror: Testimony and the Cultural Politics of Rights.* Bronx, N.Y.: Fordham University Press, 2005.

Cvetkovich, Anne. *An Archive of Feelings: Trauma, Sexuality, and Lesbian Public Culture.* Durham, N.C.: Duke University Press, 2002.

———. *Depression: A Public Feeling.* Durham, N.C.: Duke University Press, 2012.

Damasio, Antonio. *Looking for Spinoza: Joy, Sorrow, and the Feeling Brain.* New York: Houghton Mifflin Harcourt, 2003.

Dayan, Joan. "Legal Slaves and Civil Bodies." In *Materializing Democracy: Toward a Revitalized Cultural Politics,* edited by Russ Castronova and Dana Nelson, 53–94. Durham, N.C.: Duke University Press, 2000.

D'Emilio, John. "Capitalism and Gay Identity." In *Powers of Desire: The Politics of Sexuality,* edited by Ann Snitow, Christine Stansell, and Sharon Thompson, 100–13. New York: Monthly Review Press, 1983.

———. *Making Trouble: Essays on Gay History, Politics, and the University.* New York: Routledge. 1992.

———. *Sexual Politics, Sexual Communities.* Chicago: University of Chicago Press. 1983.

Derrida, Jacques. "Force of Law: The Mystical Foundations of Authority." In *Deconstruction and the Possibility of Justice,* edited by Drucilla Cornell, Michael Rosenfeld, and David Gray Carlson, 3–67. New York: Routledge, 1992.

Díaz, Francisco. *El SIDA en México: Los efectos sociales.* Mexico City: Ediciones de Cultura Popular, 1988.

Didion, Joan. *Salvador.* New York: Simon and Schuster, 1983.

Dolhinow, Rebecca. *A Jumble of Needs: Women's Activism and Neoliberalism in the Colonias of the Southwest.* Minneapolis: University of Minnesota Press, 2010.

do Mar Castro Varela, María, Nikita Dhawan, and Antke Engel, eds. *Homonormativity and Hegemony: Revisiting "The Political" in Queer Politics.* London: Ashgate, 2011.

Domínguez-Ruvalcaba, Héctor. *Modernity and the Nation in Mexican Representations of Masculinity.* New York: Palgrave, 2008.

———. "Presentacion." In Ravelo and Domínguez-Ruvalcaba, *Entre las duras aristas,* 9–20.

Domínguez-Ruvalcaba, Héctor, and Ignacio Corona, eds. *Gender Violence at the U.S.–Mexico Border: Media Representation and Public Response.* Tucson: University of Arizona Press, 2010.

Douglas, Mary. *Purity and Danger: An Analysis of Concepts of Pollution and Taboo.* 1966. Reprinted with new preface by author. New York: Routledge, 2005.

Drucker, Peter, ed. *Different Rainbows*. London: Gay Men's Press, 2000.

Duggan, Lisa. *The Twilight of Equality? Neoliberalism, Cultural Politics, and the Attack on Democracy*. New York: Beacon, 2003.

Earle, Duncan, and Jeanne Simonelli. *Uprising of Hope: Sharing the Zapatista Journey to Alternative Development*. Lanham, Md.: AltaMira, 2005.

Eber, Christine E. "Seeking Our Own Food: Indigenous Women's Power and Autonomy, San Pedro Chenalhó, Chiapas (1980–1998)." *Latin American Perspectives* 26, no. 3 (May 1999): 6–36.

Eber, Christine E., and Christine Marie Kovic, eds. *Women of Chiapas: Making History in Times of Struggle and Hope*. New York: Routledge, 2003.

Eng, David, Judith Halberstam, and José Esteban Muñoz, eds. "What's Queer about Queer Studies Now?" *Social Text* 23, nos. 3–4 (Fall–Winter 2005): 84–85.

Engster, Daniel. "Rethinking Care Theory." *Hypatia* 20, no. 3 (2005): 50–74.

Esteva, Gustavo, and Carlos Pérez. "The Meaning and Scope of the Struggle for Autonomy." *Latin American Perspectives* 28, no. 120 (2001): 121–47.

EZLN. *Documentos y comunicados, tomo uno, 1 de Enero/8 de Agosto, 1994*. Mexico City: Ediciones Era, 1994.

Federici, Silvia. *Caliban and the Witch: Women, the Body, and Primitive Accumulation*. New York: Autonomedia, 2004.

Felman, Shoshana, and Dori Laub. *Testimony: Crises of Witnessing in Literature, Psychoanalysis, and History*. New York: Routledge, 1991.

Ferguson, Ann. *Blood at the Root: Motherhood, Sexuality, and Male Dominance*. London: Pandora Press, 1989.

———. *Sexual Democracy: Women, Oppression, and Revolution*. Boulder, Colo.: Westview, 1991.

Ferguson, R. A. *Aberrations in Black: Toward a Queer of Color Critique*. Minneapolis: University of Minnesota Press, 2004.

Fernández-Kelly, María Patricia. *For We Are Sold, I and My People: Women and Industry in Mexico's Frontier*. Albany: SUNY Press, 1983.

Fineman, Martha. *The Neutered Mother, the Sexual Family, and Other Twentieth-Century Tragedies*. New York: Routledge, 1995.

Flam, Helena. "Emotions' Map: A Research Agenda." *Journal of Consumer Culture* 9, no. 3 (2009): 19–40.

Flam, Helena, and Debra King. *Emotions and Social Movements*. New York: Routledge, 2005.

Flatley, Jonathan. *Affective Mapping: Melancholia and the Politics of Modernism*. Cambridge: Harvard University Press, 2008.

Floyd, Kevin. *The Reification of Desire: Toward a Queer Marxism*. Minneapolis: University of Minnesota Press, 2009.

Folbre, Nancy, and Michael Brittman, eds. *Family Time*. London: Taylor and Francis. 2007.

Fones-Wolf, Elizabeth. *Selling Free Enterprise: The Business Assault on Labor and Liberalism: 1945–60.* Champaign: University of Illinois Press, 1995.

Forbis, Melissa M. "Autonomy and a Handful of Herbs: Contesting Gender and Ethnic Identities through Healing." In Speed, Castillo, and Stephen, *Dissident Women,* 176–202.

———. "Hacía la Autonomía: Zapatista Women Developing a New World." In Eber and Kovic, *Women of Chiapas,* 231–51.

Fortunati, Leopoldina. *The Arcane of Reproduction: Housework, Prostitution, Labor, and Capital.* New York: Autonomedia, 1989.

Foucault, Michel. *The History of Sexuality.* Vol. 1. Translated by Robert Hurley. New York: Pantheon, 1978.

Franco, Jean. "The Long March of Feminism." *NACLA Report on the Americas* 31, no. 4 (1998): 10–16.

Fraser, Leslie. "NAFTA and the War on Drugs as Competing National Security Agendas in 1990: The Triumph of Neo-liberalism and the Quest for U.S.–Mexican Integration." *Journal of Iberian and Latin American Studies* 9, no. 1 (July 2003).

Fregoso, Rosa Linda. *Mexicana Encounters: The Making of Social Identities on the Borderlands.* Durham, N.C.: Duke University Press, 2003.

Fregoso, Rosa Linda, and Cynthia Bejarano, eds. *Terrorizing Women: Feminicide in the Americas.* Durham, N.C.: Duke University Press, 2010.

Freud, Sigmund. *The Standard Edition of the Complete Psychological Works.* Vol. 14. Translated by James Strachey. London: Hogarth Press, 1957.

Fuentes, Annette, and Barbara Ehrenreich. *Women in the Global Factory.* Boston: South End Press, 1983.

Gaspar de Alba, Alicia. *Desert Blood: The Juárez Murders.* Houston, Tex.: Arte Publico, 2005.

Gevisser, Mark, and Edwin Cameron. *Defiant Desire.* New York: Routledge, 1995.

Gibler, John. "Marketing Violence in Mexico's Drug War." *NACLA Report on the Americas,* May 2011, 31–33.

———. *To Die in Mexico: Dispatches from inside the Drug War.* San Francisco: City Lights, 2011.

Gibson-Graham, J. K. *A Postcapitalist Politics.* Minneapolis: University of Minnesota Press. 2006.

Gilmore, Ruth Wilson. "Forgotten Places and the Seeds of Grassroots Planning." In Hale, *Engaging Contradictions,* 31–61.

———. *Golden Gulag: Prisons, Surplus, Crisis, and Opposition in Globalizing California.* Berkeley: University of California Press, 2007.

———. "Public Enemies and Private Intellectuals: Apartheid USA." *Race and Class* 35, no. 1 (1993): 69–79.

Giménez, Martha. "Back to Class: Reflections on the Dialectics of Class and

Identity." In *More Unequal: Aspects of Class in the United States,* edited by Michael D. Yates, 107–17. New York: Monthly Review, 2007.

Gledhill, John. "Introduction: Anthropological Perspectives on Indigenous Resurgence in Chiapas." *Identities* 15 (2008): 483–505.

Gluckman, Max. "Gossip and Scandal." *Current Anthropology* 4 (June 1963): 307–16.

González-López, Gloria. *Erotic Journeys: Mexican Immigrants and Their Sex Lives.* Berkeley: University of California Press, 2005.

González Rodríguez, Sergio. *Huesos en el desierto.* Barcelona: Editorial Anagrama, 2002.

Goodwin, Jeff. *Passionate Politics: Emotions and Social Movements.* Chicago: University of Chicago Press, 2001.

Goodwin, Jeff, James M. Jasper, and Francesca Polletta. "Introduction: Why Emotions Matter." In Goodwin, *Passionate Politics,* 1–26.

Goodwin, Jeff, and Steven Pfaff. "Emotion Work in High-Risk Social Movements." *Mobilization* 5, no. 1 (2000): 65–83.

Gordon, Avery. *Ghostly Matters: Haunting and the Sociological Imagination.* Minneapolis: University of Minnesota Press, 1997.

Gould, Deborah B. *Moving Politics: Emotion and ACT UP's Fight against AIDS.* Chicago: University of Chicago Press, 2009.

———. "On Affect and Protest." In *Political Emotions: New Agendas in Communication,* edited by Janet Staiger, Ann Cvetkovich, and Ann Reynolds, 18–44. New York: Routledge, 2010.

Government of the State of Chiapas. *Los acuerdos de San Andrés.* Spanish–Tsotsil bilingual edition. Chiapas, Mexico: Government of the State of Chiapas, 2003.

Grabham, Emily, Davina Cooper, Jane Krisinadas, and Didi Herman, eds. *Intersectionality and Beyond: Law, Power, and the Politics of Location.* New York: Routledge-Cavendish, 2009.

Gramsci, Antonio. *Selections from the Prison Notebooks.* New York: International Publishers, 1971.

Grant, Jaime M., Lisa A. Motett, and Justin Tanis. *Injustice at Every Turn: A Report of the National Transgender Survey.* 2001. http://transequality.org/PDFs/Executive_Summary.pdf.

Gray, John. *False Dawn: The Delusions of Global Capitalism.* London: Granta, 1998.

Green, James. "Desire and Militancy: Lesbians, Gays, and the Brazilian Workers' Party." In Drucker, *Different Rainbows,* 57–70.

Gregg, Melissa, and Gregory Seigworth, eds. *The Affect Theory Reader.* Durham, N.C.: Duke University Press, 2010.

Grim, Ryan. *This Is Your Country on Drugs: The Secret History of Getting High in America.* Hoboken, N.J.: Wiley, 2009.

Grossberg, Lawrence. *We Gotta Get Out of This Place: Popular Conservatism and Postmodern Culture.* New York: Routledge, 1992.

Gugelberger, Georg M. *The Real Thing: Testimonial Discourse and Latin America.* Durham, N.C.: Duke University Press, 1996.

Gutiérrez-Rodríguez, Encarnación. *Migration, Domestic Work, and Affect.* New York: Routledge, 2010.

Gutmann, Matthew. *Fixing Men: Sex, Birth Control, and AIDS in Mexico.* Berkeley: University of California Press, 2007.

———. *The Meanings of Macho: Being a Man in Mexico City.* Berkeley: University of California Press, 1996.

Halberstam, Judith. *The Queer Art of Failure.* Durham, N.C.: Duke University Press, 2011.

Hale, Charles, ed. *Engaging Contradictions: Theory, Politics, and Methods of Activist Scholarship.* Berkeley: University of California Press, 2008.

Hames-García, Michael. *Identity Complex: Making the Case for Multiplicity.* Minneapolis: University of Minnesota Press, 2011.

Haraway, Donna. "A Cyborg Manifesto: Science, Technology, and Socialist-Feminism in the 1980s." *Socialist Review* 80 (1985): 65–108.

Hardt, Michael. "Affective Labor." *boundary 2* 26, no. 2 (1999): 89–100.

Hardt, Michael, and Antonio Negri. *Commonwealth.* Cambridge: Harvard University Press, 2009.

———. *Empire.* Cambridge: Harvard University Press. 2001.

———. *Multitude: War and Democracy in the Age of Empire.* Cambridge: Harvard University Press. 2005.

Hartman, Saidiya. *Lose Your Mother: A Journey along the Atlantic Slave Route.* New York: Farrar, Straus and Giroux, 2008.

Harvey, David. "The Body as an Accumulation Strategy." *Environment and Planning D* 16 (1998): 401–21.

Haug, Frigga, et al. *Female Sexualization: A Collective Work of Memory.* Translated by Erica Carter. New York: Verso, 1987.

Hemmings, Clare. "Invoking Affect: Cultural Theory and the Ontological Turn." *Cultural Studies* 19, no. 5 (2005): 548–67.

Hennessy, Rosemary. *Profit and Pleasure: Sexual Identities in Late Capitalism.* New York: Routledge, 2000.

———. "Queer Theory: A Review of the *differences* Special Issue and Wittig's *The Straight Mind.*" *Signs* 18, no. 4 (Summer 1993): 964–73.

———. "Thinking Sex Materially: Marxist, Socialist, and Other Materialist Approaches to Sexuality." In *The Feminist Theory Handbook,* edited by Ania Plimien, Clare Hemmings, Marsha Henry, Mary Evans, Sadie Waring, and Sumi Madhok. London: Sage, 2013.

———. "The Value of a Second Skin." In *Intersections in Feminist and Queer Theory: Sexualities, Cultures, and Identities,* edited by Diane Richardson,

Janice Mc Laughlin, and Mark Casey, 116–35. Basingstoke, UK: Palgrave, 2006.

Hennessy, Rosemary, and Chrys Ingraham, eds. *Materialist Feminism: A Reader in Class, Difference, and Women's Lives.* New York: Routledge, 1997.

Herdt, Gilbert, and Cymene Howe, eds. *21st Century Sexualities: Contemporary Issues in Health, Education, and Rights.* New York: Routledge, 2007.

Herlinghaus, Hermann. *Violence without Guilt: Ethical Narratives from the Global South.* New York: Palgrave, 2009.

Hesford, Victoria. "The Politics of Love: Women's Liberation and Feeling Differently." *Feminist Theory* 10, no. 1 (2009): 5–33.

Hochschild, Arlie Russell. "Emotion Work, Feeling Rules, and Social Structure." *American Journal of Sociology* 85 (1979): 551–75.

———. *The Managed Heart: Commercialization of Human Feeling.* Berkeley: University of California Press, 1983.

———. "Review of Sex Role Research." *American Journal of Sociology* 78, no. 4 (1973): 1011–29.

———. "The Sociology of Emotion and Feeling." *Sociological Inquiry* 45, nos. 2–3 (1973): 280–307.

Hochschild, Arlie Russell, with Anne Machung. "Global Care Chains and Emotional Surplus Value." In *On the Edge: Globalization and the New Millennium,* edited by Tony Giddens and Will Hutton, 130–46. London: Sage, 2000.

———. *The Second Shift.* New York: Viking Penguin, 1989.

Horton, Myles. *The Long Haul: An Autobiography.* New York: Teachers College Press, 1997.

Horton, Myles, and Paolo Friere. *We Make the Road by Walking: Conversations on Education and Social Change.* Philadelphia: Temple University Press, 1990.

Howe, Cymene. *Intimate Pedagogies: Sexual Rights Activism in Post-revolutionary Nicaragua.* Durham, N.C.: Duke University Press, 2013.

Huffer, Lynne. "Eros in Biopower." Lecture given at the Center for the Study of Women, Gender, and Sexuality, Rice University, November 10, 2012.

———. *Mad for Foucault: Rethinking the Foundations of Queer Theory.* New York: Columbia University Press, 2010.

Institute for Research on Women and Gender. *Global Feminisms: Comparative Case Studies of Women's Activism and Scholarship.* Film transcript. Ann Arbor: University of Michigan, 2004. http://deepblue.lib.umich.edu/bitstream/2027.42/57279/6/USA_Thematic_Film.pdf.

Jackson, Stevi, Liu Jieyu, and Woo Juhyun, eds. *East Asian Sexualities: Modernity, Gender, and New Sexual Cultures.* London: Zed Books. 2008.

Jaggar, Alison M. "Feminist Politics and Epistemology." In *The Feminist Standpoint Reader: Intellectual and Political Controversies,* edited by Sandra Harding, 55–66. New York: Routledge, 2004.

———. "Love and Knowledge: Emotion in Feminist Epistemology." *Inquiry* 32 (June 1989): 151–176.

Jakobsen, Janet R. "Can Homosexuals End Western Civilization as We Know It? Family Values in a Global Economy." In *Queer Globalizations: Citizenship and the Afterlife of Colonialism,* edited by A. Cruz-Malavé and M. F. Manalansan IV, 49–68. New York: New York University Press, 2002.

Jameson, Fredric. *Archaeologies of the Future: The Desire Called Utopia.* London: Verso, 2007.

———. "The Politics of Utopia." *New Left Review* 25 (January/February 2004): 35–54.

Jasper, James. *The Art of Moral Protest: Culture, Biography, and Creativity in Social Movements.* Chicago: University of Chicago Press, 1997.

Johnson, E. Patrick, and Mae Henderson. *Black Queer Studies: A Critical Anthology.* Durham, N.C.: Duke University Press, 2005.

Joseph, Miranda. *Against the Romance of Community.* Minneapolis: University of Minnesota Press. 2002.

Kamel, Rachel, and Anya Hoffman, eds. *The Maquiladora Reader: Cross-Border Organizing since NAFTA.* Philadelphia: American Friends Service Committee, 1999.

Katzenberger, Elaine, ed. *First World, Ha Ha Ha! The Zapatista Challenge.* San Francisco: City Lights. 2001.

Kelly, Patty. *Lydia's Open Door: Inside Mexico's Most Modern Brothel.* Berkeley: University of California Press, 2008.

Kelsh, Deborah. "Desire and Class: The Knowledge Industry in the Wake of Post-structuralism." PhD diss., University at Albany–SUNY, 2000.

Kittay, Eva Feder. *Love's Labor: Essays on Women, Equality, and Dependency.* New York: Routledge, 1998.

Klatch, Rebecca. "The Underside of Social Movements: The Effects of Destructive Affective Ties." *Qualitative Sociology* 27, no. 4 (2004): 487–509.

Klein, Naomi. *No Logo.* New York: Picador, 2002.

———. "Reclaiming the Commons." *New Left Review* 9 (May–June 2001): 81–89.

Kollontai, Alexandra. *Selected Writings.* Westport, Conn.: A. Hill, 1977.

Kopinak, Kathryn. *Desert Capitalism: Maquiladoras in North America's Western Industrial Corridor.* Tucson: University of Arizona Press, 1996.

Kovic, Christine Marie, and Christine Engla Eber. *Women of Chiapas: Making History in Times of Struggle and Hope.* New York: Routledge. 2003.

Kristeva, Julia. *Powers of Horror: An Essay on Abjection.* New York: Columbia University Press, 1982.

Kushner, Tony. "A Socialism of the Skin." *Nation,* July 4, 1994, 9–14.

La Capra, Dominick. *Representing the Holocaust: History, Theory, Trauma.* Baltimore: Johns Hopkins University Press, 2000.

———. *Writing History, Writing Trauma.* Baltimore: Johns Hopkins University Press, 2000.

Laclau, Ernesto. "Bare Life or Social Indeterminacy?" In *Giorgio Agamben: Sovereignty and Life,* edited by Matthew Calarco and Steven DeCaroli, 11–22. Palo Alto, Calif.: Stanford University Press, 2007.

———. *On Populist Reason.* New York: Verso, 2007.

Lamas, Marta. *Feminismo: Transmisiones y retransmisiones.* Mexico City: Taurus, 2006.

Lancaster, Roger N. *Life Is Hard: Machismo, Danger, and the Intimacy of Power in Nicaragua.* Berkeley: University of California Press, 1994.

———. "On Homosexualities in Latin America (and Other Places)." *American Ethnologist* 24, no. 1 (1997): 193–202.

———. "Tolerance and Intolerance in Latin American Sexual Cultures." In *Passing Lines: Sexuality and Immigration,* edited by Brad Epps, Keja Valens, and Bill Johnson González, 255–74. Cambridge, Mass.: David Rockefeller Center on Latin American Studies / Harvard University Press, 2005.

Langman, Lauren. "From Subject to Citizen Consumer: Embodiment and the Mediation of Hegemony." In *The Politics of Selfhood: Bodies and Identities in Global Capitalism,* edited by Richard Harvey Brown, 167–87. Minneapolis: University of Minnesota Press, 2003.

Limas, Alfredo, and Alfredo Hernández. "Tránsitos de género e identidades sexuales en la reestructuración regional fronteriza: Ciudad Juárez de fin de siglo." *Estudios sobre las culturas contemporáneas* 6, part 2, no. 11 (2000): 9–29.

Limas, Alfredo, and Patricia Ravelo. "Feminicidio en Ciudad Juárez: Una civilización sacrificial." *El cotidiano* 18, no. 111 (2002): 47–57.

Liu, Petrus, and Lisa Rofel. "Beyond the Strai(gh)ts." Special issue, *positions* 18, no. 2 (2011).

Logan, Kathleen. "Personal Testimony: Latin American Women Telling Their Lives," *Latin American Research Review* 32, no. 1 (1997): 199–211.

Lorde, Audre. "Uses of the Erotic: The Erotic as Power." In *Sister Outsider,* 53–59. Berkeley, Calif.: Crossing Press, 1984.

Love, Heather. *Feeling Backward: Loss and the Politics of Queer History.* Cambridge: Harvard University Press, 2007.

Lowe, Lisa. "Utopia and Modernity: Some Observations from the Border." *Rethinking Marxism* 13, no. 2 (Summer 2001): 10–18.

Lugo, Alejandro. *Fragmented Lives, Assembled Parts: Culture, Capitalism, and Conquest at the U.S.–Mexican Border.* Austin: University of Texas Press, 2008.

Lugones, Maria C., and Pat Alake Rosezelle. "Sisterhood and Friendship as Feminist Models." In *Feminism and Community,* edited by Penny A. Weiss and Marilyn Friedman, 135–45. Philadelphia: Temple University Press, 1995.

Luibhéid, Eithne, and Lionel Cantú Jr., eds. *Queer Migrations: Sexuality, Citizenship, and U.S. Border Crossings.* Minneapolis: University of Minnesota Press, 2005.

Lumsden, Ian. *Homosexuality and the State in Mexico.* Mexico City: Colectivo Sol, 1991.

Lutz, Catherine. *Unnatural Emotions: Everyday Sentiments on a Micronesian Atoll and Their Challenge to Western Theory.* Chicago: University of Chicago Press, 1998.

Lynch, Kathleen, and Judy Walsh. "Love, Care, and Solidarity: What Is and Is Not Commodifiable." In *Affective Equality: Love, Care, and Injustice,* edited by Kathleen Lynch, John Baker, and Maureen Lyons, 35–53. London: Palgrave Macmillan, 2009.

Manzano, Valeria. "The Blue Jean Generation: Youth, Gender, and Sexuality in Buenos Aires, 1958–1975." *Journal of Social History* 42, no. 3 (2009): 657–76.

Marcos, Subcomandante. *Shadows of Tender Fury: The Letters and Communiqués of Subcomandante Marcos and the Zapatista Army of National Liberation.* New York: Monthly Review Press, 1995.

Marx, Karl. *Capital.* Vol. 1. Translated by Ben Fowkes. New York: Vintage, 1977.

———. *Early Writings.* Translated by Rodney Livingstone and George Benton. New York: Vintage, 1975.

———. *Grundrisse: Foundations of the Critique of Political Economy.* Translated by Martin Nicolaus. London: Penguin, 1973.

Massumi, Brian. *Parables for the Virtual: Movement, Affect, Sensation.* Durham, N.C.: Duke University Press, 2002.

Mattiace, Shannan. "Mayan Utopias: Rethinking the State." In *Mayan Lives, Mayan Utopias: The Indigenous Peoples of Chiapas and the Zapatista Rebellion,* edited by Jan Rus, Rosalva Aída Hernández Castillo, and Shannan Mattiace, 185–90. Lanham, Md.: Rowan and Littlefield, 2003.

Mbembe, Achille. "Necropolitics." Translated by Libby Meintjes. *Public Culture* 15, no. 1 (2003): 11–40.

McLean, Athena, and Annette Leibling, eds. *The Shadow Side of Fieldwork: Exploring the Blurred Borders between Ethnography and Life.* Malden, Mass.: Wiley-Blackwell, 2007.

Mejia, Max. "Mexican Pink." In Drucker, *Different Rainbows,* 43–55.

Mendoza, Breny. "The Undemocratic Foundations of Democracy: An Enunciation from Postoccidental Latin America." *Signs* 31, no. 4 (2006): 935–42.

Mignolo, Walter. *The Darker Side of Western Modernity: Global Futures, Decolonial Options.* Durham, N.C.: Duke University Press, 2011.

Miller, Francesca. *Latin American Women and the Search for Social Justice.* Hanover, N.H.: University Press of New England, 1991.

Mohanty, Chandra Talpade. *Feminism without Borders: Decolonizing Theory, Practicing Solidarity.* Durham, N.C.: Duke University Press, 2003.

Molyneux, Maxine. *Women's Movements in International Perspective: Latin America and Beyond.* London: University of London Press, 2003.

Monárrez Fragoso, Julia Estela. "The Victims of Ciudad Juárez Feminicide: Sexually Fetishized Commodities." Fregoso and Bejarano, *Terrorizing Women,* 59–69.

Monasterios, Karin. "Bolivian Women's Organizations in the MAS Era." *NACLA Report on the Americas* 40, no. 2 (2007): 33–37.

Mongrovejo, Norma. *Un amor que se atrevió a decir su nombre: La lucha de las lesbianas y su relación con los movimientos homosexual y feminista en América Latina.* Mexico City: Centro de Documentación y Archivo Histórico Lésbico, 2000.

Monsiváis, Carlos. *Amor perdido.* Mexico City: Era, 1977.

———. *Mexican Postcards.* New York: Verso, 1997.

Moody, Kim. *Workers in a Lean World: Unions in the International Economy.* London: Verso, 1997.

Mora, Mariana. "Zapatista Anti-capitalist Politics and the Other Campaign: Learning from the Struggle for Indigenous Rights and Autonomy." *Latin American Perspectives* 32, no. 4 (2007): 64–77.

Moten, Fred. *In the Break: The Aesthetics of the Black Radical Tradition.* Minneapolis: University of Minnesota Press, 2003.

Muñoz, José Esteban. *Cruising Utopia: The Then and There of Queer Futurity.* New York: New York University Press, 2009.

Naiman, Joanne. "Left Feminism and the Return to Class." *Monthly Review* 42, no. 8 (June 1996): 12–28.

Nash, June. "Women in Between: Globalization and the New Enlightenment." *Signs* 31, no. 1 (2005): 145–67.

Nash, June, and María Patricia Fernández-Kelly. *Women, Men, and the International Division of Labor.* Albany: State University of New York Press, 1983.

Negri, Antonio. "Value and Affect." Translated by Michael Hardt. boundary 2 26, no. 2 (1999): 77–88.

Ngai, Sianne. *Ugly Feelings.* Cambridge: Harvard University Press, 2007.

Nonini, Donald M., ed. *The Global Idea of the Commons.* New York: Berghahn Books, 2007.

Núñez Noriega, Guillermo. *Sexo entre varones: Poder y resistencia en el campo sexual.* 2nd ed. Hermasillo, Mexico: Colegio de Sonora, 1999.

Ojeda, Martha A., and Rosemary Hennessy, eds. *NAFTA from Below: Maquiladora Workers, Campesinos, and Indigenous Communities Speak Out on the Impact of Free Trade in Mexico.* San Antonio, Tex.: Coalition for Justice in the Maquiladoras, 2007.

Okin, Susan Moller. *Justice, Gender, and the Family.* New York: Basic Books, 1991.

Oliver, Kelly. *Witnessing: Beyond Recognition.* Minneapolis: University of Minnesota Press, 2001.

Olivera, Mercedes. "Subordination and Rebellion: Indigenous Peasant Women in Chiapas Ten Years after the Zapatista Uprising." *Journal of Peasant Studies* 32, nos. 3–4 (2005): 608–28.

———. "Violencia Femicida: Violence against Women and Mexico's Structural Crisis." *Latin American Perspectives* 33, no. 2 (2006): 104–14.

Paredes, Américo. "The United States, Mexico, and Machismo." *Journal of Folklore Institute* 8, no. 1 (1971): 17–37.

Payan, Tony. *The Three U.S.–Mexico Border Wars.* Westport, Conn.: Praeger Security International, 2006.

Pearson, Ruth. "Male Bias and Women's Work in Mexico's Border Industries." In *Male Bias in the Development Process,* edited by Diane Elson, 133–63. Manchester, UK: Manchester University Press, 1995.

Peña, Devon. "Las Maquiladoras: Mexican Women and Class Struggle in the Border Industries." *Aztlan* 11, no. 2 (1980): 159–229.

———. *The Terror of the Machine: Technology, Work, Gender, and Economy on the U.S.–Mexican Border.* Austin: University of Texas Press, 1997.

Pérez, Francisco R. "El infierno social y personal del marginado: El homosexual en la Ciudad de México." *CLA Journal* 41, no. 2 (1997): 204–12.

Petras, James. "The CIA and the Cultural Cold War Revisited." *Monthly Review* 51, no. 6 (November 1999). http://www.monthlyreview.org/1999petr .htm.

Petras, James, and Henry Veltmeyer. *Ensayos contra el orden: Los movimientos sociales y socialismo.* Cuenca, Ecuador: Facultad de Ciencias Económicas y Administrativas, 2003.

Philen, Robert C. "A Social Geography of Sex: Men Who Have Sex with Men (MSM) and Gay Bars on the U.S./Mexican Border." Journal of Homosexuality 50, no. 4 (2006): 31–48.

Philip, M. Nourbese. *Zong!* Toronto: Mercury Press, 2008.

Poletta, Francesca. *Freedom Is an Endless Meeting.* Chicago: University of Chicago Press, 2002.

Ponce, Patricia. "Sexualidades costeñas." *Desacatos: Revista de antropologia social* 6 (2001): 111–36.

Poniatowska, Elena. *El amanecer en el Zócolo: Los 50 días que confrontaron a México.* Mexico City: Editorial Planeta, 2007.

———. *La noche de Tlateloco: Testimonios de historia oral.* 2nd ed. Mexico City: Ediciones Era, 1998.

Pratt, Geraldine. *Working Feminism.* Edinburgh, Scotland: Edinburgh University Press, 2004.

Pratt, Geraldine, in collaboration with the Philippine Women's Centre of BC. "Circulating Sadness: Witnessing Filipina Mothers' Stories of Family Separation." *Gender, Place, and Culture* 16, no. 1 (2009): 3–22.

Price, Patricia L. *Dry Place: Landscapes of Belonging and Exclusion.* Minneapolis: University of Minnesota Press, 2004.

Prieto, Norma Iglesias. *Beautiful Flowers of the Maquiladoras: Life Histories of*

Women Workers in Tijuana. Translated by Michael Stone with Gabrielle Winkler. Austin: University of Texas Press, 1997.

Prieur, Annick. *Mema's House, Mexico City: On Transvestites, Queens, and Machos.* Chicago: University of Chicago Press, 1998.

Probyn, Elspeth. *Blush: Faces of Shame.* Minneapolis: University of Minnesota Press, 2005.

Prosser, Jay. *Second Skins.* New York: Columbia University Press, 1998.

Puar, Jaspir. *Terrorist Assemblages: Homonationalism in Queer Times.* Durham, N.C.: Duke University Press, 2007.

Quijada, O. *Comportamiento sexual en México.* Vol. 1. Mexico City: Editorial Tinta Libre, 1977.

Quinones, Sam. "The Dead Women of Juarez." In *Puro Border: Dispatches, Snapshots, and Graffiti from the U.S./Mexico Border,* edited by Luis Humberto Crosthwaite, John William Byrd, and Bobby Byrd, 139–58. El Paso, Tex.: Cinco Puntos Press, 2003.

Quiroga, José A. *Tropics of Desire: Interventions from Queer Latin America.* New York: New York University Press, 2000.

Radford, Jill, and Diana E. H. Russell, eds. *Femicide: The Politics of Woman Killing.* New York: Twayne, 1992.

Ramamurthy, Priti. "Why Is Buying a 'Madras' Cotton Shirt a Political Act? A Feminist Commodity Chain Analysis." *Feminist Studies* 30 (Fall 2004): 734–69.

Ramírez, Gloria Muñoz. *20 y 10, el fuego y la palabra.* Mexico City: Demos, 2003.

Ramos-Zayas, Ana Y. *Street Therapists: Race, Affect, and Neoliberal Personhood in Latino Newark.* Chicago: University of Chicago Press, 2012.

Randall, Margaret. *Sandino's Daughters Revisited: Feminism in Nicaragua.* New Brunswick, N.J.: Rutgers University Press, 1994.

Ravelo Blancas, Patricia. "Violencia sexual en Ciudad Juárez: Percepción de trabajadores de la maquila sobre el sistema de gobierno." In Ravelo Blancas and Domínguez-Ruvalcaba, 21–53, *Entre las duras.*

Ravelo Blancas, Patricia, and Héctor Domínguez-Ruvalcaba, eds. *Entre las duras armas: Violencia y victimización en Ciudad Juárez.* Mexico City: Publicaciones de la Casa Chata, 2006.

Reddy, Chandan. *Freedom with Violence: Race, Sexuality, and the U.S. State.* Durham, N.C.: Duke University Press, 2011.

Reddy, William M. *The Navigation of Feeling: A Framework for the History of Emotions.* Cambridge: Cambridge University Press, 2001.

Reding, Andrew A. *Question and Answer Series: Mexico: Update on Treatment of Homosexuals.* Washington, D.C.: North America Project World Policy Institute, 2000. http://www.worldpolicy.org/sites/default/files/uploaded/image/1999-Mexico-QAMEX00-001-LGBT.pdf.

Reed, Jean-Pierre. "Emotions in Context: Revolutionary Accelerators, Hope,

Moral Outrage, and Other Emotions in the Making of Nicaragua's Revolution." *Theory and Society* 33 (2004): 653–703.

Rei, Terada. *Feeling in Theory*. Cambridge: Harvard University Press, 2001.

Reid, Herbert, and Betsy Taylor. *Recovering the Commons: Democracy, Place, and Global Justice*. Champaign: University of Illinois Press, 2010.

Research Directorate of the Immigration and Refugee Board of Canada. *Mexico: Situation of Witnesses to Crime and Corruption and Victims of Discrimination Based on Sexual Orientation*. Immigration and Refugee Board of Canada website, February 2007, http://www.irb-cisr.gc.ca:8080/Publications/PubIP_DI.aspx?id=327.

Richard, Nellie. *Masculine/Feminine: Practices of Difference(s)*. Translated by Silvia R. Tandeciarz and Alice A. Nelson. Durham, N.C.: Duke University Press, 2004.

Rodríguez Ortiz, Efraín. *Crimines de odio por homofobia*. Mexico City: Universidad Autonomia Metropolitan, 2010.

Rofel, Lisa. *Desiring China: Experiments in Neoliberalism, Sexuality, and Public Culture*. Durham, N.C.: Duke University Press, 2007.

Rojas, Clara. "The V-Day March in Mexico: Appropriation and Misuse of Local Women's Activism." In *Making a Killing: Femicide, Free Trade, and La Frontera*, edited by Alicia Gaspar de Alba with Georgina Guzmán, 201–10. Austin: University of Texas Press, 2010.

Rosaldo, Michelle Z. *Knowledge and Passion*. New York: Cambridge University Press, 1980.

———. "Toward an Anthropology of Self and Feeling." In *Culture Theory: Essays on Mind, Self, and Emotion*, edited by Richard A. Shweder and Robert A. Levine, 137–57. New York: Cambridge University Press, 1984.

Rosaldo, Renato. *Culture and Truth: The Remaking of Social Analysis*. Boston: Beacon Press, 1989.

Rose, Hilary. "Hand, Brain, Heart: A Feminist Epistemology for the Natural Sciences." *Signs* 9, no. 1 (1983): 73–90.

———. *Love, Power, and Knowledge: Towards a Feminist Transformation of the Sciences*. Malden, Mass.: Polity Press, 1994.

Rosenberg, Jordana, and Amy Villarejo, eds. "Queer Studies and the Crisis of Capitalism." Special issue, *GLQ* 18, no. 1 (2012).

Ross, John. "Mexican Elections: The Zapatista Challenge." *Counterpunch*, November 2005.

Ruiz, Ramón Eduardo. *On the Rim of Mexico: Encounters of the Rich and Poor*. Boulder, Colo.: Westview Press, 1998.

Saldaña-Portillo, María Josefina. *The Revolutionary Imagination in the Americas in the Age of Development*. Durham, N.C.: Duke University Press, 2003.

Salzinger, Leslie. *Genders in Production*. Berkeley: University of California Press, 2003.

Sandoval, Chela. *Methodology of the Oppressed*. Minneapolis: University of Minnesota Press, 2000.

Saporta Sternbach, Nancy. "Re-membering the Dead." *Latin American Perspectives* 70, no. 18 (1991): 91–102.

Saunders, Frances Stoner. *Who Paid the Piper? The CIA and the Cultural Cold War*. London: Granta Books, 1999.

Scheper-Hughes, Nancy. *Death without Weeping: The Violence of Everyday Life*. Berkeley: University of California Press, 1993.

———. "The Primacy of the Ethical: Propositions for a Militant Anthropology." *Current Anthropology* 36, no. 3 (1995): 409–20.

Schmidt Camacho, Alicia. "Ciudadana X: Gender Violence and the Denationalization of Women's Rights in Ciudad Juárez." In Fregoso and Bejarano, *Terrorizing Women*, 275–89.

Schoenberger, Karl. *Levi's Children: Coming to Terms with Human Rights in the Global Marketplace*. New York: Grove Press, 2000.

Scott, James. C. *Domination and the Arts of Resistance: Hidden Transcripts*. New Haven, Conn.: Yale University Press, 1992.

Sears, Alan. "Queer Anti-capitalism: What's Left of Lesbian and Gay Liberation?" *Science and Society* 69, no. 1 (January 2005): 92–112.

Sedgwick, Eve Kosofsky. *Epistemology of the Closet*. Berkeley: University of California Press, 1990.

Segato, Rita Laura. "Territory, Sovereignty, and Crimes of the Second State: The Writing on the Body of Murdered Women." In Fregoso and Bejarano, *Terrorizing Women*, 70–93.

Serret, Estela. "El feminismo mexicano de cara al siglo XXI." *El Cotidiano* 16, no. 100 (2000): 42–51.

Shiva, Vandana. *Staying Alive: Women, Ecology, Development*. London: Zed Books, 1988.

Silvey, Rachel. "Envisioning Justice: The Politics and Possibilities of Transnational Feminist Film." In *Critical Transnational Feminist Praxis*, edited by Amanda Lock Swarr and Richa Nagar, 192–205. Albany, N.Y.: SUNY Press, 2010.

Sklair, Leslie. *Assembling for Development*. Boston: Unwin and Heyman, 1988.

Smith, Peter H. "Semiorganized Crime: Drug Trafficking in Mexico." In *Transnational Crime in the Americas*, edited by Tom Farer, 193–216. New York: Routledge, 1999.

Solomon, R. C. *A Passion for Justice: Emotions and the Origins of the Social Contract*. Lanham, Md.: Rowman and Littlefield, 1995.

Somer, Doris. " 'Not Just a Personal Story': Women's *Testimonios* and the Plural Self." In *Life/Lines: Theorizing Women's Autobiography*, edited by Bella Brodski and Celeste Schenl, 107–30. Ithaca, N.Y.: Cornell University Press, 1988.

Speas, Adriane. "Sexual Harassment in Mexico: Is NAFTA Enough?" *Law and Business Review*, Winter 2006, 83–110.

Speed, Shannon. "Actions Speak Louder Than Words: Indigenous Women and Gendered Resistance in the Wake of Acteal." In Eber and Kovic, *Women of Chiapas,* 47–65.

———. "Forged in Dialogue: Toward a Critically Engaged Activist Research." In Hale, *Engaging Contradictions,* 313–36.

Speed, Shannon, R. Aída Hernandez Castillo, and Lynn M. Stephen, eds. *Dissident Women: Gender and Cultural Politics in Chiapas.* Austin: University of Texas Press, 2006.

Spinoza, Baruch. *Ethics.* Translated by G. H. R. Parkinson. New York: Oxford University Press, 2000.

Spivak, Gayatri Chakravorty. "Scattered Speculations on the Question of Value." *diacritics,* Winter 1985, 73–93.

Stahler-Sholk, Richard. "Resisting Neoliberal Homogenization: The Zapatista Autonomy Movement." *Latin American Perspectives* 34, no. 2 (2007): 48–63.

———. "A World in Which Many Worlds Fit: Zapatista Responses to Globalization." Paper presented at Latin American Studies Association 22nd International Congress, 2000. http://lasa.international.pitt.edu/Lasa2000/Stahler-Sholk.PDF.

Staiger, Janet, Ann Cvetkovich, and Ann Reynolds, eds. *Political Emotions: New Agendas in Communication.* New York: Routledge, 2010.

Staudt, Kathleen. *Free Trade? Informal Economies on the U.S.–Mexican Border.* New York: Palgrave, 1998.

———. *Violence and Activism at the Border: Gender, Fear, and Everyday Life in Ciudad Juárez.* Austin: University of Texas Press, 2008.

Staudt, Kathleen, and Irasema Coronado. *Fronteras No Más: Toward Social Justice at the U.S.–Mexico Border.* New York: Palgrave, 2002.

Stephen, Lynn M. "Gender, Citizenship, and the Politics of Identity." *Latin American Perspectives* 28, no. 6 (2001): 54–69.

———. "Redefined Nationalism in Building a Movement for Indigenous Autonomy in Southern Mexico." *Journal of American Anthropology* 3, no. 1 (1997): 72–101.

———. "Sexualities and Genders in Zapotec Oaxaca." *Latin American Perspectives* 29, no. 2 (2002): 41–59.

———. "The Zapatista Opening: The Movement for Indigenous Autonomy and State Discourses on Indigenous Rights in Mexico, 1970–1996." *Journal of Latin American Anthropology* 2, no. 2 (1997): 2–41.

Stephen, Lynn M., Shannon Speed, and R. Aída Hernández Castillo. "Indigenous Organizing and the EZLN in the Context of Neoliberalism in Mexico." In Speed, Hernández, and Castillo, *Dissident Women,* xi–xx.

Stewart, Kathleen. *Ordinary Affects.* Durham, N.C.: Duke University Press, 2007.

Strejilevich, Nora. "Testimony: Beyond the Language of Truth." *Human Rights Quarterly* 28, no. 3 (2006): 701–800.

Strongman, K. T. *The Psychology of Emotion: From Everyday Life to Theory.* Chichester, UK: Wiley and Sons, 2003.

Tabuenca Córdoba, María Socorro. "Ghost Dance in Ciudad Juárez and the Beginning/End of the Millennium." In *Making a Killing: Femicide, Free Trade, and La Frontera,* edited by Alicia Gaspar de Alba with Georgina Guzmán, 95–120. Austin: University of Texas Press, 2010.

Taussig, Michael T. *Defacement: Public Secrecy and the Labor of the Negative.* Palo Alto, Calif.: Stanford University Press, 1999.

Tiano, Susan. "The Changing Gender Composition of the Maquiladora Workforce along the U.S.–Mexico Border." In *Women and Change at the U.S.–Mexico Border,* edited by Doreen J. Mattingly and Ellen R. Hansen, 73–90. Tucson: University of Arizona Press, 2006.

———. *Patriarchy on the Line: Labor, Gender, and Ideology in the Mexican Maquiladora Industry.* Philadelphia: Temple University Press, 1994.

Tompkins, Sylvan. *Affect, Imagery, Consciousness: The Complete Edition.* New York: Springer Publishing, 1962.

Torrant, Julie P. *The Material Family.* Rotterdam, Netherlands: Sense Publishers, 2011.

Torres-Ruiz, Antonio. "HIV/AIDS and Sexual Minorities in Mexico: A Globalized Struggle for the Protection of Human Rights." *Latin American Research Review* 46, no. 1 (2011): 5–30.

Vaid, Urvashi. *Virtual Equality: The Mainstreaming of Gay and Lesbian Liberation.* New York: Doubleday, 1995.

Valentine, David. *Imagining Transgender: An Ethnography of a Category.* Durham, N.C.: Duke University Press, 2007.

Valverde, Mariana. "A New Entity in the History of Sexuality: The Respectable Same-Sex Couple." *Feminist Studies* 32, no. 1 (2006): 155–62.

Van Schendel, Willem. "Spaces of Engagement: How Borderlands, Illegal Flows, and Territorial States Interlock." In *Illicit Flows and Criminal Things: States, Borders, and the Other Side of Globalization,* edited by Willem van Schendel and Itty Abraham, 38–68. Bloomington: Indiana University Press, 2005.

Van Waas, Michael. "The Multinational Strategy for Labor: Foreign Assembly Plants in Mexico's Border Industrialization Program." PhD diss., Stanford University, 1981.

Vila, Pablo. *Crossing Borders, Reinforcing Borders: Social Categories, Metaphors, and Narrative Identities on the U.S.–Mexican Frontier.* Austin: University of Texas Press, 2000.

———, ed. *Ethnography at the Border.* Minneapolis: University of Minnesota Press, 2003.

Washington, Diana. *The Killing Fields: Harvest of Women.* Los Angeles: Peace at the Border, 2006.

Weeks, Kathi. *Constituting Feminist Subjects.* Ithaca, N.Y.: Cornell University Press, 1998.

———. *The Problem with Work: Feminism, Marxism, Antiwork Politics, and Postwork Imaginaries.* Durham, N.C.: Duke University Press, 2011.

Whitlock, Gillian. *Soft Weapons: Autobiography in Transit.* Chicago: University of Chicago Press, 2007.

Wiegman, Robyn. *Object Lessons.* Durham, N.C.: Duke University Press, 2011.

Williams, Gareth. "The Mexican Exception and the 'Other Campaign.'" *South Atlantic Quarterly* 106, no. 1 (Winter 2007): 129–51.

Williams, Heather. "Mobile Capital and Transborder Labor Rights Mobilization." *Politics and Society* 27, no. 1 (1999): 139–66.

Williams, Raymond. *Marxism and Literature.* New York: Oxford University Press, 1977.

Wilson, Carter. *Hidden in the Blood: A Personal Exploration of AIDS in the Yucatán.* New York: Columbia University Press, 1995.

Wittig, Monique. *The Straight Mind and Other Essays.* Boston: Beacon Press, 1992.

Wolf, Sherry. *Sexuality and Socialism: History, Politics, and Theory of LGBT Liberation.* Chicago: Haymarket Books, 2009.

Womack, John, Jr. *Rebellion in Chiapas: An Historical Reader.* New York: New Press, 1999.

Wright, Melissa. "The Dialectics of Still Life: Murder, Women, and Maquiladoras." *Public Culture* 11, no. 3 (Fall 1999): 453–73.

———. *Disposable Women and Other Myths of Global Capitalism.* New York: Routledge, 2006.

———. "Justice and the Geographies of Moral Protest: Reflections from Mexico." *Environment and Planning D: Society and Space* 27, no. 2 (2009): 216–33.

———. "A Manifesto against Femicide." *Antipode,* 2001, 550–66.

———. "Necropolitics, Narcopolitics, and Femicide: Gendered Violence on the Mexico-U.S. Border." *Signs* 36, no. 3 (2011): 700–31.

———. "Witnessing, Femicide, and a Politics of the Familiar." In *The Global and the Intimate: Feminism in Our Time,* edited by Geraldine Pratt and Victoria Rosner, 267–88. New York: Columbia University Press, 2012.

Yúdice, George. "*Testimonio* and Postmodernism." *Latin American Perspectives* 18, no. 3 (1991): 15–31.

Ziarek, Ewa Ptonowska. "Bare Life on Strike: Notes on the Biopolitics of Race and Gender." *South Atlantic Quarterly* 107, no. 1 (2008): 89–105.

Zimmerman, C. "Learning to Stand on Shifting Sands: Sonoran Desert Capitalism and Working Alliances for Social Change." PhD diss., University of Arizona, 2005.

Žižek, Slavoj. "How to Begin from the Beginning." *New Left Review* 57 (May-June 2009): 43–55.

————. *Living in the End Times*. London: Verso, 2011.

————. *The Year of Dreaming Dangerously*. London: Verso, 2012.

Zournazi, Mary, ed. *Hope: New Philosophies for Change*. New York: Routledge, 2002.

Zugman, Kara. "The Other Campaign: The EZLN and New Forms of Politics in Mexico and the United States." *New Political Science* 30, no. 3 (2008): 347–67.

————. "Political Consciousness and New Social Movement Theory: The Case of Fuerza Unida." *Social Justice* 30, no. 1 (2003): 153–76.

Index

Abejas, Las, 185

abjection: dispossession as effect of, 142–44, 198–99; and embodiment, 128–31; of feminized bodies, 130–31, 133, 134–35, 150; identity formation and, 125, 128–31; mechanism of, 129–31; racial, 248n15; renarrating scripts of, 134, 135, 144

Abu-Lughod, Lila, 38

Acosta, Rosario, 23

activist scholarship, 76–77

ACT UP, 52–53, 145

Adorno, Theodor, 39, 208

Advocate (gay magazine), 107

affect(s): autonomy of, 42–43, 45; and capitalism, 58, 62, 63; as conveyed through signs, 49–50; in culture theory, 66; Damasio's theory of, 40–42; as essence of radical invest-ment, 55–56; feminist approach to, xviii, 38–39; historical and materialist approach to, xviii, 39, 57–58, 214; and labor of production and care, xviii–xix; as last colony of capital, 37–40; negative, 48; as ontological and epistemological, 57; quantum logic of indeterminacy, 42, 43–44, 45; recent work on, 231n2; semiautonomy of, 46; in social movement research, 52, 239n37; Spinoza's materialist formulation of, 207–8; transmission of, 47–48, 52. *See also* materiality of affect

affect-culture: and bioderegulation, 154, 156–57, 160–74, 176; in capitalism's value systems, 62; defined, 50; and disciplining of subjects, 50–52; and embodied sensations, 126, 127; felt dimension of, 241n62; as ideology, 63–64; and labels, 142; and marriage and weddings, 159; materiality of, 50, 62–63; mattering maps of, 65; mediating role of, 58, 66–67; of organizing, xii–xviii, 52–56, 67; and ontology and epistemology, 201; and open secrets (*see* open secrets); reasons it matters, 66–68; sexual identity and, xxiv, 65–66; as site of struggle, 45; and social reproduction, 59; unsta-ble signifying chains and narratives of, 50; use of term, 46; and utopian aspiration, 209–10; values binding capital to, xiv, xvii. *See also* love in the common

affective capacities, 44, 157, 205, 212; basic needs and, 58; capital's in-complete harvesting of, xx; labels channeling, 142; mind–body circuit drawing upon, 215; right to *una vida digna*, xx–xxi; sexuality and, 100, 157; as surplus, 54, 213, 214. *See also* love in the common

affective economies, 50, 243n17

affective epistemology of witnessing, 70–79

affective expertise, 63

affective investments, 48–49, 55, 63–64

affective labor, 53–56

"Affective Labor" (Hardt), 62

affective mapping, 46; bearing witness and, 78–79; conducting one's own, 80; rituals as part of, 92

trusted outsiders: affective attachments to, 217–19; limited trust of, 94–96
TRW auto parts assembly workers: labor campaigns of, 33, 34–35

una vida digna (life with dignity), xx–xxi, xxv. *See also* dignity
unconscious, the, 90–91
unemployment: in border cities, 8; crisis of masculinity provoked by, 173; turning to informal and illegal sectors for work, 26
unions: conflicts of interest in, 234n23; deals between government and, 13; official or *charro*, 9, 12, 233n12 (*see also* Confederation of Mexican Workers [CTM]); registrations for independent, 15. *See also* Duro Bag Manufacturing Company, workers' strike at
United States: bearing witness as outsider from, 94–96; homophobia against working-class Mexican gay immigrants in, 103; labor unrest in, 7; phases of neoliberal cultural politics in, 158
United University Professions, xvi
urban modernists (Levi's marketing target), 163–64
"Uses of the Erotic, The" (Lorde), 38
utopia(s): Bloch's concept of, 210–11; of Right as well as of Left, 223; utopian aspiration of organizing, 206, 208–12; utopian question, 205, 208, 223; world-transforming force of utopian language, 224–26

Valentine, David, 130, 140
Valle Hermoso, 33–34
valorization process of capitalism, 54
values: second skin as tissue of. *See* second skin
Veracruz: sexual culture in, 106
Video-Craft Mexicana, 11
Villa, Pancho, 182
violence: antigay, 25, 105, 110; contradiction between women's economic value and their social devaluation and, 21; culture of hypermasculinity and, 24–25; domestic, 21, 25, 245n14; exposing fear tactics used

against workers/organizers as, 16–17; gendered inflection of discourse of sexuality in culture of, 20; against media, 31–32; media coverage of, 19, 30; narco, 18–32, 235n42, 237n76; necropolitics and threat of, 28–29; push–pull between legal and extralegal political economies, 21–22; sexual abuse/harassment, 12, 156, 169. *See also* Ciudad Juárez, femicides in
virtual materialism: Massumi's notion of, 43, 45, 54
visibility: complex politics of, 117–18; epistemological distinction between the visible and the seeable, 139–40
Vogel, Lisa, 59
voluntary sector, 61
Vulnerable Observer, The (Behar), 71

wage(s): domestic labor as surplus labor and, 59–60, 63; maquiladora, 10, 11; minimum, 26; as open secret, 112
war on drugs, 4–5, 25–26
war on terror, 80; backlash against gay marriage and, 159; neoliberal reality discourses and, 157; sexuality and, 149; war on drugs and, 25–26
Washington, Diana, 32
wealth: common, 212–16, 224; surplus, 214–15, 224
Weeks, Kathi, 211
We Gotta Get Out of This Place (Grossberg), 48
"whatever": logic of, 157, 174; "whatever" rhetoric of postgay assimilation, 158, 163–64
"What's Queer about Queer Studies Now," 147
What's Real ad campaign (Levi's), 163–64
Wilson, Carter, 104
witnessing. *See* bearing witness
women: attacks by army and security forces on, 25; of Blanca Navidad, gender adjustments by, 200–202; of Blanca Navidad, resistance of, 191–92; Comandanta Esther before Mexican Congress, 183–84; as communal good, 213; contradictory economic valuation and social devaluation of,

Rosemary Hennessy is L. H. Favrot Professor of Humanities, a professor of English, and the director of the Center for the Study of Women, Gender, and Sexuality at Rice University. She is the author of *Profit and Pleasure: Sexual Identities in Late Capitalism* and *Materialist Feminism and the Politics of Discourse* and coeditor of *NAFTA from Below: Maquiladora Workers, Campesinos, and Indigenous Communities Speak Out on the Impact of Free Trade in Mexico* and *Materialist Feminism: A Reader in Class, Difference, and Women's Lives.*